A4
13
£200

THE WEST COAST OF
SCOTLAND

SKYE TO OBAN

A Shell Guide
by
STEPHEN BONE

SHIANT ISLES   W. *Daniell*, 1824

FABER AND FABER LIMITED
24 Russell Square, London

*First published in mcmlii
by Faber & Faber, Limited,
24, Russell Square, London, W.C.1
Printed in Great Britain by
Billing & Sons, Limited, Guildford and Esher*

LIST OF ILLUSTRATIONS

Highland Clans

Men must act together if they are to live, and the tie of kinship first bound them into tribes under a patriarchal head. The occupation of land brought new needs: land must be defended and its use regulated to the best advantage. Patriarch and elders saw to this, and in time the leader of men and ruler over land became owner of the land and lord of the dwellers upon it.

So the clan and feudal systems grew. They were much alike, but the underlying ideas differed. In feudalism, land governed human relationships; among the clans rights to land depended upon personal status. Celtic Scotland had been divided into earldoms under Mormaers and Thanes, of whom Macbeth is remembered for his ambition to rise from Thane and Earl to become King of Scotland. Kings built up their power by claiming all land as theirs, to grant out to followers who gave them military service, and lands were granted to the heads of lesser tribes, or to leaders who established themselves as chiefs by marriage or superior prowess. Celtic tradition survived in the royal title, King of Scots, and in the ideal of a king as father of his people.

The last great Celtic power was that of the Mac-Donalds in the West Highlands, founded by Somerled, Lord of Argyll and the Isles. His dominions were divided among his sons, and the clan split up into separate branches, such as the Clanranald, MacDonalds of Lochalsh, Sleat, Islay, Glengarry, Keppoch, and the MacIans of Ardnamurchan and Glencoe. Other clans acknowledged MacDonald leadership, and some chiefs held hereditary offices under the Lords of the Isles. Such were the MacLeans, MacLeods, Camerons and many others, and the Lords of the Isles wielded a dangerous power. The Isles had supported Bruce, but afterwards intrigued with England, and the Stewart kings broke up the confederacy. But kings could not be always in the west, and delegated authority to those chiefs who were most inclined to serve them. The system lent itself to abuse, but there was no other. Rights of jurisdiction, military command and even the keeping of royal castles were granted to Highland leaders, and became the stepping stones of ambition.

Chiefs either held land direct from the king, or from another chief or noble as feudal superior: if a chief did not own the lands on which his clansmen lived, they might by law owe military service to a possible enemy. If they chose to transfer their allegiance they could do so by giving bonds of manrent, but divided loyalties were often a source of strife. Powerful rivals enjoying court favour, Huntly, MacKenzie, or Argyll, bid for the support of lesser chiefs, and were accused of claiming lands and jurisdictions as a reward for suppressing disorders which they had stirred up. Forfeiture of lands was not easy to enforce against a warlike clan: it was met by the Highland claim to "kindness," security of tenure in virtue of long occupation. For centuries the MacDonalds of Keppoch

4

kept their hold on lands belonging to Mackintosh, as his "kindly tenants."

The clan system developed as a mixture of old tribal ways, giving the community rights in land, and feudalism, under which an individual owner held land of a feudal lord. A chief was the landowner in the eye of the law; his principal clansmen were his tenants or "tacksmen," paying a small rent in kind; many of them were related to him. They were his counsellors, and officers in war. Their dependants, the commonalty of the clan, farmed the land, which was worked in common, paying rent in kind and labour. The poorest clansman thought himself connected with his chief by blood, and entitled to provision of some kind, and to a proper show of affability on state occasions. Hospitality was freely dispensed by the chief, but he and his tacksmen were entitled to entertainment and service when hunting or at war, and to labour at seed time and harvest. The chief had rights of justice, and kept a retinue of personal attendants and servants, which provided for some of the warlike and reckless young men with no lands of their own. A fringe of "broken men" and homeless wanderers lived as they could, by robbery or "sorning" upon their neighbours.

The chiefship descended in the male line by primogeniture, an importation from feudalism: the tribal custom had been to divide land among sons, and to choose the chief's successor from his near relations. By feudal law women could inherit land, but no woman could discharge the duties of chief: the marriage of an heiress, to someone chosen by her feudal lord in his own interests, might deprive her kinsmen of any security in the land. For a woman to bear the title of chief would only be evidence that the clan system, as a political force, has passed away.

The chief is the head of a clan: the chieftain is a subordinate leader of a sept or family within it. Some of these grew strong and independent, paying the chief their "calps," a tribute of the best horse, or cow, due on the succession of an heir, as a sign of kinship rather than of subordination. Thus the Campbells, usually loyal to Argyll as chief, grew into a confederacy similar to that of the MacDonalds. It is quite improper to describe a Lord of the Isles, a Duke or Earl of Argyll or a Cameron of Lochiel as a chieftain.

Fosterage was an important clan custom, by which the heir of a chief or chieftain was sent at a tender age to be brought up in the family of one of the clansmen, who had to be of high character, though not necessarily wealthy. This formed a strong bond of affection on both sides, and gave the future chief an insight into the lives and feelings of his kinsmen. The duty of his foster brothers was to guard and succour him at all hazards.

The Seannachie had a prominent place in clan life; he was learned in genealogies and orders of precedence, on which much depended. The bard was historian and poet; the piper was musician and composer, who inspired fighting men with the strains of the pibroch, or wrung the hearts of mourners with the lament for the fallen. The harper enlivened social intercourse; and story, song and dance were important elements in Highland culture. Some knowledge of philosophy and the classics came through those of the gentry who had studied at grammar schools or universities, or under the auspices of the Church.

At the root of Highland disorder was the insufficiency of the land to support the population. Cattle raiding was an economic necessity to men whose life gave little scope for enterprise. It was their way of correcting the inequalities of fortune, as far removed from theft as honourable warfare was from murder. If movables were stolen or a clansman slain, the relatives exacted compensation or took vengeance: rules as to those on whom these duties fell are represented nowadays by the degree of consanguinity which entitles anyone to wear a clan tartan.

Highland chiefs were not more turbulent than the Scottish nobles, nor Highland warfare more barbarous than that of civilised nations. Clan feuds, such as those between the MacDonalds and MacLeans, the Camerons and Mackintoshes, or among the MacLeods of Lewis, brought their own punishment, for a weakened or divided clan fell an easy prey to its enemies. With changed conditions old evils die: and clan life bred also courage, steadfastness and loyalty, a high sense of honour, ready hospitality and natural good manners; and these things endure.

AUDREY CUNNINGHAM
Eilean Donan Castle, DORNIE, Inverness-shire.

Carding wool.

Gazetteer

NOTE: Some place names are given in an Anglicised form, some are given in the original Gaelic, a few are given in both. The choice of spelling is as a rule that of the Ordnance Survey.

Acharacle (*ch* as in loch, accent on *ar*). A village where trout and salmon fishers gather. Enormous peat mosses in the neighbourhood. Kintra Bay is shallow and sandy. West of the village is Ben Resipol, easiest climbed from Salen or Strontian, or a boat could be taken to the narrows of Loch Shiel. (*See* Moidart, Loch Shiel.)

Appin is the district between Loch Creran and Loch Leven. Appin railway station serves the village of Portnacroish, where Castle Stalker on an offshore rock looks very romantic; it was built in the fifteenth century by the Stewarts of Appin. South of the curious salt marsh of Loch Laich is Port Appin with the old white mansion of Airds among woods and green fields. The view from the road above Portnacroish is worth pausing to look at. Dorothy Wordsworth wrote of "the innumerable creeks and bays, the communion of land and water as far as the eye could travel."

But there is also the Appin Murder which R. L. Stevenson used as the mainspring of *Kidnapped*, and *Catriona*. In 1752 the unpopular Campbell of Glenure was shot from behind a dyke. James Stewart of the Glens—the local laird—was arrested, and a Campbell judge and a Campbell jury convicted him. It is probable that James Stewart was innocent; certain that he did not have a fair trial. He was hanged at Ballachulish Ferry, where there is now a monument protesting his innocence. It was said that the whole countryside knew the real culprit but when he wished to give himself up, they would not let him; it would be a useless sacrifice, the Campbells would hang James Stewart and nothing would stop them. The people of the district

AFFORESTATION

is proceeding steadily over enormous tracts of country. "Open country is covered with a thick blanket of trees, and the specific beauty of broad-leaved deciduous woodland is replaced by the dreary uniformity of the evergreen canopy. Young coniferous plantations, straight-edged and neat in form with precisely aligned saplings, are not beautiful objects." PROFESSOR A. G. TANSLEY.

"The human being attempting ingress may find such a monstrous wood impenetrable, or, if it has been properly trimmed and thinned, he will find the floor a dead, quiet, dark place in which there is little joy but that of shelter and stillness." DR. FRASER DARLING.

ALUMINIUM

see FORT WILLIAM *and* KINLOCHLEVEN.

AURORA BOREALIS
see NORTHERN LIGHTS.

Bagpipe

Always called "the pipes." Out of a leather bag protrude five pipes. One is to blow into, the other four make the music. The longest pipe is the big drone, the two smaller ones are the little drones, and the smallest—with the holes for fingering—is the chanter. The chanter has seven holes in front for the fingers and one behind for the thumb. It has nine notes.

Timid English musicians may be alarmed on hearing that notes number four and seven are a quarter of a tone sharp. So much for the chanter. The big drone is tuned to A, two octaves below the A of the chanter; the small drones are tuned to A, one octave below.

As the sound made by the pipes is continuous, grace notes, or "warblers," are much used and can produce an almost staccato effect. Five grace notes between two beats in a bar are usual and virtuosi have played eleven before now. There is a special syllabic notation for pipe music, but it is no longer much used.

The harp has a longer history in the Highlands and a more aristocratic connection, but the pipes were used on every sort of popular occasions —weddings, funerals, dances, work, and war.

Castle Stalker, APPIN.

speak of the Appin Murder as though it happened a few years ago.

Ardchattan. On the north shore of Loch Etive. Ruins of a priory founded by the MacDougalls of Lorne in the thirteenth century now in the grounds of a modern mansion. Robert Bruce held a parliament here, one of the last parliaments to do business in Gaelic.

Ardgour. A ferry takes cars across Loch Linnhe. This country belonged anciently to the small clan of the MacMasters. The Lords of the Isles, following a not unusual custom, rewarded a family of MacLeans by giving them someone else's land. MacLeans succeeded in expelling MacMasters, and there have been MacLeans of Ardgour ever since the fifteenth century. A fine waterfall is called MacLeans Towel. Ardgour is a very mountainous district; Garbh Bheinn, a hill topped with naked quartzite crags, is particularly imposing. The eastern side of this hill is for rock climbers only.

Ardnamurchan is remote. It can be reached by ship from Oban to Kilchoan, or by road via Ardgour and Strontian. The northern shore of this long promontory has many beautiful sandy bays. A rough but motorable road leads to Ardnamurchan Point, the westernmost point of the British mainland, 20 miles west of Land's End. The Scottish Mountaineering Club recommend Beinn na Seilg in spite of its modest height. Ardnamurchan belonged to the MacIan sept of the MacDonalds until the advancing tide of the Campbells proved too much for them. Mingarry Castle, the MacIans' stronghold, is still an imposing ruin.

Arisaig. "This Wild Country has always been a Nursery and Sanctuary of Priests. People in general of all Ranks in this barbarous place are much better acquainted with Rome, Madrid, and Paris than they are with London or Edinburgh."—*The Highlands in 1750.* The shore from Arisaig to Morar is extremely beautiful with white

Airds House, APPIN.

At the various Highland games one can hear competitions for the playing of reels, marches, strathspeys (slow dances), and pibrochs (piobaireachd), which are elaborate classical compositions in several movements. Pibrochs are not easy for an uninstructed listener.

The Emperor Nero was a piper and so were many other distinguished persons of antiquity. Probably Nero piped while Rome was burning. In the Highlands one family of pipers achieved great fame: the MacCrimmons of Skye, hereditary pipers to the Lords of the Isles. They had a silver chanter given to them by the Queen of the Fairies, and ran a school for pipers at Boreraig on Skye.

𝔅𝔞𝔫𝔰𝔥𝔢𝔢

see GLAISTIG.

BIRDS

Some species likely to interest the stranger are:

BLACK GROUSE (*or Black Cock and Grey Hen*). *Decreasing in numbers and vanished altogether from many places. The birds damage young conifers and the Forestry Commission dislikes them. The males meet in the mating season at special dancing floors called "leks" and display fantastically. The tail of the male bird is a favourite ornament for pipers' bonnets—see opposite page.*

CORNCRAKE *or* LANDRAIL. *Almost extinct in the south but still abundant in the Isles. Known to the insomniac as a monotonous voice on summer nights.*

CUCKOO. *Very common.*

DIVERS. *Black-throated and Red-throated are breeding species. If anyone has discovered a nest of the Great Northern Diver he has (rightly) kept silence about it.*

DUCKS. *Red-breasted Merganser, Smew, Eider, Common Pochard, Pintail, Mallard, Teal, Shoveler, Sheld-duck, are breeding species. The Scaup is rare. The Goosander and the Common Scoter may sometimes nest on the west coast.*

EAGLE. *A large, soaring hawk-like bird may be either an eagle or a buzzard. The eagle is bigger, flies in a more dashing way, and "barks" instead of "mewing." "His nobility has a dash of clownishness."—*WILLIAM MACGILLIVRAY. *Eagles are usually tolerated in*

Pipers of the First Highland Light Infantry.

strands made of powdered shell and coral. Skye, Rum, Eigg, and, in clear weather, Harris, look grand across the water. As in 1750 the people are still Catholics. The rebellion of 1745 began here when Charles Edward landed from a French frigate at Borrodale House.

Ballachulish. The biggest slate quarries in Scotland. Ballachulish slates are blue-grey and hand-trimmed. They often have sparkling bits of iron pyrites in them. The old lines of quarrymen's cottages, one-storied and white-washed, have new neighbours of a rather bleak suburban kind. On an island in the loch is a ruined chapel and the burial place, still sometimes used, of the MacDonalds of Glencoe and the Camerons of Callart; in the ruined chapel is a queer tomb showing a Highlander killing a mounted redcoat and inscribed "The fate of an English Dragoon who attacked D(uncan)Mc(Kenzie) at the Battle of Prest(on Pans) where he fought under Prince Charles Edward." The people of this district are mostly Episcopalians.

Ballachulish Slate.

Ballachulish Ferry. Three miles from the village of Ballachulish. There is a monument to James Stewart of the Glens "executed for a crime of which he was not guilty" (see under Appin).

North Ballachulish has three magnificent mountain views: east to

deer forests, but killed on sheep-walks and grouse moors. Chief food: hares and rabbits.

FINCHES. *Twite and Lesser Redpoll will be unfamiliar to southerners.*

GEESE. *The Grey-lag goose still breeds in a few lonely marshes. The others are winter visitors.*

GROUSE (*August 12th to December 10th*). *The Grouse (Red Grouse) is confined to Britain. It does not turn white in the winter like its nearest relative the Scandinavian Ryper. It eats heather, and grouse moors are often burned in early spring to stimulate the growth of new heather shoots. A density of one grouse to an acre has sometimes been achieved, but some suppose the frequent epidemics were due to overstocking.*

MERLIN. *A fierce little falcon that nests above the 1,000-ft. contour.*

PTARMIGAN. *Our only bird with the arctic habit of turning white in winter. Nests on mountain tops and seldom comes below 2,000 ft.*

RAVEN (*or Corbie*). *Not uncommon now it is less persecuted. Larger and heavier than a crow and with a much deeper voice.*

SWANS. *The wild Whooper Swan and Bewick's Swan come from Iceland to the Scottish coasts in the winter. Their necks do not take the S-curves of the semi-domestic Mute Swans. "Less graceful, more beautiful." No black lump on beak. Faster on land than the Mute Swan. Bewick's Swan much smaller than the Whooper.*

BOOKS

A DESCRIPTION OF THE WESTERN ISLANDS OF SCOTLAND *by* MARTIN MARTIN (1695). *Dr. Johnson read it and was inspired to go and see for himself.*

A JOURNEY TO THE WESTERN ISLES *by* SAMUEL JOHNSON.

A JOURNEY TO THE WESTERN ISLES WITH DR. JOHNSON *by* JAMES BOSWELL.

TOUR IN SCOTLAND IN 1769 *by* THOMAS PENNANT.

Many others toured the West Highlands and wrote about them. The classics for the serious student of Highland history are:

MACBAIN'S HIGHLANDERS OF SCOTLAND.

GREGORY'S HISTORY OF THE WEST HIGHLANDS.

SKENE'S CELTIC SCOTLAND.

ADAM'S CLANS, SEPTS AND REGIMENTS OF THE HIGHLANDS.

On folk lore one can read:

POPULAR TALES OF THE WEST HIGHLANDS *by* J. F. CAMPBELL.

SCOTTISH FOLK-LORE AND FOLK LIFE *by* DONALD MacKENZIE.

FOLK TALES AND FAIRY LORE *by* JAMES MacDOUGALL.

Also the appendices to the REPORT OF THE CROFTERS COMMISSION (1883).

An important but heart-breaking book is A HISTORY OF THE HIGHLAND CLEARANCES *by* ALEXANDER MacKENZIE.

There have been many recent topographical books; one of the best is HIGHWAYS AND BYWAYS IN THE WEST HIGHLANDS *by* SETON GORDON.

Two recent books by those who have farmed in the West Highlands are:

HIGHLAND HOMESPUN *by* MARGARET MARY LEIGH.

10

Bidean nam Bian, south to Ben Vair, and west to the hills of Ardgour where the grand rocky top of Garbh Bheinn is conspicuous. Southey watched a sunset from here and said, "The effect was such that I could have wished I were a believer in Ossian." Ossian's stock has risen since Southey's day.

Balmacara (*see* Loch Alsh).

Banavie. The best known view of Ben Nevis. A series of locks on the Caledonian Canal called "Neptune's Staircase" raises the canal 80 ft. A whole village of pre-fabricated timber houses from Scandinavia has grown up between Banavie and Fort William.

Ben Nevis (pronounced *Nevvis*). A track leads to the top from Achintee in Glen Nevis; a more exciting route is up the corrie of Allt a Mhuilinn to the saddle

I WENT A-SHEPHERDING *by* RICHARD PERRY.

A useful and instructive book is NATURAL HISTORY OF THE HIGHLANDS AND ISLANDS *by* F. FRASER DARLING.

Climbers and Walkers will need:

ROCK CLIMBING IN SKYE *by* A. P. ABRAHAM.

THE GUIDE BOOKS OF THE SCOTTISH MOUNTAINEERING CLUB.

HILL PATHS IN SCOTLAND *by* W. A. SMITH, *revised by* D. G. MOIR.

There are several books on Highland yachting. Try SAILING ORDERS *by* CAPT. J. R. HARVEY, R.N., *and if you want to be entertained by works of fiction there are, among others, the following:*

A LEGEND OF MONTROSE *by* SIR WALTER SCOTT.

KIDNAPPED *by* R. L. STEVENSON.

THE NEW ROAD AND JOHN SPLENDID *by* NEIL MUNRO.

THE VITAL SPARK AND PARA HANDY *by* HUGH FOULIS (NEIL MUNRO *writing under a pseudonym*).

THE BROTHERS *by* L. A. G. STRONG.

CHILDREN OF THE DEAD END *by* PATRICK MacGILL.

BUTCHERS BROOM *by* NEIL GUNN.

THE FLIGHT OF THE HERON *by* D. K. BROSTER.

THE GREEN RAY *by* JULES VERNE.

AND THE COCK CREW *by* FIONN MacCOLLA.

BEN NEVIS from the shores of LOCH EIL; the new houses are those of Annat.

BEN NEVIS from CORPACH.

between Ben Nevis and Carn Mor Dearg and thence along a very narrow ridge to the top; it is dangerous to descend this way. The top of the hill is rough boulders without a blade of grass; snow lies in patches under the northern cliffs throughout the summer. The ruins of a little hotel and a meteorological observatory litter the ground. The observatory was built in 1881 and abandoned in 1905. It had to be provisioned for six months at a time, as the track from Achintee was closed to pack ponies from November to April. It seems curious that it has never been re-opened now that reports of the upper atmosphere are so important for aircraft.

The view is, in good weather, immense. It includes almost every hilltop north of the Forth and some south of it. The meteorologists on a few rare occasions could even make out the coast of county Donegal, which is at least 120 miles away. From up here Scotland appears a desolate country indeed; nothing is visible but heather and rock.

See *Ben Nevis* edited by E. Graham MacPhee (Scottish Mountaineering Club).

Benderloch is the district between Loch Etive and Loch Creran. The village is Ledaig. The Campbell castle of Barcaldine has been restored and looks very picturesque with its pepper-pot turrets, corbie steps, and tiny barred windows. At Shian Ferry are trees and green fields and a view of mountains over the water.

Near Benderloch station is a double hillock which may, or may not, have been the Pictish city of Beregonium and the Ossianic city of Selma.

Bonawe (pronounced, and sometimes spelt, *Bunawe*). A ferry now takes cars across Loch Etive. Here are the ruins of an old blast furnace, with the date 1753 on it. Iron ore from Lancashire was smelted here by charcoal. Water power was used. The place is an interesting eighteenth-century parallel to twentieth-century Kinlochleven. Bonawe now earns

There are many novels by WILLIAM BLACK, *"like tartan-covered sofas," according to* IVOR BROWN.

Other books of local interest are mentioned in the course of this guide.

Barcaldine Castle, BENDERLOCH.

Brochs

are dry stone fortifications of an elaborate and specialised type. A broch, when complete, looked rather like the lower half of a lighthouse tower roughly built of big stones without mortar. This erection might be about 50 ft. high, it had a central shaft open to the sky, and the walls were double: an outer wall, the tremendous thickness of which at the bottom produced the lighthouse-like curve, and an inner wall, thinner and vertical. The space between the two walls was divided into five or six stories, some of the stories being divided into a number of rooms and some of them consisting merely of an undivided circular gallery going right round the broch. The floors were all made of big slabs of stone which held the whole building together. A broch is probably the most ambitious and skilful building ever made of uncemented stone.

This rather tedious explanation is necessary in order that the ruins of them may not be entirely incomprehensible; for ruins, alas! they all are within the area covered by this guide. There is one complete broch in Scotland—on the uninhabited island of Mousa in the Shetlands—but only the unusually enterprising tourist is likely to see it. There are, however, good ones on Skye and in Glenelg. At one time brochs were attributed to the Norsemen, but it is now supposed that the Norsemen, when they arrived, thought them as strange as we do. The date now given to the brochs is 100 B.C. to 100 A.D., but this is conjectural. Brochs only occur in Scotland and it is now supposed that the traditional name of "Pictish Towers" is perfectly correct. If the Picts didn't build them, who did?

Duns are rougher affairs as a rule, though the word is vague and often means any sort of prehistoric fortress, brochs included. There are galleried duns which are like primitive brochs and there are duns which

14

its living in the big granite quarries across the Loch. Above Bonawe Loch Etive is roadless and traffic goes by water.

Caledonian Canal. Surveyed by James Watt in 1773, begun by Telford in 1803, completed and opened in 1847. This was Telford's chief work in the Highlands. It cost a million and a quarter pounds in all. Scandinavian timber ships were meant to supply a large proportion of the traffic, but a heavy duty on timber in favour of Canada crippled this almost from the start. Fishing boats used the canal a lot at first and there used to be pleasure steamers, but today there is not much traffic. The locks have green lawns and trees beside them; the lock keepers' houses are bow-fronted, whitewashed, and dignified, and there are some well designed metal bridges.

Canna has terraced, green hills one of which, Compass Hill, is supposed to affect the accuracy of the compasses of ships travelling near. There is a rock by the harbour with a small castle of the Lords of the Isles. Canna used to belong to the monks of Iona and the site of St. Columba's chapel near the harbour is marked by a fragment of a carved cross. Canna has a good harbour, which seems to have been much used by the Norsemen.

Coll is a low sandy, island where farmers from Ayrshire settled. There are sandhills on the western shore. Doctor Johnson visited it and found MacLean of Coll still in possession of the middle of the island, though Campbells owned both ends. Coll is alive with black rabbits. Its population is about 300 and its harbour is very bad.

Connel Ferry has a number of villas with views, and a church which imitates Iona Cathedral. At this place Loch Etive is only 100 yards across and very shallow. The water pours out of the loch when the tide is falling and into it again when the tide is rising; the maximum difference in level is about 8 ft. Small steamers wait for slack water and adven-

are nothing but a wall of stones across the neck of a steep-sided promontory.

Vitrified forts are duns which have a peculiar mystery attached to them. They are built of rough stone like any other dun but the stone has been fused into a sort of slag by heat. This fusing is irregular and capricious. Sometimes the top of the wall is fused, sometimes the bottom, sometimes the outside, sometimes the inside. To fuse this stone must have required huge fires and it seems impossible to discover how, why, when, or by whom this vitrification was done. Dunjardil in Glen Nevis is a good and accessible vitrified fort.

It is tempting to arrange these various buildings in order of complexity and to say that the simplest and roughest are also the oldest. There is, however, no real evidence for this.

Cailleach Bheur

(pronounced Cal-yach Vair) is a formidable primitive deity fallen on evil days. She has a blue-black face, one eye, rust-red teeth and matted snow-white hair. Her dress is grey. She is immensely tall and strong. She has a hammer and when she strikes the ground it freezes hard and the grass stops growing. She is a creature of the winter and she keeps prisoner a beautiful girl with whom her son has fallen in love, but spring comes and they escape and the baffled Cailleach raises the great storms of March to keep them apart. On the 25th of March she is finally defeated and is turned into a stone until the first snows of the Autumn restore her power. Lochaber is her chief haunt. If you meet in Lochaber a huge and repulsive woman gutting fish by a stream it is probably the Cailleach.

CAMPING

"L'Ecosse semble frappée de la folie du camping. Ce ne sont, sur les prés marécageux, que des tentes pointues, comme des champignons poussés par l'humidité, et, sur les chemins, que roulottes aux couleurs éclatantes. Quelle santé ont ces hommes et ces femmes tannés et boucanés, ces petits enfants sans chaussettes, ces vieillards tout rouges qui vivent dehors, les pieds dans l'eau, par une température automnale!" PAUL HENRY BORDEAUX, 1932.

CARBIDE

One of the industries suggested for the Highlands. In 1937 a proposal to set up a factory at Corpach, supplied by a new power station at Kinlochleven, was defeated in the House of Commons.

CATTLE

"They are small, their countenances usually sour and their horns wide." Cattle were the great wealth of the Highlands and they were driven enormous distances to the Lowland markets. The old breed was always described as "black," and does not seem to have been the same as the shaggy light brown "Highland Cattle" of today. In order to increase the productivity of the Highlands it is now considered essential to increase the number of the cattle on the hills and subsidies are paid to ensure this.

16

Calves on SKYE.

turous spirits sometimes go down the falls without waiting; the channel is close to the southern bank. Over these reversible falls there is a steel railway bridge which motorists can cross for five shillings (it was ten shillings until 1936). The bridge is a single span, one of the largest in the world, and looks curiously awkward in design though presumably fitted for its purpose. (*See also* Dunstaffnage.)

Corpach has, what Fort William lacks, a view of Ben Nevis. The "Corp" in the name means what it sounds like; in the days when the Pictish kings of Inverness were buried with their fathers at Iona, Corpach was the place where the corpse was transferred to a ship for the last part of the journey. At nearby Annat wartime hutting has been used to house workers from Fort William. Annat is now unattractive. (*See also* Caledonian Canal).

Dornie. A bridge has now replaced the ferry. On Eilean Donan is an old castle of the MacRaes. It was battered by shots from H.M.S. *Worcester* in 1719 (*see* Glen Shiel for an account of the engagement), but was well restored by Col. Gilstrap MacRae. From Dornie a road goes beside Loch Long to Killilan, whence one can walk to the Falls of Glomach, or for that matter right across Scotland by Glen Cannich or Glen Strathfarrar.

Dubh Hirteach. This lonely lighthouse was made of granite blocks from Erraid. They interlock like a constructional toy and the lighthouse was first erected at the quarry, then taken to pieces again, packed into two lighters, and hurried out to the rock. The engineer was Thomas Stevenson, and his son, Robert Louis, wrote about the building in *Memories and Portraits.* In 1867—the year work was begun on the rock—it was only possible to land there twenty-seven times during the whole summer. The lighthouse took five years to build, and although the light is 140 ft. above sea level it has been cracked by the waves on one occasion.

Clans

The important clans on the west coast (from north to south) were the MacKays in the Cape Wrath neighbourhood; the MacKenzies to the south of them; the MacDonalds and MacLeods interlocked in endless feuds in Skye and the neighbouring mainland; the MacLeans, aggressive in Mull and Morven; the Camerons in Lochaber and beside Loch Eil; and the powerful Campbells gradually extending their dominions from their headquarters round Loch Awe.

The warfare between MacLeods and MacDonalds is ancient history and is forgotten completely, but the feuds between Campbells and non-Campbells are much more recent (see under Appin and Glencoe) and faint memories still linger.

(See also article at the beginning of this guide.)

Clearances

"From the lone shieling of the misty island
   Mountains divide us and the waste of seas—
Yet still the blood is strong, the heart is Highland,
   And we in dreams behold the Hebrides.

When the bold kindred, in the time long vanish'd,
   Conquered the soil and fortified the keep—
No seer foretold the children would be banish'd,
   That a degenerate lord might boast his sheep."

"The Canadian Boat-Song," 1829.   *Author unknown.*

After the "Forty-Five" the whole of the life of the Highlands underwent a complete change. Before the rebellion the chief lived surrounded by his clan, speaking the same language and having interests and tastes in common. Then came the forfeiture of the estates; the chiefs fled abroad, lost touch with their country and when, years later, the estates were restored to the sons of the old chiefs, they were restored to aliens who had not even a language in common with their poverty-stricken clansmen. The Highlands were in a bad way. The new chiefs and the English proprietors who had by purchase and marriage acquired Highland estates, found them poor, miserable, and encumbered with debts. Sheep farming was a way of making money, and with quite unbelievable callousness many of the landlords forced their helpless tenants to leave the homes of their ancestors and then did pretty well for themselves, feeding sheep among the ruins. No imaginative person can to-day look unmoved on the humble heaps of stones that can be found in almost every glen in the Highlands. The horrible story can be read at length in MacKenzie's *History of the Highland Clearances.* The emigration began at the end of the eighteenth century, reached huge proportions after the Napoleonic Wars and was further helped by the potato famine of 1846. Most of the emigrants went to Glasgow or Canada, which may be said to have been built out of the ruins of the Highlands. The loss of population from the Highland counties has been placed at 200,000. The Highlands have never really recovered from the clearances. Sheep later gave place to deer and the decay of the country progressed one stage further.

18

BEN NEVIS and the old Gondolier *which used to take passengers on the CALEDONIAN CANAL.*

Dunstaffnage Castle. Here the Scots, newly arrived from Ireland, are supposed to have established their headquarters from 500 to 843, when they were united with the Picts. They then removed their capital to Scone and took with them their Coronation Stone now under the throne in Westminster Abbey. The MacDougalls held Dunstaffnage in the early middle ages, but Bruce captured it and appointed a Campbell hereditary "captain." There is a Captain of Dunstaffnage to-day.

The present ruin is not very remarkable, though some of it dates from Bruce's time. On the ramparts is a brass gun from the Tobermory wreck. The situation is beautiful, though rather over-

CLEGS

(or Horse-flies). They will not trouble you after the beginning of August, but this is the only cheerful thing I know about them.

CLIMBING

as distinct from scrambling and walking can best be indulged in on Ben Nevis, the hills of Glencoe, Garbh Bheinn in Ardgour, and particularly the Coolins. The Scottish Mountaineering Club publish excellent guide books and maps to these districts. There is one phrase which recurs in these guide books and will act as a spur: "As far as is known, nothing has been attempted here."

Columba

see IONA.

LOCH DUICH.

grown with trees. The chapel near the castle is said to contain the bones of various early monarchs.

Duror. A railway station and a few houses. There is a standing-stone in front of Achara House. A minister of Duror, the Rev. James MacDougall, published some interesting collections of folk-lore.

Easdale. The village is partly on the Island of Seil and partly on Easdale Island. It was a slate-quarrying village with rows of white cottages. The slate quarries are now filled with green sea water and only a few cottages are white and inhabited, many are in various stages of greyness and dissolution. The situation is remarkable and there is a magnificent view from the high ground. Between 1842 and 1862 nearly half a million pounds' worth of slates were taken from Easdale. The method used was to drive wedges of wood into the rocks at low water; the wood swelled when the tide rose, and the rocks split. Quarrying has been going on here at least since the beginning of the seventeenth century. *Nether Lorn and its Neighbourhood*, by Patrick H. Gillies, is an interesting book about this district.

Eigg has many crofts and is a pleasing contrast to the melancholy desert of Rum. The Sgùrr of Eigg looks odd and is odd. Lava from a huge volcano flowed down a valley and solidified there into extremely hard pitchstone; rain, frost, and sun have removed the whole landscape—volcano, valley and all—but the pitchstone was so hard that it remained; and now instead of flooring a valley it roofs a hill. Eigg belonged to the MacDonalds—the Clanranald branch of the clan—but about 1590 the whole population was wiped out by MacLeods in a peculiarly horrible massacre, and the island was re-settled from the mainland (*see* Sir Walter Scott's *Tales of a Grandfather*). "Singing sands" in Laig Bay are curious; they make a queer noise, not unmusical, when trodden on. The people of Eigg are Catholics. *The Cruise of The*

DUROR Church.

EASDALE.

Betsey, by Hugh Miller, has a good account of Eigg.

Erraid *or* **Earraid** (accent on first syllable). A little island whence the Dubh Hirteach lighthouse was hewn and where to-day the lighthouse men live when off duty. Robert Louis Stevenson came here when his father was building the lighthouse and wrote of Erraid as Aros in the *Merry Men* (only he placed a farm on the island), again under its own name in *Kidnapped*, and finally in *Memories and Portraits*.

Fladdachuan. "There's abundance of sea-fowl that come to hatch their Young in the Isle; the Coulterneb [Puffin] is very numerous here, it comes in the middle of March, and goes away in the middle of August: it makes a Tour round the Isle Sunways, before it settles on the Ground, and another at going away in August; which Ceremony is much approved by the Tenant of the Isle, and is one of the chief

RUM from EIGG.

CROFTERS

are yearly tenants of Highland farms the rent of which does not exceed fifty pounds a year. In practice few crofters pay anything like this rent. A croft consists usually of three to ten acres of arable land as well as grazing rights for a fixed number of sheep on the open hillside. A crofter holds his land on a yearly tenancy but the landlord cannot give him notice to quit if he pays his rent, cultivates the land himself, and keeps buildings and land from deteriorating. The crofter, however, can terminate his tenancy on a year's notice. The Land Court can be asked by either crofter or landlord to fix a "fair rent." A crofter's right to occupy and cultivate his croft descends from father to son, or can be willed away. In Ireland it can be sold, but not in Scotland.

Some maintain that an adequate living can still be had from a croft even without various government subsidies, but the fact remains that the crofting population is diminishing.

Ranching near FORT WILLIAM. A recent revival of the cattle rearing which was once the chief occupation of the Highlanders.

Crofts at STAFFIN BAY, SKYE.

Arguments he made use of for making the like round, as he sets out to Sea with his boat." *Martin.* There is no tenant now to imitate the superstitious practices of the sea-birds.

Fort William is a little tourist town below Ben Nevis. From the town the Ben is out of sight, but it is Fort William's chief attraction all the same. The foreshore of Loch Linnhe is taken up with railway sidings, and the town consists of one long, very miscellaneous street, with villas perched on the hillside above. Knitted goods, tartans, and walking sticks in abundance. The West Highland Museum contains a remarkable historical collection, including a "secret" portrait of Charles Edward, a portrait which appears to be a meaningless collection of daubs until one gazes not at the painting but at its reflection in a polished cylinder.

The history of Fort William begins with a fort built by King William III to overawe the men of Lochaber: Camerons, Stewarts and MacDonalds, Jacobites to a man. William's fort was demolished to make way for the railway; a bit of the rampart and the derelict governor's house can be seen between the goods station and the loch. The panelling from this house is in the museum.

The ancient history of the district is to be found at Inverlochy, where there are the ruins of the old castle. Boethius—from Aberdeen—maintained that here there was once a great city remarkable for the resort of Frenchmen and Spaniards, ruled by King Achaius, a person of sufficient importance to conclude pacts of mutual assistance with Charlemagne. A glance at a map shows what a good eye Achaius had for a strategic site. Two battles have been fought here. In 1431 Donald Balloch defeated an army sent by James V, and in February, 1645, Montrose defeated Argyll; near the town are some cairns commemorating this second battle of Inverlochy. MacDonalds are said to add a stone whenever they pass, Campbells to remove one. Scott

CULDEES

Were members of a religious order instituted by St. Maelruin in Dublin in 787. They were hermits, and ruins of their cells can be found in the most extraordinary places, particularly on Atlantic islets where it is impossible to land nine days in ten. With the rest of the old Celtic church the Culdees were suppressed in the twelfth century.

DEER

STAGS: 12*th August to* 12*th October.*
HINDS: 10*th November to* 31*st March.*

The man who shoots a stag or a hind at other times is not breaking any law, only a gentleman's agreement. The deer go to the mountain tops in June when the clegs begin to bite. "Deer" in the Highlands means Red Deer. There are a few Fallow Deer on Mull and near Arisaig, and Roe Deer live in many wooded districts.

Red deer.

Devil

Demons seem to be common in the Highlands, but the Devil is not often met with. He can be raised by the horrible process of the Taghairm. You roast cats alive. After one or two die in this manner a fiend will come and ask you to stop—the Devil is King of the Cats. If you go on, a superior fiend will come until finally, at dawn or thereabouts, the Devil himself will appear, willing to grant anything you want if you will leave the cats alone. The Taghairm is best done in a ruined church.

DUNS

(*see under* BROCHS).

gives an anti-Campbell account of the battle in *A Legend of Montrose*, and Neil Munro in *John Splendid* gives a pro-Campbell account. To-day Inverlochy is industrial. The British Aluminium Company have built an immense erection of blood-coloured corrugated iron, where they smelt aluminium by water-power. There are streets of new semi-detached houses. Some of the pros and a lot of the cons of Highland industrialism can be studied at Inverlochy. (*See also* Ben Nevis and Glen Nevis.)

Garvelloch Isles *or* **Isles of the Sea.** Three islets in a row where the Firth of Lorne becomes the Atlantic Ocean. All are uninhabited, but on the southernmost, Eileach an Naoimh, there are some very ancient ruins. A stone with a rough cross on it is said to mark the grave of Eithne, mother of Columba. Other carved stones have been stolen. This island is probably the Hinba mentioned several times in Adamnan's *Life of Columba*.

Glencoe has not been improved by a Kingston-by-pass of a road which has been driven through it in an unnecessarily brutal manner. Brilliant streamlined charabancs purr up and down. But the glen is still as grim as ever, once one takes two steps off the road. On the north side Aonach Eagach is a continuous wall, on the south side six rocky hills tower above the glen. These are, starting from the foot, Bidean nam Bian (3,766 ft.), the Three Sisters of Glencoe, Buchaille Etive Beg (3,129 ft.), and Buchaille Etive Mor (3,345 ft.). There are stiff rock climbs on all of them. Near the top of the glen is "the Studdy" (studdy =an anvil), where one traditionally pauses to admire the view; from it a path goes over to Dalness at the head of Loch Etive. A little further on a walker can go to Kinlochleven by the "Devil's Staircase," the wreck of one of Wade's roads.

Glencoe is, of course, notorious for the massacre of the Mac-Donalds in 1692. It shocked the

GLENCOE.

Each Uisge

(or Water Horse) is a fiend that lives in a loch. It appears in two forms. Sometimes a handsome young man makes love to girls, the girl is fortunate if she finds in time that he has water weeds in his hair or horse hoofs. If she doesn't notice this she is taken to the loch and eaten. At other times a beautiful horse, very gentle and ingratiating, approaches children playing beside the loch; a child gets on its back and the demon instantly leaps into the loch and devours its victim. There are also water bulls and kelpies, which are much the same. The kelpies, however, have the curious and unpleasant speciality of leaping from behind on to lonely horsemen and folding them in a wet embrace.

EAGLES

(*see* BIRDS).

EXTINCT BEASTS AND BIRDS

Brown bears became extinct in the Highlands before 1100, Reindeer and elks before 1300, beavers before 1600. The last wolf was killed in 1743. The goshawk and the kite were exterminated about fifty years ago, the polecat more recently.

The Fairies

Highland fairies are almost all women. They have no queen and no names or titles. They live inside green hillocks and seem to spend most of their time singing and dancing; fiddlers and pipers are decoyed into their mounds to give them music. They also kidnap women to act as nurses and often leave their own children instead of human ones. They conscience of the Highlands as nothing else has, before or since, for the murderers used the sacred laws of hospitality to commit the crime. The man on the spot who carried it through was Campbell of Glenlyon, and behind him is a line of men increasing in rank and, possibly, decreasing in culpability until one reaches King William himself. Queen Victoria said, "Let me hope King William knew nothing of it." Let us hope so, too. The deliberate planning of this massacre must be one of the basest things in history. The letters still exist.

The place where the village of the MacDonalds stood has never been re-occupied; the village of Glencoe, where there are several new Scandinavian houses, is now down near the loch where the River Coe flows through shady pools. On the hillside above is a big modern mansion that until recently was roofed with vermilion tiles; a public benefactor who bought it has now replaced them with slates. Above the mansion is the queer little Sgùrr na Ciche (the Pap of Glencoe) (2,430 ft.) with an interesting view. The people of Glencoe are almost all Episcopalians.

Glenelg. A few houses remain of all the hundreds that once filled these glens. Glenelg can be reached by a very rough and adventurous road over the Bealach Ratagain (1,115 ft.). The difficulty of this road is one of the reasons why the car ferry to Skye has been suspended. This ferry to Skye was much used in the past and many thousand cattle must have swum across on their way to the markets in the Lowlands, though the current in the narrows is so strong that small steamers often anchor here waiting for the tide to turn. Ships call at Genelg pier on their way to Kyle of Lochalsh and Mallaig. South of Genelg is Glenbeg with two brochs. From the head of Glenbeg one can climb Ben Screel (Beinn Sgriol) 3,039 ft. high.

Glenfinnan. At the head of Loch

MacDonald Burial Place, LOCH LEVEN.

travel invisibly in eddies of wind, but if anyone throws into these eddies their left shoe, earth from a molehill, or a naked knife, the fairies have to drop whatever it is that they have stolen. They milk deer (perhaps a memory of the reindeer which existed in Scotland until the early middle ages). The flowers, which fade on earth in the autumn, bloom again in the underworld; the cuckoo sings there through the winter. The fairies have sometimes an alarming dog as big as a bullock and dark green; dogs of this earth hate it and them. The underworld is a place of great gaiety but it is timeless and much easier to enter than to leave; it is faintly sinister. Fairy women are beautiful but there is often something slightly wrong with them. If, on Mull, a lovely woman dressed in green, but with only one nostril, asks the traveller for a pinch of snuff he would do well to be cautious.

FAIRY EGGS,

or sea nuts, are like big, flattish horse-chestnuts, very hard and light. They are sometimes found thrown up by the sea on the west coast of Scotland. They used to be prized and worn to keep off the evil eye; then someone thought of planting them, and they grew into a flower called Mimosa Scandens, which flourishes in the West Indies. So the Gulf Stream is evidently no myth.

Searching for fairy eggs is a pleasant occupation, though the chances of success are small. You can see some in the West Highland Museum at Fort William.

Fionn's Questions:

"What is redder than blood?
The face of a worthy man when strangers come and no meat by him to give them.
What is sharper than a sword?
A foe's reproach
What is the best jewel?
A knife."

J. F. Campbell's TALES OF THE WEST HIGHLANDS.

GLENFINNAN Viaduct.

Shiel. Here is a fine railway viaduct and a monument, erected in 1815, marking the place where Charles Edward called the clans together at the beginning of the forty-five. Among the plantations to the west of the loch is a large modern catholic church with a bell picturesquely hung between two supports. There are big hills all round. From Glenfinnan onwards for 20 miles the Mallaig road is not one for a fussy or nervous motorist, but it is exceptionally beautiful.

Glen Nevis, between tremendous craggy walls, is a very beautiful glen. It has two waterfalls and a vitrified fort. It is a *cul-de-sac*, except for a pedestrian energetic enough to walk over the moors to the railway station at Corrour.

Glen Shiel (nothing to do with Loch Shiel) "a dark and gloomy defile." On the south side is the Saddle (3,317 ft.) not despised by rock-climbers. On the north are the Five Sisters of Kintail, the chief of which—Sgùrr Fhuaran (Scour Ouran) (3,505 ft.)—rises in one continuous slope from sea level to the top. One just has to keep on and on and on Round the corner, above Croe Bridge, is Beinn Fhada (which is also spelt, more phonetically, Ben Attow) (3,383 ft.). "There must be many good rock climbs on the northern aspect of this mountain, but apparently nothing has yet been tried," says the guide book of the Scottish Mountaineering Club; Beinn Fhada means "long mountain" and it is long. There is plenty of exercise for the legs hereabouts, for after climbing the hills one can walk to the Falls of Glomach where a river plunges into a chasm 500 ft. deep; or across to Glen Affric and down it to Invercannich (about 30 miles). In 1719 there was a battle in Glen Shiel. Two Spanish ships had landed 300 Spanish soldiers. MacRaes and MacKenzies joined them, but the other clans had a depressingly clear recollection of the failure of the Jacobite rising of 1715 and stayed at home. Troops were rushed from Inver-

Forty-Five

means 1745; the date of Charles Edward Stuart's attempt to regain for his father the sovereignty of Great Britain and Ireland. This rebellion has been the subject of innumerable books and almost everything there is to be said about it has been said already. Remarkable though the events of 1745 and 1746 were, it is, however, the tragic results of these years that are of greater interest to us to-day. It may be said that the Highlands have never really recovered from what happened more than two hundred years ago.

The course of the Forty-Five was as follows:

The French agreed to help James the Old Pretender (or James III and VIII) to seize the throne of Britain. A French fleet set out but was driven back by the English fleet and lost many ships in a storm. The French would not try again in spite of the desperate attempts to persuade them made by Charles Edward, son of James. Seeing this was hopeless Charles Edward pawned his jewels, chartered two ships, and set off for Scotland unknown to his father or the French court. On the voyage they fell in with an English man-of-war and after a long fight one of Charles's ships was so damaged she had to turn back. On the 2nd of August with one ship and no army Charles landed near Arisaig. The Highland chiefs met him and the general feeling was one of hopelessness. But Charles talked them round, on the 19th of August the standard was raised at Glenfinnan, and Charles, with an army of 1,200 men, which rapidly increased, marched away from the Highlands to conquer the south. He captured Perth; then Edinburgh, where he set up a court; then on to Lancaster and Preston and Derby. When the Highland army reached Derby the court at London were already packing their luggage. But this astonishing raid into England was useless. The English Jacobites drank toasts but would not fight, the Highlanders wanted to get home. The retreat began on the 6th of December. For four months the Highland army retreated north with the English army following slowly behind. On the 16th of April, 1746, the Highlanders turned and fought at Culloden, near Inverness. They were routed.

Charles escaped. He made for the same place near Arisaig where he had landed nine months before and found a ship to take him to the Outer Isles. It was a bad move. The English had command of the sea, and in the small area of the islands he would soon have been captured but for Flora MacDonald, who disguised him as her maid and brought him safely to Skye, through the blockade. On Skye he had various narrow escapes until on the 5th of July he got back to the mainland For the next fortnight he hid in various caves in the Morar and Arisaig districts, hemmed in by a chain of sentries and camps which had been established from Loch Hourn to Loch Eilt. On the 21st of July he got through the chain near the head of Loch Hourn. On the 1st of August he was hiding somewhere in the great woods of Glen Affric. On the 15th of August he was near Loch Arkaig. On the 28th of August he struck east to Ben Alder, where Cluny MacPherson hid him in the famous "cage" on the mountain side. On the 13th of September he heard that a French ship was at Arisaig and he set off once more for this district. On the 19th of September he and many of his followers sailed from Loch nan Uamh in a French ship, called, ironically, *L'Heureuse*.

FOXES

are technically "vermin" and are shot.

GAELIC

see article.

28

MORVEN. *LOCH LINNHE in the foreground.* LOCH SUNART *in the distance.* CREACH BHEINN *in the centre.*

ness, frigates sailed into Loch Duich, and the Hanoverians crushed the rising without much difficulty.

Iona. "Narrest this (Isle of Mull) be twa myles of sea, layes the Isle the Erische call I colm kill, that is Sanct Colm's Isle, ane faire mayne Isle of twa myle and mair and ane myle braid, fertill and fruitfull of corn and store and guid for fishing. Within this ile there is a monastery of Mounkes and ane uther of nuns, with a paroche kirke, and sundrie uther chapells dotat of auld be the kings of Scotland and Clandonald of the Iyles." Dean Munro in 1592.

Today there is less to see on the island of Iona than there was in 1592, but there are still the ruins of the nunnery, bright with flowers and the graveyard where more than fifty kings and innumerable clan chiefs are buried "because this sanctuary was wont to be the maist honourable and ancient place that was in Scotland in thair dayes." The restored cathedral church is conspicuous on a hill above the village and nearby are the monastery ruins which are being gradually restored to serve as headquarters for the recently formed Iona Community. Of all the carved stone crosses on the island three survive.

The buildings now standing on Iona are of great interest, but the small island itself has an interest which is perhaps greater still. Its connection with the life of St. Columba is very detailed and intimate. On this small green hill Columba had a vision of angels, on this stone he sat to say goodbye to the brethren, and so on. Every stone and stream has a name and a legend; Dr. Johnson was entirely correct when he said of Iona "To abstract the mind from all local emotion would be impossible if it were endeavoured and would be foolish if it were possible."

The village, once near the western shore, now faces east across the Sound of Iona. The centre of the island is cultivated and so is the north-east portion, the rest consists of little heathery ups and downs. There is a machar with beautiful white sands on the western shore and another at the northern end.

IONA Cathedral and St. Martin's Cross.

The most considerable hill is behind the cathedral—Dun I (pronounced ee)—and from its summit one can see all the islands of the Inner Hebrides, and in clear weather South Uist as well. But one cannot see Ireland and this was the reason Columba came here, landing at Port na Churaich (Curragh harbour) at the south end of the island on May 12th (Whit Saturday) 563. Either as penance or because it made him intolerably homesick he had vowed to settle out of sight of his native country and his first act on landing was to climb to the headland above the bay and convince himself that Ireland really was below the horizon. The headland is called Carn Cul ri Eirinn (Hill of turning the back to Ireland).

When Columba landed Scotland was four separate nations. The Scots, Columba's kinsmen, were new-comers from Ireland, they held Argyllshire and were Christians. The kingdom of Strathclyde extended from Lanarkshire to Lancashire, the people spoke some ancient Welsh dialect and had at least heard Christian preaching ever since Ninian set up his church in Galloway in the year 390. South-east Scotland was held by the Angles who worshipped Thor and Odin and who spoke a northern form of Anglo-Saxon. The fourth nation was that of the Picts who spoke Pictish—whatever that was—and worshipped Gods of their own, it was much the largest of the four nations and had a powerful king named Brude who lived at Inverness. Columba became the apostle to the Picts. His life was spent travelling in Brude's dominions founding churches and monasteries, but Iona always remained his headquarters. Most of our early missionary saints are dim names, but Columba's life was written by his kinsman and successor Adamnan and his personality emerges remarkably clearly even after fourteen centuries.

After thirty years of unceasing activity Columba died on Iona at the age of seventy-two. In the same year Augustine landed in Kent, bringing with him the Roman Christianity which backed by the powerful Northumbrian kings, was ultimately to displace the Celtic Church.

Originally Iona must have been a safe and peaceful place, secure from the warfare of the mainland, but, when the Vikings appeared in these waters, Iona, as a matter of course, became one of their objectives. The first massacre took place on the sands of Martyrs Bay in 806. Iona had become a dangerous outpost and about the year 818 the primacy of Scotland was transferred from Iona to the newly founded abbey of Dunkeld (near Perth). Iona henceforward ceases to be of importance in Scottish history, but becomes a place of pilgrimage and "sepulture." Many kings were buried here including the great Kenneth MacAlpine (died 860) Duncan (died 1040) and MacBeth (died 1057). The oldest existing building on the island—the roofless St. Oran's chapel—dates from 1070 when Margaret, wife of King Malcolm Canmore, restored the decayed monastery. Soon after Iona was made a part of the diocese of Sodor and Man under the primacy not of Dunkeld but of Trondhjem in Norway. Reginald Lord of the Isles finally put an end to the Celtic Church of Iona in 1203, when he brought the Benedictines to the island and founded a monastery and a nunnery, the ruins of which still exist. In 1247 the Abbots of Iona once more acknowledged the Bishop of Dunkeld as their superior. The earliest part of the present cathedral dates from this time. About 1500 the cathedral was largely reconstructed, but in 1561 the reformers in Scotland ordered it to be dismantled. It is said that at the same time some three hundred stone crosses were thrown into the sea.

In 1899 the eighth Duke of Argyll, the owner of the whole island, gave the cathedral ruins to the Church of Scotland on condition that any recognised Christian denomination might apply for its use for the celebration of its full office of worship. This arrangement is believed to be unique in the world. The cathedral was restored between the years 1902 and 1910, and the eighth duke and his duchess were buried in it under an elaborate marble tomb.

To complete this history of Iona a note must be added about the Iona Community, at present busily restoring the monastic buildings adjoining the cathedral. The Community dates from 1938 when Dr. George Macleod was minister of the notorious district of Govan in Glasgow. For three months each summer the community live on Iona; many are craftsmen helping in the restoration of the abbey buildings, most of the others are ministers newly ordained who join for two years. They wish "to make reverent experiment in new organization and new approaches to worship." There is also an Iona Youth Trust, and in July and August some four hundred young people —chiefly from industrial Glasgow —attend a succession of holiday conferences.

In the summer Iona is visited also by many excursionists from Oban, who spend an hour and a half ashore. They see the ruins of the nunnery (thirteenth century), they see the tall thin MacLean's cross (fifteenth century) standing by the roadside, they enter the little graveyard of St. Oran where some carved tombs remain of the kings and chiefs once buried here. In the middle of the graveyard they see St. Oran's chapel (eleventh century) with its carved Norman door. In front of the cathedral stands the fine cross of St. Martin (tenth century) and the—perhaps older—St. John's cross, recently restored. The west front of the cathedral is 1910. Most of the rest dates from about 1500, but some of it is as old as the thirteenth century. Columba's tomb on the north side of the entrance to the nave may, however, actually be Columba's tomb.

31

Those who want to spend longer on Iona would be wise to make plans well ahead. There is not much accommodation on the island, and it is usually booked months in advance. The tourist ships from Oban only come in the summer. In winter one must ferry from Oban to Mull, cross Mull, and ferry once more. In bad weather, even in summer, Iona can be completely isolated.

The best small book about Iona is perhaps *Iona, a History of the Island*, by F. M. McNeill. Further reading should include two large books: *Iona, Its History and Antiquities*, by Macmillan and Brydall (1898), and *The Story of Iona*, by E. C. Trenholme (1909); also *Vita Sanctae Columbae*, by Adamnan (translated W. Huyshe).

Inverlochy (*see* Fort William).

Kerrera (accent on first syllable) has the ruins of Gylen Castle, built by MacDougalls, at its southern end. Alexander II died of a fever at Kerrera in 1249 when leading a fleet against the Norsemen of the Isles. Kerrera is lumpy and green, the southern end is a wilderness of tumbled rocks. The obelisk at the north end commemorates David Hutcheson, who founded the steamship company which is now MacBrayne's. Lobsters are sent from Kerrera to Piccadilly.

Kilbride (south of Oban) has a restored cross 11½ ft. in height near the old churchyard. A Latin inscription gives the date 1516.

Kilmelfort. Frequented by trout and salmon fishers. Near here is the Pass of Melfort, a deep, wooded ravine. The old road, which wound along the bottom, has been closed because falling stones were so dangerous. The new road keeps above the ravine and only at one point is there a view down into it.

Kinlochleven. Industrial and smoky. Scarlet-roofed semi-detached, in rows. For a few hundreds yards one might be in Coatbridge or Falkirk. British Aluminium Company's works belch fumes which contain fluorine. This has had a bad effect on vegetation, but seems to

32

GILPIN

"*A mountain is of use sometimes to close a distance by an elegant, varied line: and sometimes to come in as a second ground, hanging over a lake, or forming a skreen to the nearer objects. To each purpose the Scotch mountains are well adapted. The distances of this country, with all their uniformity, have at least one praise, as we have often had occasion to observe, that of being bounded by a grand chain of blue mountains: and when these mountains approach, their shapes are generally such as may with little alteration be transferred to canvas.*"

"*The lakes of Scotland are as various as its mountains: but they partake with them of the barrenness of the country. In the neighbourhood of water one should expect something more of vegetation. In general, however, the Scotch lakes are very little adorned. You see fine sweeping lines, bays, recesses, islands, castles and mountain skreens; all of which, except the castles, are in the best style. But with these embellishments you must be content: wood you seldom find; at least in any degree of richness or proportion.*"

William Gilpin's TOUR IN SCOTLAND.

Glaistig

A supernatural female, not so ugly nor so powerful as the great Cailleach Bheur. There was a glaistig attached to the castles of most chiefs; she wept before a funeral or was seen washing a shroud; before a wedding she could be heard rejoicing. Like the fairies, she wore green and she had long, yellow hair. She did house work mysteriously while everyone slept and milk was poured out on the ground as an offering to her. A banshee is a sort of glaistig that specialises in wailing and shroud washing. Banshees have never been known to be cheerful, whereas this seems to be the normal state of mind of an ordinary glaistig.

GOLF

The course at Oban is well known; most of the others in our area are unpretentious but pleasant enough. They vary from courses like those of Portree, Kyle of Lochalsh, Fort William, and Mallaig to courses where one has to chase cattle away from all the greens before playing.

GROUSE

(*see* BIRDS.)

HEATHER

Three species are common:
CALLUNA VULGARIS: *Ling* or *Heather*—with tiny flowers which are rose-coloured.
ERICA CINEREA: *Bell Heather*—with larger egg-shaped flowers of a strong purple colour.
ERICA TETRALIX: *Cross-leaved Heath*, *Marsh Heather*, or *French Heather*—with flowers larger still and rosy red, the leaves arranged up the stem in groups of four.
All these can have white flowers.

PORTREE at low tide.

have none on human beings (it is even said to improve their teeth!) But even without the yellow smoke Kinlochleven is unattractive.

The road from Kinlochleven to Ballachulish was made by German prisoners in the first war; before that "the Devil's Staircase" was used, a high and difficult track that zigzagged over the hills from Glencoe, originally constructed by General Wade. When the works at Kinlochleven were being built, a number of navvies, tramping to find work, were overtaken by a snowstorm on the Devil's Staircase and lost their lives. (See *Children of the Dead End*, by Patrick MacGill.) A careful piece of researh icnto social conditions at Kinlochleven has recently been published: *From Croft to Factory*, by Mary Gregor and Ruth Crichton (1946). A footpath from Kinlochleven to Fort William has been clearly signposted by the Scottish Rights of Way Society.

Kintail is the district at the head of Loch Duich. "The commons here are MacRaes and are by far the most Fierce, Warlike and Strongest Men under Seaforth": *The Highlands in* 1750. Kintail Forest now belongs to the National Trust for Scotland. (*See also* Glen Shiel.)

Knoydart. The district between Loch Hourn and Loch Nevis. Very mountainous. Can only be reached on foot or by boat. It belonged of old to a branch of the MacDonnells of Glengarry. (*See under* Loch Hourn and Loch Nevis.)

Kyle of Lochalsh. The railway terminus and port of call for steamers to Mallaig, Portree, Stornoway, etc. A ferry for cars runs to Kyleakin on Skye. A miscellaneous and planless village but with a view of Skye.

Ledaig (*see* Benderloch).

Lismore. Long and narrow and low and green. Can be reached from Oban or Port Appin. Chiefly remarkable for having been the seat of the Bishop of Argyll and the Isles. The extremely humble little cathedral is now the parish

Heather is burnt in the spring in order that grass may grow for the sheep. Grouse eat heather and sheep eat grass, and bitter arguments sometimes arise.

𝕶𝖊𝖑𝖕𝖎𝖈

see EACH UISGE.

MACHAIR

(accent on first syllable). In various parts of the west coast and the islands one comes on flat areas of sandy soil between the rocky hills and the sea. Sometimes these little plains are cultivated, as at Arisaig. Sometimes they provide grazing for cattle (and innumerable rabbits). The machairs are dry, and the soil, though light, has plenty of lime. Flowers like the dark-blue chalk milkwort grow there. The machairs are one of the chief beauties of the West Highlands and the Hebrides. They exist on Colonsay, Iona, Coll, Tiree, and on the mainland near Arisaig and Morar.

MIDGES

" . . . terribles insectes, plus petits que des poux et plus cruels que des moustiques, car ils piquent tout le corps, sans sifflement avertisseur."—PAUL HENRI BORDEAUX.

See CONTROL OF MIDGES, *published by Department of Health for Scotland (H.M.S.O., 1946), though its conclusions are not cheerful.*

Light a smudge fire, smoke black shag, and if you know of an "Insect Repellent" by all means use it.

CASTLE STALKER, LISMORE and MULL (a very low spring tide).

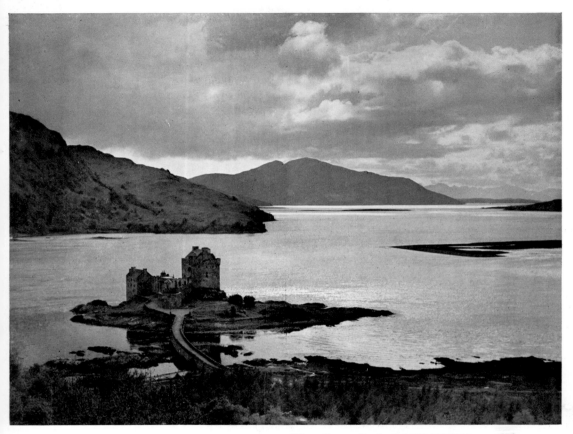

Eilean Donan Castle, LOCH DUICH.

church. The bishop had a castle, like any other chief; it was at Auchindown on the western shore. Lismore is unusual in the West Highlands in being made of limestone.

Lochaber. Means "the meeting of the lochs," and is applied to the districts of Glen Nevis, Glen Roy and Glen Spean. It is an old mistake to suppose that the upper part of Loch Linnhe is called "Loch Aber."

Loch Aline (*see* Morven).

Loch Alsh. The southern shore is steep and bleak, the northern one has little green capes and bays. It once supported a large population of Mathesons; in Glen Udalain, now empty, they could muster seven hundred men. Balmacara and the neighbourhood belong to the National Trust for Scot-

SKYE from KYLE OF LOCHALSH.

land (*see* Kyle of Lochalsh and Dornie).

Loch Awe is confusing, as, owing to a recent geological change, the water runs out at what is obviously the wrong end. This new exit is the Pass of Brander, a strange, gloomy valley, not particularly picturesque, but certainly odd. The southern end of the loch is pleasant but unexciting. The northern end has the magnificent hill of Cruachan. There are two ruined castles on islands: Ardconnel of the Campbells and a MacNaughton stronghold on Innis Fraoch. There are two island burial grounds: Innis Sherrich and the MacArthurs' burial place on Innishail with old carved tombs. The artist P. G. Hamerton camped on Innishail and wrote a book about it: *A Painter's Camp in the Highlands* (1862). There is also an island with a modern mansion-house, and a peninsula—nearly an island—with the famous ruins of Kilchurn Castle, that must have been painted a thousand times. Gilpin says, "This castle was built by the Lady of one of the Campbells who went to the Holy Wars. Here in solitary retirement she mourned his absence and waited his return." Wordsworth wrote a famous sonnet about it. The war cry of the Campbells was "It's a Far Cry to Lochow" (or Loch Awe), boasting the impregnability of this central stronghold.

Loch Duich has a road along the northern shore which, for no very obvious reason, climbs to 506 ft. From up here there is a view. The big hills at the head of the loch are the Five Sisters of Kintail (*see under* Glen Sheil). Down below is Eilean Donan Castle (*see under* Dornie).

Loch Hourn. A road leads from Invergarry past Tomdown to the head of Loch Hourn. There it stops. Big hills come straight down into the loch on all sides. Upper Loch Hourn is very narrow, lower Loch Hourn is wider and has two hills like gateposts at the entrance: Beinn Sgriol (3,196 ft.) and Ladhar Bheinn

MOUNTAINS

A TABLE OF HEIGHTS

				EASIEST CLIMBED FROM
BEN NEVIS	..	..	4406	Fort William or Banavie.
(*BEN MACDHUI* ..		..	4296)	
AONACH BEG	..	..	4060	Banavie.
CARN EIGE	..	..	3877	Glen Affric.
MAM SOUL	..	..	3862	
BIDEAN NAM BIAN	..		3766	Glen Coe or Glen Etive.
BINNEIN MOR (MAMORE)	..		3700	Glen Nevis or Kinloch-
(*SNOWDON*	..	..	3560)	leven.
BEN CRUACHAN	..	..	3689	Dalmally or Bonawe.
BEN STARAV	..	..	3541	Kinlochetive.
SCOUR OURAN ..				
(SGURR FHUARAN)	..	..	3505	Glen Shiel.
SGURR NA CICHE	..	..	3410	The head of Loch Nevis.
BEN ATTOW (BEINN FHADA)		3383	Kintail.
BEN VAIR	..	..	3363	Ballachulish or Duror.
BUCHAILLE ETIVE MOR	..		3345	Glencoe.
THE SADDLE	..	..	3317	Glen Shiel.
SGURR ALASDAIR (COOLINS)	..		3309	Glen Brittle (Skye).
(*SCAFELL PIKE*	..	..	3210)	
BEN SCREEL (BEINN SGRIOL)		3196	Glenelg.
BEN MORE (MULL)	..	..	3185	Salen or Kinloch.
BLAVEN (SKYE) ..	..	..	3042	Loch Slapin.

NORSEMEN

The first Viking raid in the Hebrides was in 794. A hundred years later the Norsemen were well established in the Orkneys and elsewhere, and the Scottish coasts were suffering from continual attacks. During the tenth and eleventh centuries the Scots gradually lost Caithness, Sutherland, Wester Ross, and the Islands; in 1102 the Western Isles were formally made over to Magnus of Orkney. In 1249 Alexander II took the offensive once more against the Norsemen of the Isles but he died of a fever at Oban and his fleet sailed home; it was not until 1263 that his great successor, Alexander III, fought and won the Battle of Largs, which finally broke the Norse power and made possible the re-conquest of the Isles.

The Norse ruled the Hebrides for approximately four hundred years, but left surprisingly little behind except place names and a considerable racial admixture. Many of the northern clans were racially more Scandinavian than Celtic and many of the Norsemen became Celticised; the ferocious Magnus Barelegs, for instance, received his name from his shocked fellow countrymen when he stepped ashore at Trondhjem in highland dress.

NORTHERN LIGHTS

can often be seen in the dark nights of Winter, though they are actually more frequent in spring and autumn than in mid-winter. They usually appear as a faint glow along the northern horizon, or they look like a row of dim, vertical searchlights. In these latitudes they are almost always colourless. They sometimes take other forms, I saw one on Skye that was a flickering arch from horizon to horizon passing straight overhead, and sometimes they justify their old name of "the merry dancers." They are electrical outbursts and are usually followed by a magnetic storm; when one sees the northern

RIVER LOCHY.

(3,343 ft.). There are footpaths from the head of Loch Hourn to Arnisdale and so, by a rough road, to Glenelg; and to Inverie on Loch Nevis by way of Barrisdale; but the loch itself is the usual road.

Loch Morar is remarkable for its amazing depth: 1,080 ft. It is the deepest hole anywhere on the European plateau, except for the submarine valley that skirts southern Norway. A small road starts up the northern shore of the loch but rapidly becomes impassable for motors and continues as a beautiful bridle path to Tarbert where one can cross to Loch Nevis and perhaps return to Mallaig by the mail launch. The upper part of Loch Morar is among big hills, the lower end has a number of islands, on one of which a seminary for Catholic priests was founded about 1700 and transferred to Moidart a little later.

Loch Nell. An attractive little loch behind Oban. The "Serpent Mound"—a big heap of boulders at the south-west corner—is odd and unexplained; the idea of serpent worship seems to have been dropped.

Loch Nevis (nothing to do with Ben Nevis). At the head of the loch are some very grand hills. The conspicuous cone is Sgùrr na Ciche (3,410 ft.) The only reasonably easy way to climb it is to get a motor boat to the head of Loch Nevis. There is a bridle path to the south of Sgùrr na Ciche which leads to Loch Arkaig. Loch Nevis separates MacDonalds from MacDonnells.

Loch Shiel is more like two lochs than one. The upper part is a typical Highland loch among big hills. Sgùrr Ghiubsachain, particularly, is grand. Twelve miles down, the loch narrows and there is an island burial place still sometimes used by both protestants and catholics. The ruined chapel on this island has an altar with an ancient little square handbell standing on it. Below the island the loch widens again but its axis is different, it now runs almost due east and west, and the shores are huge peat bogs, quite flat.

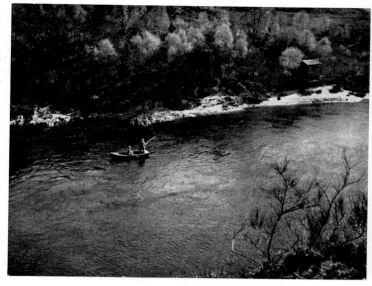

Fishing on RIVER LOCHY.

lights one does not expect good wireless reception. As you probably know, it's the sunspots that do it; or rather some mysterious disturbance in the sun reaches a maximum with remarkable regularity every $11\frac{1}{3}$ years, and produces sunspots; the atmosphere of the earth responds by producing the northern lights; and really not very much more is known about them than that.

ORPHANS

In a Highland village many of the children one sees are not related to the villagers but are orphans from a large town. When the orphans are in a minority they become Highland children and the result is satisfactory; when, however, the orphans are too many all the children in the village begin to talk with the accent of the Glasgow slums, and the result is less satisfactory.

Ossian

James MacPherson's "translations" of Ossian's poems were published between 1760 and 1762. They were received with astonishment and enthusiasm, particularly in France and Germany. It is hard to remember that, before the publication of MacPherson's *Ossian*, no one had ever thought of the Highlands as romantic. In England and Scotland a furious controversy started, one side maintaining that the "translations" were a fake from beginning to end, the other side maintaining their genuineness. Englishmen were particularly inclined to regard them as a fake, for, after the Forty-Five, the Highlanders were unpopular in England and it was considered unpatriotic to suggest that they were anything else than half-naked, illiterate savages. MacPherson himself was unlikely to convince anybody of anything, he was obstinate and unreliable, and the "original Gaelic manuscripts" he finally produced were extremely suspicious. Nevertheless there has been a considerable reaction in

The loch separates protestant MacLeans from catholic MacDonalds and Argyllshire from Inverness-shire. Much fished.

Lorne is approximately the country south of Loch Etive and west of Loch Awe. The old Lords of Lorne were MacDougalls but Lorne came into Campbell hands by marriage.

Luing (pronounced Ling) is rather inaccessible now there is no steamer service. One has to take the ferry from Seil across Cuan Sound where the tide runs at 9 knots during the springs. On Luing lived Alexander Campbell, who spent the last years of his life carving an astonishing tomb, covered with long inscriptions declaring very emphatically, if rather irrelevantly, his views on life, death, and those in authority. He died in 1829 and was buried under it. In 1936 the survivors of a wrecked Russian ship managed to reach the tiny islet of Belnahua, which has houses on it though they are now uninhabited. Their disappointment at finding the island deserted must have been intense, but they lit a great fire and men from Luing went out and took them off. Belnahua was once a slate quarry. It must have been the smallest inhabited island in Great Britain. The Luing slate quarries are the only ones now active south of Oban. At Cullipool on Luing there is a huge sea-water pond full of captive lobsters.

Mallaig (accent on the first syllable). A rather messy little place, the terminus of the railway and the headquarters of a number of drifters. Herring-gutting is done mechanically, and the herrings are turned into kippers in the big sheds near the harbour. Ships go to Armadale, Glenelg, Kyle of Lochalsh, Portree, Stornoway, etc., and in the summer to Loch Scavaig to land passengers for Coruisk. Motor launches go to Eigg, Rum, Moidart, etc., and up the big sea lochs of the mainland. The motorist is more restricted. The only road out of Mallaig is the road by which one comes in.

MacPherson's favour. It is now supposed that he took a large number of Gaelic traditional poems dealing with that band of heroes called the Fine and strung them together, no doubt adding and altering very considerably. MacPherson's *Ossian* bears some relation to Tennyson's *Idylls of the King*. A number of genuine traditional poems about the Fine have been discovered by folk-lore enthusiasts since the days of MacPherson and have gone a long way to rehabilitate him.

As for Ossian himself, J. F. Campbell is worth quoting: "I neither believe that MacPherson composed *Ossian*, nor that Ossian composed all the poems that bear his name. I am quite content to believe Ossian to have been an Irishman, a Scotsman, or a myth, on sufficient evidence."

Picts

Are supposed to have been Celts (see CELTS).
Built Brochs (see BROCHS).
Had a king called Brude converted by Columba (see under IONA).
Had their capital at Inverness (see a future guide).
United with the Scots in 844.

PORK, EELS AND RABBITS

Strong prejudice exists in the Highlands against these. The prejudice against pork is often found in other parts of Scotland, but does not exist in England, Ireland, or Scandinavia. Its origin is rather mysterious, especially since there is no prejudice against bacon. These foods are also forbidden to Jews, but it seems unlikely that this is anything more than a coincidence.

Kippers at MALLAIG.

A MALLAIG Drifter.

Moidart (accent on first syllable) is accessible by road—a rough and narrow one—from Ardgour via Strontian. A lot of this neighbourhood is covered with thick woods of conifers and baronial 1860 mansion houses. Castle Tirrim (or Tioram) is a ruin on an island in Loch Moidart. At low tide when the sands of Loch Moidart are bare one can walk to the castle. It was a MacDonald stronghold; Donald the Cruel who lived here had a huge toad as a familiar; he tried to get rid of the toad but found that it was easier to raise the Devil than to lay him. The end of Castle Tirrim was a strange one: Allan Mór MacDonald of Moidart set out to join the old Pretender in 1715, but had a presentiment that he would not return, so he fired his own castle, went off, and was killed. There is a beautiful walk of about twelve miles along the coast from the shores of Loch Moidart to the railway at Lochailort. To do this journey by car one must travel not twelve miles but seventy-six. A direct road from Moidart to Loch Ailort would transform (for good or ill) the whole of this part of the coast.

Morar (accent on first syllable). There are a few houses on and near the main road. The River Morar used to pour down two waterfalls from the loch into the sea, but the upper and more remarkable one has been destroyed to provide electricity. At the mouth of the river are famous white coral sands. This country is all MacDonald and all Catholic. On an island in the loch was once a famous college for priests, and the Catholic church here has some eighteenth-century vestments and a little seventeenth-century chalice and paten. Morar is both beautiful and accessible, and is becoming popular (*see also* Loch Morar).

Morven. Can be reached by a bad road from Ardgour or by ship from Oban to Loch Aline. There is a small hamlet at the entrance to Loch Aline—with an ancient cross—and a huge house at the head of the loch, otherwise this

POTATOES

Now the staple food of the crofters. Potatoes displaced oats about the beginning of the nineteenth century. The terrible potato famine of 1845 caused almost as much distress in the Highlands as in Ireland. "Death or America" was the choice, often Hobson's choice.

RAILWAYS

Oban, Mallaig and Kyle of Lochalsh are railheads.

One reaches Oban from Euston (London), Buchanan St. (Glasgow) or Princes Street (Edinburgh). From Oban a branch line runs northwards to Ballachulish.

One reaches Mallaig from King's Cross (London), Queen St. (Glasgow) or Waverley (Edinburgh) pausing on the way at Fort William.

One reaches Kyle of Lochalsh from Inverness.

There is striking and beautiful scenery beside all these railway lines, especially the two first. Road travellers miss some of the best Highland landscapes.

RAIN

is not unknown in the West Highlands. Its abundance has, however, sometimes been exaggerated. The wettest place in Scotland comes in our area, but it is unlikely that the visitor will spend long there. It is the top of Ben Nevis, with a rainfall (and snowfall) of 151 inches per annum (Styhead Pass in Cumberland has 185 inches). The driest place in our area is Tiree with a rainfall of little more than 40 inches. Coll, Iona, the Small Isles, and the end of Trotternish, have less than 60; Oban has just over 60; the Coolins, Ben More of Mull and the upper part of all the big sea lochs on the mainland have from 90 to 130. May and June are almost always the driest months in the Highlands. The north and north-west winds are the driest winds; when a west wind veers it is a good sign, when it backs it is a bad one. The barometer can usually be relied on to foretell a westerly or south-westerly gale, but an easterly one sometimes seems to take it by surprise.

Religion

At one time there were at least seven distinct Presbyterian Churches in Scotland and practically every parish possessed at least three of them: the Established Church, the Free Church, and the United Presbyterian Church (the U.P.s). In 1900 the two last combined and formed the United Free Church of Scotland, but a few congregations (in Skye and Ross-shire mainly) remained obdurate and still maintain a separate existence, calling themselves the Free Church, but often called by others "the Wee Frees." In 1929 the Established Church and the United Free Church combined and are now the United Established Church of Scotland. The history of the Presbyterian Church in Scotland thus consists of a period of endless secessions on minute shades of opinion, usually on matters of church government rather than on matters of doctrine, followed by a period of general reunion.

The coast from Loch Eil to Loch Hourn—including Moidart, but not Morven or Ardnamurchan—is Roman Catholic, and so are the

big tract of country is a practically uninhabited sporting estate. In 1930, when St. Kilda was evacuated, most of its 35 inhabitants settled in Morven and were employed by the Forestry Commission. On the shore of the Sound of Mull are the ruins of Ardtornish Castle. They are unremarkable ruins, but this was the headquarters of the earlier Lords of the Isles and Scott's poem has made the name famous. Five miles from Loch Aline pier is Fiunary where the manse has held a succession of Macleods. Norman MacLeod senior (Tormoid) wrote one of the most famous of all Gaelic songs " Farewell to Fiunary." His son (also Norman MacLeod) published *A Highlznd Parish* (1867), an interesting book about this district.

Small Isles. The Catholic cathedral, by Sir Giles Gilbert Scott, stands on the sea-front at Oban.

The Episcopal Church of Scotland is the equivalent of the Church of England, though it is a quite separate organization. The coast from Oban to Fort William is mainly "Episcopalian." The unfinished Episcopal cathedral of Argyll and the Isles is at Oban.

UIG, SKYE.

MULL

Mull is volcanic. It is "the most complicated igneous centre as yet accorded detailed examination anywhere in the world according to the Geological Survey. The end of the Ross of Mull is knobbly pink granite, Ben More and its neighbours are also granite but dome-shaped, the rest is terraced hills of dark basalt. Huge cliffs on the southern shore. Most of the hills very grassy. The Ross of Mull has a relatively low rainfall, but Ben More is perhaps the cloudiest hill in the Highlands. Gaelic is much spoken. " Ane grate rough ile, noch the les it is fertile and fruitful." Various small clans. MacQuarries, MacFadyens, and MacGillivrays were ousted from their possessions by the MacLeans. MacLeans in turn were conquered by Campbells after a horrible six years' war in the reign of James VII. The MacLeans, however, were by no

Castle Duart, MULL.

TOBERMORY, MULL

MULL

means subdued; they were "out" under their chiefs in 1689, 1715, and 1745. They were (and are) Protestants despite their devotion to the Stuarts.

"The MacLeans were Remarkable among the Highlanders for a Lively, Handsome, Forward People, though not so tall as the Camerons or Stuarts, but they were to a very great Degree Extravagant, Proud and Inconsiderate" (or reckless). *The Highlands in 1750*.

Between 1841 and 1871, 4,171 families left Mull. Many of these emigrants set out for America but never reached it; cholera broke out on the ships and the passengers died in hundreds. *The Beautiful Isle of Mull*, by Thomas Hannen is interesting.

Ardmeanach. This is the promontory between Loch Scridain and Loch na Keal. On the shore is the huge MacKinnon's Cave which can only be entered on foot at low tide.

Bunessan (accent on "ess"). A pleasant little village where cargo steamers call. Holborn Viaduct and the Albert Memorial were both built from quarries near here, but few buildings are now made of pink granite.

Calgary. Emigrants from this now deserted bay named Calgary (Alberta) after their home on Mull.

Carsaig. Cliffs 800 ft. high; some show basalt columns and wave-worn arches. Sapphires have been found here. Carsaig is a remote village, even for Mull.

Duart. The castle of the chief of the clan MacLean. "A strengthy place bigged on ane craig at the sea syde." Rebuilt—very well—by Sir Fitzroy MacLean of Duart, 25th chief, who died in 1936 at the age of 101.

Loch Buie. The home of the MacLaines of Loch Buie, who refused to accept MacLean of Duart as head of the clan and assert their independence by spelling their name differently. One of them—Hugh, with the Little Head—fought a battle with his father and was killed. He now rides to foretell a death in the family. His little head is due to his having lost half of it in his

energetic parricidal attempt. The fine old 18th-century house of Loch Buie stands near the ruins of the castle it superseded.

Salen. Has a steamer pier. There is an annual show held at Salen which is the chief event of the year for most Mull people. Telford's road to Kinloch is exciting, it curves about on the brink of precipices. The footpath to Kinloch goes beside the charming little Loch Bà and over the shoulder of Ben More. Near Salen is Pennygown, where the ruined burial ground has some old carved stones.

Tobermory. The only town in Mull—about 800 inhabitants—was built in 1788 for the herring fishery, but the herring went and the town declined. The situation is rather like that of Oban on a small scale. There are pleasant wooded walks to the lighthouse and to some waterfalls in the grounds of Aros house. At the bottom of the harbour is the famous wreck of the Spanish Ship *Florida* (or *Florencia*). She came into Tobermory for water and a refit after the rout of the Armada and was well received by MacLean of Duart, who employed the Spaniards to ravage Ardnamurchan for him. Later he quarrelled with them and managed

somehow to blow up 700 of them on board their ship. Various stories exist, some more romantic than others. There were said to have been huge sums in gold on board, but persistent attempts at salvage have recovered, as far as is known, only a beautiful bronze cannon and a lot of odds and ends. The latest attempt at salvage, using modern methods, is in the hands of the Royal Navy.

Peat cutting.

TOBERMORY.

BLAVEN, from SGURR NAN GILLEAN, SKY

A Victorian lithograph view of OBAN before it was developed.

Oban is a tourist town of some 5,000 inhabitants. It has a deep, safe harbour used by trawlers, steamers to the islands, and yachts. Mr. Seton Gordon says: "Oban is the town with the finest view, not only in Scotland but, I should say, in the British Isles." For some tastes, however, Oban is rather shut in; the island of Kerrera, which makes the harbour such a good one, also cuts off any view of the open sea.

Steamships and the tourists have made the town of Oban. Sir Walter Scott's "Lord of the Isles" was published in 1814 and had an immediate effect on the tourist trade; the Iona and Staffa tour became established; it was done partly by four-oared boats and partly by fishing smacks of 8 tons or less and took, as a rule, four days. But it was the steamers, beginning about 1852, that really brought Oban prosperity, which was once more increased in 1880 when the railway to Glasgow was opened. Oban to-day has little of architectural interest, but the wooded hill of Dunollie gives the

McCaig's Tower, OBAN.

Argyll Hotel, OBAN.

47

town a certain distinction and the bay is charming. Dunollie Castle is a ruin. It was built by the Mac-Dougalls and, rather remarkably, still belongs to them. Wordsworth visited the castle and wrote a sonnet on a captive eagle he saw there. Two years later he returned. The eagle had gone but he saw a picture of it done with coloured pebbles and he wrote a sonnet about that. The traveller to-day can go and see the mosaic eagle and write a sonnet about it if he likes. At the mansion house behind Dunollie Castle lives the present head of the clan MacDougall. One great treasure is kept in the house: the brooch of Lorne which was torn from the shoulder of King Robert Bruce in a fight near Tyndrum.

Oban has two strange wrecks on the hilltops behind the town. One is an unfinished hydro; the other is a grandiose structure begun in 1900 by a wealthy Oban banker named McCaig but left unfinished after his death. The completed building was to have had a roof and to have been adorned with statues of the builder and his family.

At Ganavan sands, 2 miles from Oban, are the only bathing boxes in the whole of the West Highlands.

The Argyllshire Gathering takes place at Oban in the second week of September and lasts two days. The pipe competitions are usually good.

Onich. A pleasant village on the high road, its back to the hill and its front to the loch. View down Loch Linnhe to Morven and Mull.

Pabbay. "It excells in Pasturage, the Cows in it afford near double the Milk that they yield in Skie. In the Dog-Days there's a big Fly in this Isle, which infests the Cows, makes them run up and down, and discomposes them exceedingly." *Martin.*

The name means "Priest's Island." There is one farm, and a great many fossils of the upper lias.

Raasay. A long narrow island belonging to the Department of

RIGHTS OF WAY

Scottish Rights of Way Society (Secretary, G. D. Cheyne, 32 Rutland Square, Edinburgh) is at present busy signposting hill tracks in the West Highlands.

SALMON

10th February to 1st November.

𝔖𝔥𝔦𝔢𝔩𝔦𝔫𝔤 (*or* 𝔖𝔥𝔢𝔞𝔩𝔦𝔫𝔤)

a hut occupied in the summer when the cattle were driven to the upland pastures. There are no shielings in the Highlands now, but one comes on ruins of them in the most improbable places.

𝔖𝔢𝔞 𝔖𝔢𝔯𝔭𝔢𝔫𝔱

Lieut.-Commander Gould, the chief advocate for the sea serpent, records two appearances of marine monsters off Skye, in 1872 and 1893. The various eye-witnesses' accounts are remarkably convincing. There is also another appearance recorded off Coll in 1808 when a sea creature of some kind put a whole fishing fleet to flight.

The 1872 monster was seen in the Sound of Sleat by the Rev. John MacRae and the Rev. David Twopeny, Vicar of Stockbury, Kent. "It gave the impression of a creature crooking up its back to sun itself." The account is long and circumstantial and the parsons watched the beast for the best part of a couple of days. Mr. Twopeny says, very sensibly: "It should be noticed that the inhabitants of that western coast are quite familiar with the appearances of whales, seals, and porpoises, and, when they see them, they recognize them at once." This is sometimes forgotten by town folk.

The 1893 monster was seen in Loch Alsh by Dr. Farquhar Matheson, who practised in Soho Square, London, and his wife. He says: "I saw clearly that it was a large sea-monster—of the saurian type I should

Brochel Castle, RAASAY.

48

RUM on a bad day.

Agriculture for Scotland which has planted many trees. The climate is mild and eucalyptus trees and fuchsias flourish. Raasay House was new when Johnson and Boswell stayed there in 1773. It is now a hotel. There is iron ore on Raasay and the wrecked buildings near the steamer pier belonged to the company that used to work it. Raasay anciently belonged to a rather dim clan called MacSwan, but they were ousted by MacLeods who arrived from the Outer Isles and for 500 years these MacLeods held their lands without gaining or losing a single acre. Unlike the Mac-Leods of Skye, those of Raasay were friendly with the Mac-Donalds, indeed they had a curious sort of blood brother-hood with them. Brochel Castle, in the north-west of the island, was the ancient stronghold of the MacLeods of Raasay. The little flat-topped hill in the middle of Raasay is a landmark for miles. It is called Dun Caan.

Rona *or* South Rona. "This little Isle is the most unequal rocky piece of Ground to be seen anywhere; there's but very few Acres fit for digging, the whole is covered with long Heath and some mixture of Grass; it is reckoned very fruitful in Pastur-age: most of the rocks consist of the *Hectic* stone and a con-siderable part of 'em is of a Red Colour." *Martin.*

Rum, as George Blake says, "bears the Highland burden of the deer." It was "cleared" of its 400 inhabitants in 1826. It is a sport-ing estate and tourists are not allowed. Some of the hills are made of Gabbro like the Coolins on Skye.

Scarba. "It rises, from the east and south-east, gradually into hills and valleys towards the top of it, of which hills and valleys some of them very gramineous and are computed good for nourishing lanigerous cattle. The top of the mountain is very rugged and is almost useless, owing to the number of water ponds, and also to its producing no grass, owing to the conglaciousness of

think. It was brown in colour, shining, and with a sort of ruffle at the junction of the head and neck. It moved its head from side to side and I saw the reflection of the light from its wet skin. I saw no body, only a ripple of water where the line of the body should be. I should judge, however, that there must have been a large base of body to support such a neck. It was not a sea serpent, but a much larger and more substantial beast."

Both accounts read convincingly but they hardly seem to be des-criptions of the same kind of creature.

Second Sight

Dr. Johnson was very interested in this subject. He says: "The *Second Sight* is an impression made either by the mind on the eye, or by the eye on the mind, by which things distant or future are perceived, and seen as if they were present. A man on a journey far from home falls from his horse; another who is perhaps at work about the house, sees him bleeding on the ground, commonly with a landscape of the place where the accident befalls him. Another seer, driving home his cattle, or wandering in idleness, or musing in the sunshine, is suddenly surprised by the appearance of a bridal ceremony, or funeral procession, and counts the mourners or attendants, of whom, if he knows them, he relates the names, if he knows them not, he can describe the dresses. Things distant are seen at the instant when they happen. Of things future I know not that there is any rule for determining the time between the sight and the event.

"This receptive faculty, for power it cannot be called, is neither voluntary nor constant. The appearances have no dependence upon choice: they cannot be summoned, detained, or recalled. The impression is sudden, and the effect often painful.

"By pretension to second sight, no profit was ever sought or gained. It is an involuntary affliction, in which neither hope nor fear is known to have any part. Those who profess to feel it do not boast of it as a privilege, nor are they considered by others as advantageously dis-tinguished. They have no temptation to feign; and their hearers have no motive to encourage the imposture.

"The foresight of the seers is not always prescience: they are impressed with images, of which the event only shows them the meaning. They tell what they have seen to others, who are at that time not more knowing than themselves, but may become at last very adequate witnesses, by comparing the narrative with its verification."

Dr. Johnson concludes by saying what many others must have said: "I never could advance my curiosity to conviction; but came away at last only willing to believe."

SHARKS

Basking sharks are sometimes met with in the summer. They have a habit of loitering about near the surface of the water and, although not man-eaters, they are sometimes 20 ft. long, or more, and can swamp a small boat with ease. Fortunately they are usually very lazy while basking. Leave them alone.

TEMPERATURE

"Sub-tropical" plants are grown in many gardens on the West coast. This is made possible by the absence of winter frosts. The average January temperature of Skye is 41°F., about the same as Dorset. On the hilltops things are different. The summit of Ben Nevis, for instance, is usually 15 degrees colder than Fort William below it.

RUM *from* ARISAIG.

Painting by Stephen Bone.

the air in general. The west side is generally inaccessible with rocks and precipices, insurmountable by wild goats in general, excepting birds of prey, of which there are a great many that dwell among the stupendous cliffs, which are very dangerous to the quadrupeds called lambs, owing to their carnivorous nature (I mean eagles)." Archibald Sinclair, schoolmaster at Kilbrandon, quoted by P. H. Gillies in *Nether Lorn*.

Seil was a slate-quarrying island, but there is no work going on now (*see* Easdale). Clachan Bridge by Telford spans Seil Sound and joins the island to the mainland, it is one high arch of stone, and has been called "the only bridge across the Atlantic." Seil Sound is a curious salt-water river with a reversible flow.

Quarrymen's cottages, SEIL.

51

Shiant Isles. Precipitous islands half way between Skye and Harris. Now uninhabited. The islands belong to Mr. Compton MacKenzie and were once—and may still be—the home of the famous Blue Men of the Minch: mermen of a bloodthirsty nature who caught hold of ships and pulled them under. Mr. Donald MacKenzie in *Scottish Folk-Lore and Folk-Life* has a remarkable theory about these Blue Men and who they really were.

Skerryvore. A lighthouse built in 1844 by the uncle and the father of Robert Louis Stevenson, who describes the rock as "a pleasant assemblage of shelves, and pools, and creeks, about which a child might play for a whole summer day without weariness." In the winter it is different; the force of the breakers has been measured and during winter storms has been found to be nearly 3 tons to the square foot.

CLACHAN bridge connecting the island of SEIL with the mainland.

SKYE

Skye is a large island, more than 70 miles by road from end to end. Its population is about 10,000. The one town is Portree, with 1,600 inhabitants. The landscape is almost entirely mountainous, but the mountains, although all volcanic, belong to several very different types:

1. The Black Coolins (or simply The Coolins or Cuillins, "Cuchullins" is definitely wrong) including Blaven, are spiky masses of an astonishingly harsh dark rock called gabbro. Hardly a blade of grass grows on them. They are quite unlike any other hills in Britain and most visitors to Skye come for the purpose of climbing these jagged peaks, or, at least, of sitting at the bottom and looking at them.

BROADFORD, SKYE.

SKYE

BRACADALE and the COOLINS, SKYE.

2. The Red Hills, including Lord MacDonald's Forest, are pink granite and buried to their ears in screes. They are almost all neatly conical, like the sand in the bottom of an hour-glass.

3. The Hills of Trotternish, culminating in the Storr Rock, are a long ridge—heathery slopes on the west, huge precipices on the east. This imposing escarpment is made of basalt spread over the softer jurassic rocks. This dark basalt extends over all northern Skye, forming the flat-topped MacLeods Tables and some colossal sea cliffs. These basalt hills, like those in Mull and Morven, are terraced and very grassy.

4. The end of Sleat is made of that extremely ancient bedrock on which Scotland is founded: the Lewisian Gneiss. "Ovally swollen up from granitic dough," it is lumpy, heathery country with many little lochs in the hollows.

5. East of the road from Broadford to Isle Ornsay the hills are like the hills of the mainland and made of the same material, Torridonian sandstone.

Much of the centre of Skye, even where it is not mountainous, is just a heathery wilderness, but crofting townships are strung along most of the roads and hidden away in various remote places. Skye is very treeless except on the Sound of Sleat and near Dunvegan.

The Norsemen gave Skye many of its place names and many of its inhabitants must be Norse in origin. MacLeod, for instance, is Norse. When the Norsemen went, three clans divided Skye. MacDonalds held the two opposite ends, Trotternish and Sleat; MacKinnons held Strath; and the MacLeods held all the northwest. The MacDonalds of Sleat boasted that "in the house of MacDonald the Slates are always the top," called themselves "Of the Isles," and claimed headship of the huge and heterogeneous clan. MacDonalds and MacLeods were constantly at feud—the two chief episodes being a hideous massacre of MacDonalds on the Isle of Eigg and an equally hideous massacre of MacLeods at Trumpan on Skye. MacKinnons were relatively peaceful people. Dr. Johnson found their chiefs' house the merriest house in the Highlands.

The Skye chiefs fought for the Stuarts on every possible occasion except the last. They fought with their clansmen for Charles II,

53

SKYE

James VII, and James VIII, but when the '45 came the chiefs had been persuaded to the other side. Not the clansmen. MacDonald tried to raise the clan for George: the clan stayed at home. MacLeod raised a thousand men, but it was Charles Edward they went to fight for, in spite of their chief. After the tragedy of Culloden, Charles Edward fled to the Outer Isles but it was considered safer that he should double back to the mainland. The romantic story of how he travelled to Skye disguised as Flora MacDonald's maidservant, how he crossed Skye tramping the hills and hiding in caves, and how at last he reached the mainland pursued as closely as ever, is well known.

In the nineteenth century the history of Skye is the usual melancholy one of poverty, famine, evictions, and emigration. In 1882 the people felt their wrongs to be such that they resisted a huge force of police sent to make some arrests near Portree. There was a fight: "The Battle of the Braes." No one was killed but twelve policemen were hurt and the prisoners were refused a trial by jury. A gunboat called—not altogether inappropriately — the *Jackal*, was sent to Portree. But the grievances were still there and in the autumn the landlord and the crofters were in conflict again. The landlord asked for two companies of soldiers: mercifully he didn't get them. The County Council appealed for police reinforcements from elsewhere, but public opinion was now overwhelmingly on the side of the crofters, events of this kind had been happening in other parts of the Highlands, and a commotion arose which ended by producing the Royal Commission of 1883. This gave wide publicity to the incredibly tyrannous powers of the Highland landlords and produced subsequent legislation (*see* account in "The Former Days," by Norman Maclean).

There have been serious efforts to establish new crofts on Skye, and in some parts—Bracadale for instance—the crofting population

has actually increased, but the Skye population as a whole is dwindling. The arrival of tourists in large numbers has meant that many remote crofts now take lodgers in the summer. Here and there one comes on houses thatched with rushes, but there are no real "black houses" left on Skye today—houses, that is to say, without chimneys or ceilings. Since the end of the war many prefabricated wooden houses have been imported from Sweden; they are excellent in many ways but have a very alien look. Agile black-faced sleep roam most of the Skye hills; there is little attempt to preserve game nowadays. Skye is Gaelic speaking and Presbyterian. It is one of the strongholds of the "Wee-Frees," very strict and Sabbatarian people. Skye ferries and buses do not run on Sundays.

Armadale (*see* Sleat).

Bracadale. Three miles south of the village is Dun Taimh—a broch with a fine view and a memorial of Victoria's Jubilee in the middle of it. Loch Bracadale is an immensely complicated shape; at the western end of it are some isolated rocks called MacLeod's Maidens and some impressive caves that must be explored by boat. A striking view of the ins and outs of Loch Bracadale and the numerous crofts of this neighbourhood can be had from the township of Roag at the north-western end. Near Roag is Orbost house, a fine early nineteenth century house, pedimented and urned, looking south to the mountains of Rum. The rough road which leads from Bracadale direct to Portree across very empty moorland passes near Allt Mor, a striking ravine.

Broadford. Crofts surround the bay. The Red Hills rise behind them. At the foot of the Red Hills is the ruined house of Coirechat-achan, where the MacKinnons entertained Johnson and Boswell. A road leads off from Broadford along Strath Suardal, formerly cultivated from end to end, to Torran and Elgol. (*See under* these names.) In Strath Suardal

is the ruined church and the graveyard of Kilchrist (Cill Chriosd) where many Mac-Kinnons are buried.

The Coolins. In the bowels of a long-vanished volcano lava cooled under pressure and turned into a hard, dark rock called gabbro. The volcano has gone, worn away by the weather, except for its hard core which still remains with an almost Dolomitic outline and a surface like coarse emery paper. Glaciers have ground the lower slopes smooth and left boulders lying about, but the tops are jagged and splintered peaks, and are not to be climbed without a good deal of care and attention. For serious rock-climbers the Scottish Mountaineering Club have published guide books and maps which are very unlikely ever to be bettered. This guide book can only bow politely and hand you over to them, you will be well looked after. If you are less ambitious it would be advisable to be content with climbing Blaven from Torran or Sgùrr nan Gillean from Sligachan. Both have noble views. Anything else should be undertaken with caution, for mist can suddenly make an easy walk into something very formidable indeed. The Coolins should not be underestimated.

The semi-circle of the Coolins can be approached from Sligachan, Elgol, or Glen Brittle. From Sligachan the nearest hill, Sgùrr nan Gillean, is about 4 miles away over a wet moor; it is easiest climbed on the south-east side from the top of Glen Sligachan, but even this is not too easy. From Elgol one has a wet walk of about 7 miles to Coruisk in the centre of the semi-circle, or one can take a boat to the head of Loch Scavaig. Glen Brittle is nearest to the Coolins, particularly to Sgùrr Alasdair, the highest of them—but don't think it is only an afternoon stroll.

Apart from the Coolins proper stands another hill which has an obvious family resemblance: Blaven. Owing to its isolation it looks even more imposing than the others. It is easiest climbed

54

SKYE

SGÚRR NAN GILLEAN in the COOLINS.

from the shore of Loch Slapin, up the Allt Dunaiche to the sky-line and so to the top; the "saddle" of Blaven should only be tried when absolutely dead sober and with nails in one's shoes. It's simple enough, but there is a very nasty drop.

Duirinish. The westernmost peninsula of Skye. The cliffs of basalt are enormous at Dunvegan Head and Waterstein Head. The two flat-topped "MacLeod's Tables" (Healaval More and Healaval Beg) are the landmarks of this district. The crofting valley of Glendale was the scene of riots in 1884. Beyond Glendale is Milovaig with a pier and some boats—a remote and picturesque place. At Boreraig on Loch Dunvegan (there are other Boreraigs on Skye) the most famous of all pipe schools used to be instructed by the MacCrimmons, hereditary pipers to MacLeods of MacLeod.

Dunvegan. A few houses, an hotel, and the ancient castle of the MacLeods of MacLeod. It is supposed that Dunvegan castle has been continuously occupied by MacLeods since the thirteenth century, when Leod son of Olaf the Black, king of the Isle of Man, married the heiress of Macarailt (Haraldson) governor of Skye under the King of Norway. (It will be observed that we are in the period when the island and chiefs were Norse.) Who owned the castle before the days of Macarailt is unknown, but it seems almost certain that there was a stronghold here from very early times. The earliest part of the existing buildings, however, seems only to belong to the fourteenth century; this is the big square tower at the northern end of the rock. In the sixteenth century the eighth chief built the picturesque "Fairy Tower" at the opposite end of the rock, and in 1623 the famous Rory More, sixteenth chief, joined the two together. In 1810 the gatehouse was added—origin-

SKYE

Peaks of BLAVEN and LOCH SLAPIN, SKYE.

ally the only approach to the building was from the sea—and finally in the nineteenth century the whole building was tidied up and supplied with the pepper-pot turrets, then thought essential to a Scottish castle.

There are some good portraits in the castle and some remarkable relics, of which the most astonishing is the Fairy Flag (Bratach Sith) said to have been given to Iain, fourth chief, about the end of the fourteenth century by his wife. His wife was a fairy and her marriage to a mortal was only for a limited number of years. When she received a summons to rejoin her own people she gave her husband this silk flag, which could be waved three times in battle and each time would bring victory to the MacLeods. It has already been waved twice. The flag is now a tattered fragment of brownish silk with some very curious red darns. Archæologists, dubious about this story, have noticed that the silk is apparently of Near Eastern manufacture and have wondered whether it might not be some relic brought back from the crusades. Other relics include the Dunvegan cup, a wooden cup set with jewels and adorned with silver. There is a tradition that the cup belonged to Niall of the Black Knees, King of Ulster in the tenth century, but the ornamentation with gold and jewels is certainly more recent. There is also Rory More's drinking horn. It was an ordeal horn which had to be drained at one draught—it holds nearly half a gallon.

The Dunvegan Cup.

SKYE

An excellent guide book is on sale at the entrance. The castle is open to the public two days a week. The old graveyard in Dunvegan village contains many MacLeod tombs and a monument to " that inimitable poetess Mairi Naighean Alasdair Ruaidh, who died in the year 1675 aged 105 years."

Elgol on Loch Scavaig. An impressive view of the Coolins. A boat can be obtained to Loch Coruisk, or one can walk there along the shore via The Bad Step : a narrow ledge which needs a steady head.

Kyleakin. A rare thing in the Highlands : a picturesque village. Its curious situation makes it so rather than its architecture. Castle Moil or Maol, a mere fragment, was built by a Norse princess who used to stretch a chain across the sound and levy tolls. It subsequently passed into the hands of the MacKinnons. The hills of the Applecross Forest look very fine across the water. "*I went a-Shepherding,*" by Richard Perry, is about this neighbourhood.

Portree is not a particularly interesting town. The Royal Hotel was there in 1746, and in one of the rooms the hunted Charles Edward said good-bye to Flora MacDonald. The town is mostly built on a plateau, 60 ft. or so above the harbour. The annual Mod, the musical festival, is usually held in Portree; and the Skye Gathering is one of the best of such things; it is less Mayfair and more Highland than most. Portree has woollen mills where tweeds and blankets are made.

Quiraing (*see* Trotternish).

Sleat (pronounced Slate). Knobby Lewisian gneiss (see above). Even Doctor Johnson noticed the big trees of Armadale. Armadale Castle is 1815 Gothic. A rough road crosses the peninsula from the Sound of Sleat to the remote crofting townships of Tarskavaig and Tokavaig and the romantic ruin of Dunskaith Castle which, even for a Hebridean castle, is remarkable for the number of its legends — Ossianic, supernatural and merely bloodthirsty. Near Dunskaith is Ord, where Alexander

Crofters' houses, SKYE, as they used to be.

QUIRAING, SKYE.

Smith ("Summer in Skye") lived.

Sligachan. A lonely hotel, one of the best places for the exploration of the Coolins. Footpaths lead from Sligachan to Glen Brittle; via Drumhain to Coruisk; via Coire na Creiche to Coruisk across the spine of the Coolins; and via Camasunary to Elgol. At the north side of the entrance to

Loch Sligachan are the crofting townships where the "Battle of the Braes" was fought in 1882.

Staffin (*see* Trotternish.)

Talisker. The famous whisky is made at Carbost on Loch Harport (there are two Carbosts on Skye). Near here is Port nan Long, where a settlement of Harris crofters make tweed.

SKYE

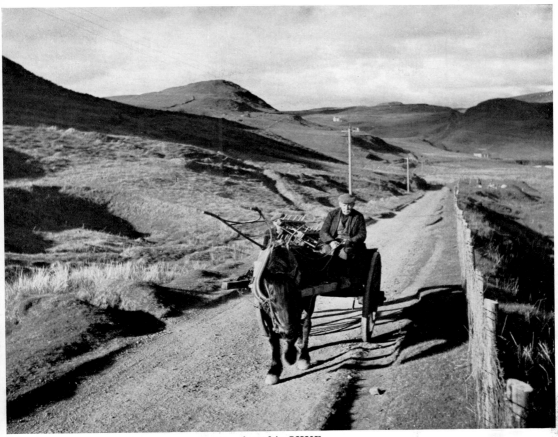

A road in SKYE.

Torran is a small crofting township with probably the finest view of the finest hill in Great Britain: Blaven across Loch Slapin.

Trotternish. The long backbone of Trotternish is a good walk for the energetic. The highest point is the Storr (2,360 ft.) with a remarkable view. Below it is the Old Man of Storr—a startling-looking pinnacle of black trap. It is 160 ft. high, about the same height as London's Nelson's Column. It leans alarmingly. On the shore at Rigg is a big arched boulder, Eaglais Breagach (The False Church) where the small but disgusting clan of MacQuithens once performed the Taghairm (*see* Devil). The road up the east coast of Trotternish from Portree to Staffin is narrow and very rough but exceedingly picturesque. It passes the striking waterfall of the river Lealt, where diatomite was once mined, and the picturesque neighbourhood of Loch Mealt, where there is a striking view of columnar cliffs. Beyond Staffin is the Quiraing, an extraordinary place of towers and spires of stone, only to be explored on foot.

The western shore of Trotternish is fertile country and many battles have been fought for its possession. At the northern end is Duntulm castle, built by the MacDonalds. Duntulm Farm belonged to the hereditary doctors of the Lords of the Isles—the chief always paid for the eldest son's medical training. A few miles south of this is Kilmuir, where Flora MacDonald is buried with others of her clan. South again is Uig, the largest of many crofting townships, situated on a pleasant little bay. At Kingsburgh Flora MacDonald lived with her husband, MacDonald of Kingsburgh; Boswell and Johnson visited her there.

Vaternish (*or* Waternish). The promontory between Loch Dunvegan and Loch Snizort. Many crofts at Stein and Loch Bay. At Trumpan is a curious little green peninsula where one can see a few rough stones—the ruins of the church in which MacDonalds burnt MacLeods in 1590 or thereabouts.

The COOLINS from ARISAIG.

Sir Muirhead Bone.

61

The Small Isles: Rum, Figg, Canna and Muck.

Soay (south of Skye). To prevent confusion with the St. Kilda Soay this one is sometimes called Soay Brittle. There are ten or twelve crofts on the island, which is most easily reached from Elgol on Skye or by motor launch from Mallaig.

Staffa. Really very surprising indeed. Many caves to be explored, but Fingals Cave is the only one with walls made of columnar basalt. Some of the caves are said to penetrate the island, but this is doubtful. The island is now uninhabited, but there are ruins of a chapel and several families once lived here.

Strontian (pronounced *stron-tee-an*). Disused lead mines near the village. The mineral strontium was first isolated here.

Taynuilt. A pleasant village adjoining Bonawe. Cruachan (3,689 ft.) can be climbed from here. There is also a charming woodland road up Glen Nant and across moorlands to Taychreggan on Loch Awe where it stops.

Treshnish Isles. Now uninhabited and a great haunt of seabirds. Both Carnburg Mor and Carnburg Beag were fortified and garrisoned, first by MacDougalls, then by MacLean of Duart, and then by the Crown. The island of Lunga has the remains of crofts. The Dutchman's Cap (or Bac Mor), the oddest of them all, can only be approached in very calm weather, yet even here are the remains of buildings.

Tyree (or Tiree) has a certain number of visitors in the summer. It is green, treeless, and windswept with sandy beaches and many crofts. The rainfall is only about 40 in. compared with Glencoe's 120. It belonged formerly to the MacLeans of Duart but now belongs to the Duke of Argyll. There is a strange prehistoric dwelling at Kilkenneth on the west coast. Neither Tyree nor Coll has any sort of a harbour and landing is often impossible. "The Isle of Coll produces more Boys than

The pier at SOAY.

TINKERS

although nomadic are not gipsies. True gipsies are rare in the Highlands; their place is taken by the tinkers who hawk goods, do a little casual labour, play on the pipes, etc. They almost all have names like Stewart, Cameron and MacDonald, and they are the lineal descendants of some of the broken and landless clans or of the crofters driven from their homes by the "clearances" of the nineteenth century.

TROUT

1st March to 15th October.

Urisk

a supernatural creature particularly fond of waterfalls. He usually looks like a sort of satyr, "half human, half goat, with abnormally long hair, long teeth, and long claws." The urisk longs for human company and sometimes manages to make friends, but its well-meant efforts to scrape acquaintance with lonely travellers usually scare them out of their wits.

WATERFALLS

When it rains, visit a waterfall. A really good waterfall is worth a long expedition. It is also likely to become a thing of the past, for hydro-electricians frequently express horror at "water running to waste." However, before they get to work on them it is worth visiting among many others:

The Falls of CRUACHAN (among thick woods).

A fall at the top of GLENCOE beside the new road.

MACLEAN'S TOWEL (not far from the ARDGOUR ferry. A pleasant name).

Two falls in GLEN NEVIS (very good).

The Falls of MUCCOMIR near Gairlochy.

STAFFA.

Girls and the Isle of Tyree more Girls than Boys; as if Nature intended both these Isles for mutual Alliances, without being at the trouble of going to the adjacent Isles or Continent to be matched." *Martin.*

Ulva.

"O! I'm the chief of Ulva's Isle,
    And this Lord Ullin's daughter."
Campbell, who wrote this much-recited poem, lived for a while on Mull as tutor to a laird's son. The chiefs of Ulva's Isle were MacQuarries and Doctor Johnson was entertained by one of them at Ulva House. A later MacQuarrie from Ulva was Governor of New South Wales from 1809 to 1821, and the town of Sydney is largely his creation.

The RIVER SPEAN (not what it was before the Lochaber Power Scheme). The lower fall at MORAR (the upper fall, the more picturesque of the two, has now been destroyed).

The FALLS OF GLOMACH, $7\frac{1}{2}$ miles from Croe Bridge in Kintail. The FALLS OF THE LEALT in Trotternish, Skye.

WILD CAT

Not a tame pussy but a ferocious miniature tiger. A different species to the domestic cat and quite untamable. A certain number of wild cats exist precariously in the remoter mountains of Inverness-shire and Ross-shire; their numbers touched bottom about 1900, they have increased since then. They are large tabbies, but bigger and leggier than most domestic cats and they have a club-shaped tail with a black tip. They eat any flesh or fowl up to and including lambs.

YOUTH HOSTELS

Scottish Youth Hostels Association, 7 Bruntsfield Crescent, Edinburgh, 10.

Gaelic

The stranger in the Highlands, for the first time among Gaelic-speaking people, must feel that he is on alien soil, unless he bears in mind that, not such a very long time ago in the world's history, the Celtic language—of which Gaelic is the Scottish version—was the native language of the British Isles and, even now is the native language of several thousand people there.

Up to comparatively recent times it covered the whole of Scotland. Gaelic was spoken in Galloway as late as the reign of Mary, Queen of Scots, and in isolated instances survived into the middle of the eighteenth century, thus coming quite near to the lifetime of Robert Burns. To-day, although the language is still spoken by thousands of people, the actual area in which it is a native language is the Highlands and Islands.

I suppose the average Englishman, or lowlander, derives his ideas of the Highlands from the genius of Sir Walter Scott. And, though certain aspects of Highland life are vividly and unsurpassedly described by him, his conception of highland and lowland, never the twain meeting, of Celt and Saxon, is not true to fact. In the racial sense of the word the whole of Scotland is of the same Celtic stock. The division between highland and lowland is largely an artificial one, derived from historical circumstances. There is an underlying unity which should bind all Scots together, in whatever part of Scotland they live, whether highland or lowland. (The term "lowland" in any case, seems a little misleading when, on a first journey in Scotland you discover that the lowlands contain mountains nearly 3,000 ft. high, and lovely moorland country such as is found in Galloway.) The genius of Sir Walter Scott will always make his novels readable (though his Gaelic is terrible!), but actually a better picture of Highland life, and one showing a deeper insight into Highland ways of thought, will be found in the novels of Dr. Neil Munro, whose native language was Gaelic, and who habitually thought in that idiom.

This article is not intended to be a condensed grammar of Gaelic, nor is it meant to introduce the reader to the complex structure of the language, but to call his attention to the fact that the language exists, and forms an integral part of the life and manners of the Highlands. As the language has survived in these parts, so has its folk-lore, songs and customs—the heritage of an ancient people.

A study of the language, however, will well repay anyone who undertakes it. Knowing something of the language is of inestimable advantage to the stranger —an Open Sesame to much that would otherwise remain closed to him. There are several simple books by which a working knowledge of the language can be gained, though to master the language completely requires several years of patient study.

To the scholar the study is of surpassing interest.

It presents the almost unique opportunity of studying a language in all its changes over 1,000 years. Old Irish can still be studied, right up to the living Gaelic and Erse. German philologists were among the first to see the advantages of this, and much valuable work has been done in the past and is still being done by them. To the scholar it has also the attraction of an unexhausted field of study. So many fields of scholarship seem to have had the last word said in them, and one who wishes to pursue further studies in them has to hunt for a subject. (Hence the curious titles of many Ph.D. and B.Litt. theses.) In Celtic there are still great problems of philology to be solved, and many interesting manuscripts to be translated.

One of the advantages of an even comparatively slight knowledge of the language is that many place names become intelligible. (This is rather a contrast to England, where the names of many of the villages seem to defy all reason.) Thus Ballachulish is the town on the narrows. Ben More is the great mountain, etc. Though here the beginner should be warned that there is no study which contains greater pitfalls than that of place names; and that, while many names are obvious in their meaning, there is no greater happy hunting ground for the amateur and the crank than those whose meaning is not quite so obvious.

Coming fresh to the Highlands one of the pleasantest experiences is to hear the well spoken English of the average Highlander. He learns English at school as a second language, and speaks it with the dignity that is natural to his native language, adding something to its charm by his quaint use of word and phrase. His use of genders can be sometimes quite confusing; grandfathers, boats, railway engines, and many other things may all be called "she."

The future of the language seems at the present time to be rather dark, though there are strong movements in Scotland which may stem the tide of the steady decline of Gaelic. There are many explanations for this decline, but the most obvious one is the apparent inability of the language to adapt itself to modern industrial civilisation (though this is not necessarily to the credit of the said civilisation).

It is so essentially a part of another culture whose roots are set in different ideals and values (which some may have the temerity to think still worthy of consideration), that it is hard to see how it can flower in an alien soil.

For those who mean to make a study of Gaelic there is a whole world undreamed of, a literature of rare distinction from earliest times; poetry, music and folk-lore to occupy one for a lifetime. A language of subtlety and beauty that preserves for our civilisation a breath of that charm which comes from the childhood of the world.

JOHN CHAPPELL SPROTT.

THE IDEA
OF THE HOLY

THE IDEA
OF THE HOLY

An Inquiry into the non-rational factor
in the idea of the divine and its
relation to the rational

BY

RUDOLF OTTO

TRANSLATED BY

JOHN W. HARVEY

Professor of Philosophy in the
University of Leeds

SECOND EDITION

GEOFFREY CUMBERLEGE
OXFORD UNIVERSITY PRESS
LONDON   NEW YORK   TORONTO
1950

Oxford University Press, Amen House, London E.C.4

GLASGOW NEW YORK TORONTO MELBOURNE WELLINGTON
BOMBAY CALCUTTA MADRAS CAPE TOWN

Geoffrey Cumberlege, Publisher to the University

First Edition (ten impressions)   *1923*
Second Edition   *1950*

PRINTED IN GREAT BRITAIN

DEDICATED TO
THEODOR VON HÄRING

Das Schaudern ist der Menschheit bestes Teil.
Wie auch die Welt ihm das Gefühl verteuere,
Ergriffen fühlt er tief das Ungeheuere.

CONTENTS

TRANSLATOR'S PREFACE

TO THE SECOND EDITION

I

THE complete reprinting of this translation of Rudolf Otto's *Das Heilige* enables me to include in a revised preface a tribute prompted by personal friendship and gratitude to the author, whose death in 1937 deprived the world of western Christendom of one of its most notable and individual religious thinkers. At the same time I have taken the opportunity, in reviewing the fortunes of his book in its English version during the twenty-six years since the translation was first published, to attempt to meet one or two misunderstandings which seem rather tiresomely persistent.

Rudolf Otto was born at Peine in Hanover in 1869, and his career at first was the normal one of a University teacher of theology; he passed through the University to become *Privat-Dozent* in Systematic Theology at Göttingen in 1897, and seven years later attained the status of *Ausserordentlicher Professor* in the same University, until in 1914 he was appointed to an official Chair at Breslau. In the meantime he had published his first book, translated in 1909 under the title *Religion and Naturalism*. It is a forcibly stated argument for the autonomy of the human spirit and the insufficiency of a naturalistic science to explain or comprehend spiritual experience. He had made himself thoroughly conversant with the scientific outlook of the nineteenth century and the tendencies in it, mechanism, neo-Darwinism, and the like, which were or might be inimical to religion. But there is nothing of special originality in the book. The significant year for the development of his own distinctive contribution to religious thinking was, I suspect, 1910, when he set out on a long journey to the East which was to take him round the world. Otto had already travelled in Europe: he knew England and France and Italy, and got on well with foreigners. But the long sojourn in the East in 1910–11 must have meant much more to him. He visited North Africa, Egypt and Palestine,

India, China, and Japan, returning in due time by way of the
United States. In this and in later visits to the Near East
and India (1925, 1927–8) he not only deepened an already
profound study of the great religions of the East but was able
to realize at first hand what in the religious experience which
they enshrine is specific and unique and what on the other
hand is common to all genuine religions, however diversely
expressed in sacred writings, ritual, or art. He brought to the
interpretation of the religious practices and beliefs of many
lands an imaginative sympathy that was receptive without
ceasing to be critical. One of the special interests in the last
ten years of his life was the establishment at Marburg of a
museum for the comparative study of religions, not as dead
curiosities but as living faiths.

From the time of this first Eastern journey Christianity
must have stood for Otto against a background not so much
of west-European science as of the great world-religions of
which he held it to be the culmination. In 1917 he was appointed to a Chair of Theology at Marburg-on-the-Lahn,
quaintest and most fascinating of German university towns,
and there he resided till his death. He had never married,
but lived with a widowed sister and her daughter, and the
household was a charmingly devoted one. And it was in this
year 1917 that *Das Heilige* appeared. It is no doubt Otto's
most central and important work. Those that followed it
were all within the framework of its ideas, some of them
being amplifications working out more fully points of the
argument, others manifesting further the interest in Indian
and other religions which is so unmistakable in the present work. Certainly *Das Heilige* appeared at an opportune
moment, and its success was immediate. It ran rapidly
through a number of editions and was translated into many
languages, including Japanese. What Otto had to say did
appear, in the phrase of George Fox, to 'speak to the condition' of many thoughtful people in that decade of disillusion
that followed the First World War. It is noteworthy that he
was one of the first German scholars to be invited after the
war to lecture in the United States. Widely read as his books
were, however, he never attempted to found a 'school', partly

because his influence cut across the denominational divisions, partly because he was much more a religious philosopher than a dogmatic theologian, but most of all because his whole bias of mind was towards emphasizing what religious men have in common rather than what divides them.

Marburg University has always had the name of a centre of conservative and nationalist sentiment, and, it may be added, this reputation may well be perpetuated since (in 1946) the remains of Hindenburg and of Frederick the Great were transferred for reinterment in the great Marburg church of St. Elizabeth. Otto, however, was international and liberal in grain. He had served for a few momentous years (1913–18) as a member of the Prussian Parliament, but his heart was not, I am sure, in politics. He concerned himself with the political questions of the Weimar Republic not with any personal zest but as a matter of civic duty. This led him to adhere to the pathetically small party of Democrats or Progressives rather than to Social Democracy, for which, I think, he never felt much sympathy. The advent to power of Hitler and the Nazis must have outraged his deepest political convictions. He had become Professor Emeritus in 1929, so he had no active part to play in any academic resistance to the Third Reich, but one might certainly have expected that he would have been whole-heartedly on the side of the Confessional Movement of resistance to the subtle Nazification of the Lutheran Church. In fact, however, he felt, at first at any rate, little sympathy for this movement of protest, and for a time had hopes that the 'German Christian' movement might live up to its name and effect a rejuvenation in the religious life of his country which he felt was sorely needed. That hope cannot have survived for long. The political and neo-pagan development in Germany had become to him more and more heartbreaking, and when death came to him in March of 1937 as the result of a tragic accident, the grievous loss to his friends may have been to himself a merciful release. He must have foreseen clearly the inevitable catastrophe that loomed ahead, and caught the sound of Niagara thundering beyond the upper rapids.

II

I well remember my own first meeting with Otto, some-time in the very early twenties. It was an impression so surprising as almost to be daunting. This, whatever he was, was almost the opposite of the German *Gelehrter* as one commonly found him, and far removed indeed from the traditional figure of caricature (if indeed the latter was ever typical of the German professor at all), bearded and be-spectacled, dreamy and pedantic. Otto's figure was tall and erect and suggested the soldier rather than the scholar, with his Kaiser moustaches and his tight, light, military-looking jacket fastened high at the neck. Nor was a diffident foreigner reassured by the touch of formality in his address, which later one came to recognize as merely the scrupulous respect he paid to the strict grammar of courtesy. But in a very short time the thin film of ice was effectively broken, and his, and his household's, unaffected friendliness had quite won his visitor's heart, aided by the dry humour that played about persons as well as things, shrewdly yet without malice, and was one of his most endearing qualities. There followed walks together in the lovely woodland country around Marburg, and talks upon every sort of topic, philosophical and political and educational and literary. I was soon deeply interested in *Das Heilige*, and it was an exciting privilege to hear the doctrines of this and other books expounded by their author. And if some lucky quotation or illustration appealed to him it evoked the most prompt and ungrudging recognition.

The first visit was followed by several others during the next few years. As his reputation spread farther afield his house became a place where visitors from foreign lands were more and more often to be found: now it would be a young American theologian, now a pastor from Sweden, now a scholar from India. To all he extended the same patient and cordial courtesy. But his health was wretched: he was a constant sufferer from asthma and racking headaches. Only when he was at his physically best could he enjoy his favour-ite walks in the forest across the valley, ending up, perhaps, with coffee at an *Aussichtsturm* restaurant. During the walk there would be moments when in the course of the conversation the soldierly figure would come to an unexpected stop, as though 'stung by the splendour of a sudden thought', and his expression would grow grave and tense. It was as though a commander had suddenly glimpsed a new possibility in tactics or strategy; only here the tactics were dialectical, not military, and the campaign that of the quest for religious truth.

But for his poor health Otto would, before he died, have delivered a course of Gifford Lectures, and his subject would have been the ethical basis of theism. Had he been able to do so, he would almost certainly have corrected certain misconceptions as to his teaching to which I shall refer later. But as it was, he was able in the years before the Hitler régime closed down upon Germany to pay an all-too-short visit to this country in 1927, and delivered some lectures at King's College, London, on Mysticism. The first began with a deprecating remark to the effect that for a foreigner to speak of Mysticism in England was to bring owls to Athens or, as we should say, coals to Newcastle. Otto sometimes spoke with a delightfully impish humour of the theological *naïveté* sometimes shown by our professional instructors in religion; but he had a profound respect for the British contribution to Christian thought and teaching in the lives of saints, mystics, and poets, as well as religious thinkers.[1] He was very fond of reading English books, light as well as serious, and I remember how keenly appreciative he was of two English classics to which I introduced him, the poems of Blake with their supernatural thrill and *Wuthering Heights* with its sombre torment of passion. In the latter he found, and surely rightly, a supreme example of 'the daemonic' in literature.

Rudolf Otto was not only a great scholar and interpreter of religions; he was also a great liberal (in the deepest sense that means one who loves and prizes freedom); a great

[1] The Dean of St. Paul's (Dr. W. R. Matthews) who presided at these lectures in London, and who after Otto's death paid the tribute of an address in his memory at Marburg, writes that Otto 'formed the opinion that England was still the most religious country in the world, and he attributed this very much to the influence of the *Book of Common Prayer*. He was very anxious to produce a Book of Common Prayer for the German people.'

well-wisher and understander of England; and, most of all, a
great and true Christian. Yet he was none the less German
through and through. And so when we are told that all
Germans are inherently and incorrigibly prepared to pros-
titute honest scholarship in the service of some ideology; that
they are congenitally incapable of understanding the meaning of liberty; that they can never comprehend, still less truly
appreciate, England or the English; and that beneath a
Christian veneer every German is a pagan in grain: then
those who have been fortunate enough to have the friendship
of such a man as Rudolf Otto are not likely to accept these
glib generalizations with any excessive credulity.

III

When the present translation of *Das Heilige* appeared
twenty-six years ago it received an appreciative and generous
welcome in many and diverse quarters, and the steady demand for the book ever since is the best evidence that Otto's
work has been recognized by readers of very different denominational affiliations as still meeting a real need in the
field of religious philosophy. But since the original book was
published thirty-two years ago the climate of thought has
noticeably changed, and were he alive to-day the author
would certainly have wished that his argument should be so
presented to a new generation of readers as to avert the distortion and wrong emphasis which interpreters, in many
respects friendly, have often tended to give to it. I wish
briefly to notice one or two of these distortions, which have
been regrettably persistent.

In my original preface to the translation I mentioned
three respects in which I thought that Otto's book should be
a valuable corrective to contemporary tendencies. I noted
that it had appeared at a time when a much more vigorous
and a much more sympathetic study of religion had been
gaining ground, but that this very sympathy might tend to
misleading conclusions if on the one hand it led to missing
what was common to religious experience in different climes
and different times, in its normal and more representative
forms, through an undue attention to the more interesting

and exceptional case: and also if it 'became so far absorbed in the subjective states of mind manifested in religious experience' as to ignore or half-ignore the objective significance of them. The first danger was illustrated by some of those whose special study of Mysticism led them into a one-sided account of religion as a whole: 'they do not see the wood for the trees; or, more accurately, they fail to get a true view of the common nature of the trees in their structure and growth through an undue preoccupation with certain particularly striking examples'. The second danger might be symbolized by the attempt to give a true description of the tree without regarding the sources that sustain its life or the fact that it is growing upward towards the light. And then there was a third danger—that of so far humanizing our conception of the divine and the sacred that a severance is brought about between the divine as immanent and as transcendent, between God as rational and moral Person and God (if indeed in this view the name could also be applied here) as Majesty and Mystery and superhuman Otherness.

In the intervening period I think it would be true to say that whereas the first of these errors has not proved very serious—and Otto's book has, no doubt, done much to avert it—the other two still persist tenaciously. And by what I can only judge to be a perverse misunderstanding Otto's book is sometimes taken to favour and commend aberrations which he recognized to be mischievous and against which he expressly warns the reader. At the same time I think it must be admitted that, if only by his choice of terms for the expression of his own doctrine, Otto did in some degree abet this misunderstanding.

Taking first the aberration towards an unduly subjectivist interpretation of religion, it is a complete error to suppose that Otto is mainly concerned to plead for, or indeed primarily interested in, the vindication of the emotional aspect of religion. There have, indeed, been periods and milieus when such a plea was necessary, when religious emotion was regarded as a sign of fanaticism or 'enthusiasm'. But in England at any rate, when theology in the nineteenth century passed from a rationalizing to an ethical atmosphere, a good

b

deal had been done to restore the balance by admitting
emotion into its account at least in the sense of that 'moral
passion' of which Mr. Shaw has written or that 'enthusiasm
of Humanity' which Seeley found at the heart of the Gospel
of Jesus. Matthew Arnold and J. A. Froude are both typical
nineteenth-century voices in their uncompromising acceptance of the paramount importance of ethics in religion, but
the former in his famous definition could speak of religion
as 'morality touched with emotion', while the latter could
write of religion as 'the consecration of the whole man, of
his heart, his conduct, his knowledge and his mind', where
'heart' is clearly to be understood as a man's capacity for
emotion. And even if there was need seventy years ago to
urge that *feeling* in this sense has an essential place in religion,
there was far less need when Otto wrote thirty years ago, and
there is perhaps still less to-day, when the claims of man's
emotional and affective life are being so effectively asserted.

When, therefore, Otto uses so frequently expressions like
'the numinous *feeling*' (*das numinose Gefühl*) he must not be
taken to be merely repeating the claim of 'affect', subjective
emotion, to a place in any genuine religious experience. But
it would certainly have been better had he always preferred
the alternative phrase 'the feeling *of* the numinous'. The
word 'numinous' has been widely received as a happy contribution to the theological vocabulary, as standing for that
aspect of deity which transcends or eludes comprehension in
rational or ethical terms. But it is Otto's purpose to emphasize
that this is an objective reality, not merely a subjective feeling
in the mind; and he uses the word *feeling* in this connexion
not as equivalent to emotion but as a form of awareness that
is neither that of ordinary perceiving nor of ordinary conceiving. Certainly he is very much concerned to describe as
precisely and identify as unmistakably as possible, by hint,
illustration, and analogy, the nature of the subjective feelings
which characterize this awareness; but that is because it is
only through them that we can come to an apprehension of
their object.

The ambiguity attaching both to the English *feeling* and
the German *Gefühl* should not therefore mislead us. We do

after all speak of feeling the beauty of a landscape or feeling the presence of a friend, and our 'feeling' in these cases is not merely an emotion engendered or stimulated in the mind but also a recognition of something in the objective situation awaiting discovery and acknowledgement. It is analogously to such uses that Otto speaks of the 'feeling of the numinous' or (less aptly) the 'numinous feeling'. As one of his compatriots, the philosopher Rickert, put it: 'by the "numinous" is indicated not the psychological process but its object, the Holy'.

So far then, from stressing the place of the subjective state of mind in the religious experience, Otto's emphasis is always upon the objective reference, and upon subjective feelings only as the indispensable clues to this.

IV

The other misunderstanding may be dealt with the more briefly inasmuch as Otto wrote a special foreword for the second impression of this translation (see p. xxi), in which he took the opportunity to make his own standpoint unmistakably clear in a few lines. He *was*, as has been said, really opposing the subjectivist trend in religious thought: he was definitely *not* opposing the attempt of reverent minds to interpret the divine nature in rational and ethical categories. He was urging, on the contrary, that the rational and moral is an essential part of the content of what we mean by holy or sacred: only it is not the whole of it. There is an overplus of meaning which is non-rational, but neither in the sense of being *counter to* reason on the one hand nor *above* reason on the other. The two elements, the rational and the non-rational, have to be regarded (in his favourite simile) as the warp and the woof of the complete fabric, neither of which can dispense with the other.

This is, indeed, made so clear in the text of the book that one can hardly but suspect carelessness or obtuseness in those critics who have persisted in mistaking Otto's meaning. Here again, however, his choice of words perhaps did something to further the error. I have sought to mitigate the unfortunate suggestion of the key-word 'irrational' in the original

by rendering it 'non-rational', but the implication of a re-
pudiation of reason has not perhaps been entirely dissipated.
Another phrase is perhaps more misleading: 'das ganz An-
dere', the 'wholly other', the quite different. This is a phrase
that has occupied a more prominent place in some of the
writings of the neo-Calvinist school of theology associated
with the names of Barth and Brunner, and there it is used
in a way which to many does seem to break completely and
utterly with the religious claim that the divine Spirit may
enter into communion with the spirit of man. But Otto, who
was, I think, the first to make this religious use of the phrase,
is not open to the criticism of exaggerating and isolating the
divine transcendent Otherness. God for him is not, so to
speak, *wholly* 'wholly other'. That aspect of Deity, the mysterious overplus surpassing all that can be clearly understood
and appraised, is asserted emphatically against any excessive
anthropocentric tendency to scale down the Sacred and Holy
to the measure of our human reason. But it is an aspect
only, one note that has to be preserved in (to use another
favourite phrase) the 'harmony of contrasts'. And here it
seems to me that his teaching is more wholesome (and may I
add, more Christian?) than that of those who would stress
exclusively the one note or the other and so oversimplify the
harmony into a monotone. Every such one-sided interpretation can only, and must inevitably, provoke its opposite
extreme, and indeed we have seen this happen. Had Otto
ever been able to deliver the course of Gifford Lectures upon
the religious basis of ethics which he was planning, I think he
would have been able to give a final statement of his position
in this matter which would have done much to bring together
points of view, each based on authentic experience, which
cannot fall irreconcilably apart without disaster to religion.

    And yet, for those who read it fairly, all had been said
clearly enough in this book. And for that matter the double
note was sounded long ago by Pascal in his *Pensées*, in a passage which it is strange that Otto did not quote, but which
admirably expresses his own attitude: 'If one subjects everything to reason our religion will lose its mystery and its
supernatural character. If one offends the principles of

reason our religion will be absurd and ridiculous. . . . There are two equally dangerous extremes, to shut reason out and to let nothing else in.'

Since Otto wrote this book thirty-two years ago, and even since he died twelve years ago, new improvements have appeared to deflect and complicate, as well as to enrich, the current of religious and philosophical thought. In the one case we need only think of such distinguished names as Barth and Brunner, Niebuhr, Berdiaiev, and Maritain; in the latter, of the defiant challenge of Logical Positivism and the still very esoteric enigma of 'Existentialism'. Those who knew Rudolf Otto well, who profited themselves from his eager intellectual sympathy, his penetration of mind, and his deep reverence for truth, can have no doubt that had he lived he would have learned much from such movements, positively or negatively, and that he would himself have had an important contribution to make to the discussions which have arisen about them. Nor is there any doubt that he would have been among those who are striving to re-knit the torn fabric of Christendom by re-establishing intercourse among the Christian churches, and a truer understanding by them all of the significance of the Christian Faith. But I believe that this book, born during the stress and travail of the First World War, has a vital message in it that will outlive the tragic aftermath of the second. His principal legacy to his own generation, it remains very relevant to the religious perplexities of to-day.

JOHN W. HARVEY

October 1949

NOTE ON APPENDIXES, &c.

THIS translation was originally made from the ninth German edition of *Das Heilige*, from which Appendixes I–IX are taken. One of the German appendixes, on 'Myth and Religion in Wundt's *Völkerpsychologie*', and some other matter which seemed of less interest to English than to German readers, were omitted with the concurrence of the author; on the other hand Appendix X, 'The Expression of the Numinous in English', was added by the translator.

Appendix XI was added to this translation in its fifth impression (1928), together with additions to the text at the close of Chapters VIII and IX, from the fourteenth German edition.

The appendixes of the later editions of *Das Heilige*, as had been pointed out in a Translator's Note to the third English impression, had by this time grown so numerous that they were published with additional matter in a separate volume entitled *Aufsätze das Numinose betreffend* (*Essays concerning the Numinous*). One of these, 'The Resurrection as a Spiritual Experience', was added to this translation as Appendix XII. Some other supplementary matter was published as *Religious Essays, A Supplement to the Idea of the Holy*, by R. Otto, translated by Brian Lunn (Oxford University Press, 1931); and to give the reader some indication in what directions *The Idea of the Holy* has been thus supplemented, the Table of Contents of *Religious Essays* has been included here as Appendix XIII.

FOREWORD BY THE AUTHOR

TO THE FIRST ENGLISH EDITION

IN this book I have ventured to write of that which may be called 'non-rational' or 'supra-rational' in the depths of the divine nature. I do not thereby want to promote in any way the tendency of our time towards an extravagant and fantastic 'irrationalism', but rather to join issue with it in its morbid form. The 'irrational' is to-day a favourite theme of all who are too lazy to think or too ready to evade the arduous duty of clarifying their ideas and grounding their convictions on a basis of coherent thought. This book, recognizing the profound import of the non-rational for metaphysic, makes a serious attempt to analyse all the more exactly the *feeling* which remains where the *concept* fails, and to introduce a terminology which is not any the more loose or indeterminate for having necessarily to make use of *symbols*.

Before I ventured upon this field of inquiry I spent many years of study upon the *rational* aspect of that supreme Reality we call 'God', and the results of my work are contained in my books, *Naturalistische und religiöse Weltansicht* (Eng. Tr. 'Naturalism and Religion', London, 1907), and *Die Kant-Friesische Religions-Philosophie*. And I feel that no one ought to concern himself with the 'Numen ineffabile' who has not already devoted assiduous and serious study to the 'Ratio aeterna'.

This foreword gives me a very welcome opportunity to express my thanks to the translator for his care, his remarkable delicacy of interpretation, and for the valuable supplementary pages he has added. An English critic has said that 'the translation is much better than the original'; and to this I have nothing to object.

RUDOLF OTTO

MARBURG
1923

CHAPTER I

THE RATIONAL AND THE NON-RATIONAL

IT is essential to every theistic conception of God, and most of all to the Christian, that it designates and precisely characterizes deity by the attributes spirit, reason, purpose, good will, supreme power, unity, selfhood. The nature of God is thus thought of by analogy with our human nature of reason and personality; only, whereas in ourselves we are aware of this as qualified by restriction and limitation, as applied to God the attributes we use are 'completed', i.e. thought as absolute and unqualified. Now all these attributes constitute clear and definite *concepts*: they can be grasped by the intellect; they can be analysed by thought; they even admit of definition. An object that can thus be thought conceptually may be termed *rational*. The nature of deity described in the attributes above mentioned is, then, a rational nature; and a religion which recognizes and maintains such a view of God is in so far a 'rational' religion. Only on such terms is *belief* possible in contrast to mere *feeling*. And of Christianity at least it is false that 'feeling is all, the name but sound and smoke';[1]—where 'name' stands for conception or thought. Rather we count this the very mark and criterion of a religion's high rank and superior value—that it should have no lack of *conceptions* about God; that it should admit knowledge—the knowledge that comes by faith—of the transcendent in terms of conceptual thought, whether those already mentioned or others which continue and develop them. Christianity not only possesses such conceptions but possesses them in unique clarity and abundance, and this is, though not the sole or even the chief, yet a very real sign of its superiority over religions of other forms and at other levels. This must be asserted at the outset and with the most positive emphasis.

But, when this is granted, we have to be on our guard against an error which would lead to a wrong and one-sided interpretation of religion. This is the view that the essence

---

[1] Goethe, *Faust*.

of deity can be given completely and exhaustively in such 'rational' attributions as have been referred to above and in others like them. It is not an unnatural misconception. We are prompted to it by the traditional language of edification, with its characteristic phraseology and ideas; by the learned treatment of religious themes in sermon and theological instruction; and further even by our Holy Scriptures themselves. In all these cases the 'rational' element occupies the foreground, and often nothing else seems to be present at all. But this is after all to be expected. All language, in so far as it consists of words, purports to convey ideas or concepts;— that is what language means;—and the more clearly and unequivocally it does so, the better the language. And hence expositions of religious truth in language inevitably tend to stress the 'rational' attributes of God.

But though the above mistake is thus a natural one enough, it is none the less seriously misleading. For so far are these 'rational' attributes from exhausting the idea of deity, that they in fact imply a non-rational or supra-rational Subject of which they are predicates. They are 'essential' (and not merely 'accidental') attributes of that subject, but they are also, it is important to notice, *synthetic* essential attributes. That is to say, we have to predicate them of a subject which they qualify, but which in its deeper essence is not, nor indeed can be, comprehended in them; which rather requires comprehension of a quite different kind. Yet, though it eludes the conceptual way of understanding, it must be in some way or other within our grasp, else absolutely nothing could be asserted of it. And even mysticism, in speaking of it as τὸ ἄρρητον, the ineffable, does not really mean to imply that absolutely nothing can be asserted of the object of the religious consciousness; otherwise, mysticism could exist only in unbroken silence, whereas what has generally been a characteristic of the mystics is their copious eloquence.

Here for the first time we come up against the contrast between rationalism and profounder religion, and with this contrast and its signs we shall be repeatedly concerned in what follows. We have here in fact the first and most distinctive mark of rationalism, with which all the rest are bound up.

It is not that which is commonly asserted, that rationalism is the denial, and its opposite the affirmation, of the miraculous. That is manifestly a wrong or at least a very superficial distinction. For the traditional theory of the miraculous as the occasional breach in the causal nexus in nature by a Being who himself instituted and must therefore be master of it—this theory is itself as massively 'rational' as it is possible to be. Rationalists have often enough acquiesced in the possibility of the miraculous in this sense; they have even themselves contributed to frame a theory of it;—whereas anti-rationalists have been often indifferent to the whole controversy about miracles. The difference between rationalism and its opposite is to be found elsewhere. It resolves itself rather into a peculiar difference of *quality* in the mental attitude and emotional content of the religious life itself. All depends upon this: in our idea of God is the non-rational overborne, even perhaps wholly excluded, by the rational? Or conversely, does the non-rational itself preponderate over the rational? Looking at the matter thus, we see that the common dictum, that orthodoxy itself has been the mother of rationalism, is in some measure well founded. It is not simply that orthodoxy was preoccupied with doctrine and the framing of dogma, for these have been no less a concern of the wildest mystics. It is rather that orthodoxy found in the construction of dogma and doctrine no way to do justice to the non-rational aspect of its subject. So far from keeping the non-rational element in religion alive in the heart of the religious experience, orthodox Christianity manifestly failed to recognize its value, and by this failure gave to the idea of God a one-sidedly intellectualistic and rationalistic interpretation.

This bias to rationalization still prevails, not only in theology but in the science of comparative religion in general, and from top to bottom of it. The modern students of mythology, and those who pursue research into the religion of 'primitive man' and attempt to reconstruct the 'bases' or 'sources' of religion, are all victims to it. Men do not, of course, in these cases employ those lofty 'rational' concepts which we took as our point of departure; but they tend to take these concepts and their gradual 'evolution' as setting the main problem of their inquiry, and fashion ideas and notions of lower value, which they regard as paving the way for them. It is always in terms of concepts and ideas that the subject is pursued, 'natural' ones, moreover, such as have a place in the general sphere of man's ideational life, and are not specifically 'religious'. And then with a resolution and cunning which one can hardly help admiring, men shut their eyes to that which is quite unique in the religious experience, even in its most primitive manifestations. But it is rather a matter for astonishment than for admiration! For if there be any single domain of human experience that presents us with something unmistakably specific and unique, peculiar to itself, assuredly it is that of the religious life. In truth the enemy has often a keener vision in this matter than either the champion of religion or the neutral and professedly impartial theorist. For the adversaries on their side know very well that the entire 'pother about mysticism' has nothing to do with 'reason' and 'rationality'.

And so it is salutary that we should be incited to notice that religion is not exclusively contained and exhaustively comprised in any series of 'rational' assertions; and it is well worth while to attempt to bring the relation of the different 'moments' of religion to one another clearly before the mind, so that its nature may become more manifest.

This attempt we are now to make with respect to the quite distinctive category of the holy or sacred.

CHAPTER II

'NUMEN' AND THE 'NUMINOUS'

'HOLINESS'—'the holy'—is a category of interpretation and valuation peculiar to the sphere of religion. It is, indeed, applied by transference to another sphere—that of ethics—but it is not itself derived from this. While it is complex, it contains a quite specific element or 'moment', which sets it apart from 'the rational' in the meaning we gave to that word above, and which remains inexpressible—an ἄρρητον or *ineffabile*—in the sense that it completely eludes apprehension in terms of concepts. The same thing is true (to take a quite different region of experience) of the category of the beautiful.

Now these statements would be untrue from the outset if 'the holy' were merely what is meant by the word, not only in common parlance, but in philosophical, and generally even in theological usage. The fact is we have come to use the words 'holy', 'sacred' (*heilig*) in an entirely derivative sense, quite different from that which they originally bore. We generally take 'holy' as meaning 'completely good'; it is the absolute moral attribute, denoting the consummation of moral goodness. In this sense Kant calls the will which remains unwaveringly obedient to the moral law from the motive of duty a 'holy' will; here clearly we have simply the *perfectly moral* will. In the same way we may speak of the holiness or sanctity of duty or law, meaning merely that they are imperative upon conduct and universally obligatory.

But this common usage of the term is inaccurate. It is true that all this moral significance is contained in the word 'holy', but it includes in addition—as even we cannot but feel—a clear overplus of meaning, and this it is now our task to isolate. Nor is this merely a later or acquired meaning; rather, 'holy', or at least the equivalent words in Latin and Greek, in Semitic and other ancient languages, denoted first and foremost *only* this overplus: if the ethical element was present at all, at any rate it was not original and never constituted the whole meaning of the word. Any one who uses it to-day does undoubtedly always feel 'the morally good' to be implied in 'holy'; and accordingly in our inquiry into that element which is separate and peculiar to the idea of the holy it will be useful, at least for the temporary purpose of the investigation, to invent a special term to stand for 'the holy' *minus* its moral factor or 'moment', and, as we can now add, minus its 'rational' aspect altogether.

It will be our endeavour to suggest this unnamed Something to the reader as far as we may, so that he may himself feel it. There is no religion in which it does not live as the real innermost core, and without it no religion would be worthy of the name. It is pre-eminently a living force in the Semitic religions, and of these again in none has it such vigour as in that of the Bible. Here, too, it has a name of its own, viz. the Hebrew *qādôsh*, to which the Greek ἅγιος and the Latin *sanctus*, and, more accurately still, *sacer*, are the corresponding terms. It is not, of course, disputed that these terms in all three languages connote, as part of their meaning, *good, absolute goodness*, when, that is, the notion has ripened and reached the highest stage in its development. And we then use the word 'holy' to translate them. But this 'holy' then represents the gradual shaping and filling in with ethical meaning, or what we shall call the 'schematization', of what was a unique original feeling-response, which can be in itself ethically neutral and claims consideration in its own right. And when this moment or element first emerges and begins its long development, all those expressions (*qādôsh*, ἅγιος, *sacer*, &c.) mean beyond all question something quite other than 'the good'. This is universally agreed by contemporary criticism, which rightly explains the rendering of *qādôsh* by 'good' as a mistranslation and unwarranted 'rationalization' or 'moralization' of the term.

Accordingly, it is worth while, as we have said, to find a word to stand for this element in isolation, this 'extra' in the meaning of 'holy' above and beyond the meaning of goodness. By means of a special term we shall the better be able, first, to keep the meaning clearly apart and distinct, and second, to apprehend and classify connectedly whatever subordinate forms or stages of development it may show. For this purpose I adopt a word coined from the Latin *numen*.

Omen has given us 'ominous', and there is no reason why from *numen* we should not similarly form a word 'numinous'. I shall speak, then, of a unique 'numinous' category of value and of a definitely 'numinous' state of mind, which is always found wherever the category is applied. This mental state is perfectly *sui generis* and irreducible to any other; and therefore, like every absolutely primary and elementary datum, while it admits of being discussed, it cannot be strictly defined. There is only one way to help another to an understanding of it. He must be guided and led on by consideration and discussion of the matter through the ways of his own mind, until he reach the point at which 'the numinous' in him perforce begins to stir, to start into life and into consciousness. We can co-operate in this process by bringing before his notice all that can be found in other regions of the mind, already known and familiar, to resemble, or again to afford some special contrast to, the particular experience we wish to elucidate. Then we must add: 'This *X* of ours is not precisely *this* experience, but akin to this one and the opposite of that other. Cannot you now realize for yourself what it is?' In other words our *X* cannot, strictly speaking, be taught, it can only be evoked, awakened in the mind; as everything that comes 'of the spirit' must be awakened.

CHAPTER III

THE ELEMENTS IN THE 'NUMINOUS'

Creature-Feeling

THE reader is invited to direct his mind to a moment of deeply-felt religious experience, as little as possible qualified by other forms of consciousness. Whoever cannot do this, whoever knows no such moments in his experience, is requested to read no farther; for it is not easy to discuss questions of religious psychology with one who can recollect the emotions of his adolescence, the discomforts of indigestion, or, say, social feelings, but cannot recall any intrinsically religious feelings. We do not blame such an one, when he tries for himself to advance as far as he can with the help of such principles of explanation as he knows, interpreting 'aesthetics' in terms of sensuous pleasure, and 'religion' as a function of the gregarious instinct and social standards, or as something more primitive still. But the artist, who for his part has an intimate personal knowledge of the distinctive element in the aesthetic experience, will decline his theories with thanks, and the religious man will reject them even more uncompromisingly.

Next, in the probing and analysis of such states of the soul as that of solemn worship, it will be well if regard be paid to what is unique in them rather than to what they have in common with other similar states. To be *rapt* in worship is one thing; to be morally *uplifted* by the contemplation of a good deed is another; and it is not to their common features, but to those elements of emotional content peculiar to the first that we would have attention directed as precisely as possible. As Christians we undoubtedly here first meet with feelings familiar enough in a weaker form in other departments of experience, such as feelings of gratitude, trust, love, reliance, humble submission, and dedication. But this does not by any means exhaust the content of religious worship. Not in any of these have we got the special features of the quite unique and incomparable experience of solemn worship. In what does this consist?

Schleiermacher has the credit of isolating a very important element in such an experience. This is the 'feeling of dependence'. But this important discovery of Schleiermacher is open to criticism in more than one respect.

In the first place, the feeling or emotion which he really has in mind in this phrase is in its specific quality not a 'feeling of dependence' in the 'natural' sense of the word. As such, other domains of life and other regions of experience than the religious occasion the feeling, as a sense of personal insufficiency and impotence, a consciousness of being determined by circumstances and environment. The feeling of which Schleiermacher wrote has an undeniable analogy with these states of mind: they serve as an indication to it, and its nature may be elucidated by them, so that, by following the direction in which they point, the feeling itself may be spontaneously felt. But the feeling is at the same time also qualitatively different from such analogous states of mind. Schleiermacher himself, in a way, recognizes this by distinguishing the feeling of pious or religious dependence from all other feelings of dependence. His mistake is in making the distinction merely that between 'absolute' and 'relative' dependence, and therefore a difference of degree and not of intrinsic quality. What he overlooks is that, in giving the feeling the name 'feeling of dependence' at all, we are really employing what is no more than a very close analogy. Anyone who compares and contrasts the two states of mind introspectively will find out, I think, what I mean. It cannot be expressed by means of anything else, just because it is so primary and elementary a datum in our psychical life, and therefore only definable through itself. It may perhaps help him if I cite a well-known example, in which the precise 'moment' or element of religious feeling of which we are speaking is most actively present. When Abraham ventures to plead with God for the men of Sodom, he says (Gen. xviii. 27): 'Behold now, I have taken upon me to speak unto the Lord, which am but dust and ashes.' There you have a self-confessed 'feeling of dependence', which is yet at the same time far more than, and something other than, *merely* a feeling of dependence. Desiring to give it a name of its own, I propose to call it 'creature-consciousness' or creature-feeling. It is the emotion of a creature, submerged and overwhelmed by its own nothingness in contrast to that which is supreme above all creatures.

It is easily seen that, once again, this phrase, whatever it is, is not a *conceptual* explanation of the matter. All that this new term, 'creature-feeling', can express, is the note of submergence into nothingness before an overpowering, absolute might of some kind; whereas everything turns upon the *character* of this overpowering might, a character which cannot be expressed verbally, and can only be suggested indirectly through the tone and content of a man's feeling-response to it. And this response must be directly experienced in oneself to be understood.

We have now to note a second defect in the formulation of Schleiermacher's principle. The religious category discovered by him, by whose means he professes to determine the real content of the religious emotion, is merely a category of *self*-valuation, in the sense of self-depreciation. According to him the religious emotion would be directly and primarily a sort of *self*-consciousness, a feeling concerning oneself in a special, determined relation, viz. one's dependence. Thus, according to Schleiermacher, I can only come upon the very fact of God as the result of an inference, that is, by reasoning to a cause beyond myself to account for my 'feeling of dependence'. But this is entirely opposed to the psychological facts of the case. Rather, the 'creature-feeling' is itself a first subjective concomitant and effect of another feeling-element, which casts it like a shadow, but which in itself indubitably has immediate and primary reference to an object outside the self.[1]

---

[1] This is so manifestly borne out by experience that it must be about the first thing to force itself upon the notice of psychologists analysing the facts of religion. There is a certain naïveté in the following passage from William James's *Varieties of Religious Experience* (p. 58), where, alluding to the origin of the Grecian representations of the gods, he says: 'As regards the origin of the Greek gods, we need not at present seek an opinion. But the whole array of our instances leads to a conclusion something like this: It is as if there were in the human consciousness *a sense of reality, a feeling of objective presence*, a *perception* of what we may call "*something there*", more deep and more general than any of the special and particular "senses" by which the current psychology supposes existent realities to be originally revealed.' (The italics are James's own.) James

Now this object is just what we have already spoken of as 'the numinous'. For the 'creature-feeling' and the sense of dependence to arise in the mind the 'numen' must be experienced as present, a *numen praesens*, as is in the case of Abraham. There must be felt a something 'numinous', something bearing the character of a 'numen', to which the mind turns spontaneously; or (which is the same thing in other words) these feelings can only arise in the mind as accompanying emotions when the category of 'the numinous' is called into play.

The numinous is thus felt as objective and outside the self. We have now to inquire more closely into its nature and the modes of its manifestation.

is debarred by his empiricist and pragmatist standpoint from coming to a recognition of faculties of knowledge and potentialities of thought in the spirit itself, and he is therefore obliged to have recourse to somewhat singular and mysterious hypotheses to explain this fact. But he grasps the fact itself clearly enough and is sufficient of a realist not to explain it away. But this 'feeling of reality', the feeling of a 'numinous' *object* objectively given, must be posited as a primary immediate datum of consciousness, and the 'feeling of dependence' is then a consequence, following very closely upon it, viz. a depreciation of the *subject* in his own eyes. The latter presupposes the former.

CHAPTER IV

'MYSTERIUM TREMENDUM'

The Analysis of 'Tremendum'

WE said above that the nature of the numinous can only be suggested by means of the special way in which it is reflected in the mind in terms of feeling. 'Its nature is such that it grips or stirs the human mind with this and that determinate affective state.' We have now to attempt to give a further indication of these determinate states. We must once again endeavour, by adducing feelings akin to them for the purpose of analogy or contrast, and by the use of metaphor and symbolic expressions, to make the states of mind we are investigating ring out, as it were, of themselves.

Let us consider the deepest and most fundamental element in all strong and sincerely felt religious emotion. Faith unto salvation, trust, love—all these are there. But over and above these is an element which may also on occasion, quite apart from them, profoundly affect us and occupy the mind with a wellnigh bewildering strength. Let us follow it up with every effort of sympathy and imaginative intuition wherever it is to be found, in the lives of those around us, in sudden, strong ebullitions of personal piety and the frames of mind such ebullitions evince, in the fixed and ordered solemnities of rites and liturgies, and again in the atmosphere that clings to old religious monuments and buildings, to temples and to churches. If we do so we shall find we are dealing with something for which there is only one appropriate expression, *'mysterium tremendum'*. The feeling of it may at times come sweeping like a gentle tide, pervading the mind with a tranquil mood of deepest worship. It may pass over into a more set and lasting attitude of the soul, continuing, as it were, thrillingly vibrant and resonant, until at last it dies away and the soul resumes its 'profane', non-religious mood of everyday experience. It may burst in sudden eruption up from the depths of the soul with spasms and convulsions, or lead to the strangest excitements, to intoxicated frenzy, to transport, and to ecstasy. It has its wild and demonic forms and can sink to an almost grisly horror and shuddering. It has its crude, barbaric antecedents and early manifestations, and again it may be developed into something beautiful and pure and glorious. It may become the hushed, trembling, and speech-less humility of the creature in the presence of—whom or what? In the presence of that which is a *mystery* inexpressible and above all creatures.

It is again evident at once that here too our attempted formulation by means of a concept is once more a merely negative one. Conceptually *mysterium* denotes merely that which is hidden and esoteric, that which is beyond conception or understanding, extraordinary and unfamiliar. The term does not define the object more positively in its qualitative character. But though what is enunciated in the word is negative, what is meant is something absolutely and intensely positive. This pure positive we can experience in feelings, feelings which our discussion can help to make clear to us, in so far as it arouses them actually in our hearts.

1. *The Element of Awefulness*

To get light upon the positive '*quale*' of the object of these feelings, we must analyse more closely our phrase *mysterium tremendum*, and we will begin first with the adjective.

Tremor is in itself merely the perfectly familiar and 'natu-ral' emotion of *fear*. But here the term is taken, aptly enough but still only by analogy, to denote a quite specific kind of emotional response, wholly distinct from that of being afraid, though it so far resembles it that the analogy of fear may be used to throw light upon its nature. There are in some languages special expressions which denote, either exclusively or in the first instance, this 'fear' that is more than fear proper. The Hebrew *hiqdīsh* (hallow) is an example. To 'keep a thing holy in the heart' means to mark it off by a feeling of peculiar dread, not to be mistaken for any ordinary dread, that is, to appraise it by the category of the numinous. But the Old Testament throughout is rich in parallel expres-sions for this feeling. Specially noticeable is the '*ēmāh* of Yahweh ('fear of God'), which Yahweh can pour forth, dispatching almost like a daemon, and which seizes upon a man with paralysing effect. It is closely related to the δεῖμα πανικόν of the Greeks. Compare Exod. xxiii. 27: 'I will send my fear before thee, and will destroy all the people to whom thou shalt come . . .'; also Job ix. 34; xiii. 21 ('let not his fear terrify me'; 'let not thy dread make me afraid'). Here we have a terror fraught with an inward shuddering such as not even the most menacing and overpowering created thing can instil. It has something spectral in it.

In the Greek language we have a corresponding term in σεβαστός. The early Christians could clearly feel that the title σεβαστός (*augustus*) was one that could not fittingly be given to any creature, not even to the emperor. They felt that to call a man σεβαστός was to give a human being a name proper only to the *numen*, to rank him by the category proper only to the *numen*, and that it therefore amounted to a kind of idolatry. Of modern languages English has the words 'awe', 'aweful', which in their deeper and most special sense approximate closely to our meaning. The phrase, 'he stood aghast', is also suggestive in this connexion. On the other hand, German has no native-grown expression of its own for the higher and riper form of the emotion we are considering, unless it be in a word like *erschauern*, which does suggest it fairly well. It is far otherwise with its cruder and more debased phases, where such terms as *grausen* and *Schauer*, and the more popular and telling *gruseln* ('grue'), *gräsen*, and *grässlich* ('grisly'), very clearly designate the numinous element. In my examination of Wundt's Animism I suggested the term *Scheu* (dread); but the special 'numinous' quality (making it 'awe' rather than 'dread' in the ordinary sense) would then, of course, have to be denoted by inverted commas. 'Religious dread' (or 'awe') would perhaps be a better designation. Its antecedent stage is 'daemonic dread' (cf. the horror of Pan) with its queer perversion, a sort of abortive offshoot, the 'dread of ghosts'. It first begins to stir in the feeling of 'something uncanny', 'eerie', or 'weird'. It is this feeling which, emerging in the mind of primeval man, forms the starting-point for the entire religious development in history. 'Daemons' and 'gods' alike spring from this root, and all the products of 'mythological apperception' or 'fantasy' are nothing but different modes in which it has been objectified. And all ostensible explanations of the origin of religion in terms of animism or magic or folk-psychology are doomed from the outset to wander astray and miss the real goal of their inquiry, unless they recognize this fact of our nature—primary, unique, underivable from anything else—to be the basic factor and the basic impulse underlying the entire process of religious evolution.[1]

Not only is the saying of Luther, that the natural man cannot fear God perfectly, correct from the standpoint of psychology, but we ought to go farther and add that the natural man is quite unable even to 'shudder' (*grauen*) or feel horror in the real sense of the word. For 'shuddering' is something more than 'natural', ordinary fear. It implies that the mysterious is already beginning to loom before the mind, to touch the feelings. It implies the first application of a category of valuation which has no place in the everyday natural world of ordinary experience, and is only possible to a being in whom has been awakened a mental predisposition, unique in kind and different in a definite way from any 'natural' faculty. And this newly-revealed capacity, even in the crude and violent manifestations which are all it at first evinces, bears witness to a completely new function of experience and standard of valuation, only belonging to the spirit of man.

Before going on to consider the elements which unfold as the '*tremendum*' develops, let us give a little further consideration to the first crude, primitive forms in which this 'numinous dread' or *awe* shows itself. It is the mark which really characterizes the so-called 'religion of primitive man', and

---

[1] Cf. my papers in *Theologische Rundschau*, 1910, vol. i, on 'Myth and Religion in Wundt's *Völkerpsychologie*', and in *Deutsche Literaturzeitung*, 1910, No. 38. I find in more recent investigations, especially those of R. R. Marett and N. Söderblom, a very welcome confirmation of the positions I there maintained. It is true that neither of them calls attention quite as precisely as, in this matter, psychologists need to do, to the unique character of the religious 'awe' and its qualitative distinction from all 'natural' feelings. But Marett more particularly comes within a hair's breadth of what I take to be the truth about the matter. Cf. his *Threshold of Religion* (London, 1909), and N. Söderblom's *Das Werden des Gottesglaubens* (Leipzig, 1915), also my review of the latter in *Theol. Literaturzeitung*, Jan. 1915.

there it appears as 'daemonic dread'. This crudely naïve and primordial emotional disturbance, and the fantastic images to which it gives rise, are later overborne and ousted by more highly developed forms of the numinous emotion, with all its mysteriously impelling power. But even when this has long attained its higher and purer mode of expression it is possible for the primitive types of excitation that were formerly a part of it to break out in the soul in all their original naïveté and so to be experienced afresh. That this is so is shown by the potent attraction again and again exercised by the element of horror and 'shudder' in ghost stories, even among persons of high all-round education. It is a remarkable fact that the physical reaction to which this unique 'dread' of the uncanny gives rise is also unique, and is not found in the case of any 'natural' fear or terror. We say: 'my blood ran icy cold', and 'my flesh crept'. The 'cold blood' feeling may be a symptom of ordinary, natural fear, but there is something non-natural or supernatural about the symptom of 'creeping flesh'. And any one who is capable of more precise intro-spection must recognize that the distinction between such a 'dread' and natural fear is not simply one of degree and intensity. The awe or 'dread' *may* indeed be so overwhelm-ingly great that it seems to penetrate to the very marrow, making the man's hair bristle and his limbs quake. But it may also steal upon him almost unobserved as the gentlest of agitations, a mere fleeting shadow passing across his mood. It has therefore nothing to do with intensity, and no natural fear passes over into it merely by being intensified. I may be beyond all measure afraid and terrified without there being even a trace of the feeling of uncanniness in my emotion.

We should see the facts more clearly if psychology in general would make a more decisive endeavour to examine and classify the feelings and emotions according to their qualita-tive differences. But the far too rough division of elementary feelings in general into pleasures and pains is still an obstacle to this. In point of fact 'pleasures' no more than other feelings are differentiated merely by degrees of intensity: they show very definite and specific differences. It makes a specific difference to the condition of mind whether the soul is merely in a state of pleasure, or joy, or aesthetic rapture, or moral exaltation, or finally in the religious bliss that may come in worship. Such states certainly show resemblances one to another, and on that account can legitimately be brought under a common class-concept ('pleasure'), which serves to cut them off from other psychical functions, generically different. But this class-concept, so far from turning the various subordinate species into merely different degrees of the same thing, can do nothing at all to throw light upon the essence of each several state of mind which it includes.

Though the numinous emotion in its completest development shows a world of difference from the mere 'daemonic dread', yet not even at the highest level does it belie its pedigree or kindred. Even when the worship of 'daemons' has long since reached the higher level of worship of 'gods', these gods still retain as *numina* something of the 'ghost' in the impress they make on the feelings of the worshipper, viz. the peculiar quality of the 'uncanny' and 'aweful', which survives with the quality of exaltedness and sublimity or is symbolized by means of it. And this element, softened though it is, does not disappear even on the highest level of all, where the worship of God is at its purest. Its disappearance would be indeed an essential loss. The 'shudder' reappears in a form ennobled beyond measure where the soul, held speechless, trembles inwardly to the farthest fibre of its being. It invades the mind mightily in Christian worship with the words: 'Holy, holy, holy'; it breaks forth from the hymn of Tersteegen:

> God Himself is present:
> Heart, be stilled before Him:
> Prostrate inwardly adore Him.

The 'shudder' has here lost its crazy and bewildering note, but not the ineffable something that holds the mind. It has become a mystical awe, and sets free as its accompaniment, reflected in self-consciousness, that 'creature-feeling' that has already been described as the feeling of personal nothingness and submergence before the awe-inspiring object directly experienced.

C

The referring of this feeling numinous *tremor* to its object in the numen brings into relief a property of the latter which plays an important part in our Holy Scriptures, and which has been the occasion of many difficulties, both to commentators and to theologians, from its puzzling and baffling nature. This is the ὀργή (*orgé*), the Wrath of Yahweh, which recurs in the New Testament as ὀργὴ θεοῦ, and which is clearly analogous to the idea occurring in many religions of a mysterious *ira deorum*. To pass through the Indian Pantheon of gods is to find deities who seem to be made up altogether out of such an ὀργή; and even the higher Indian gods of grace and pardon have frequently, beside their merciful, their 'wrath' form. But as regards the 'wrath of Yahweh', the strange features about it have for long been a matter for constant remark. In the first place, it is patent from many passages of the Old Testament that this 'wrath' has no concern whatever with moral qualities. There is something very baffling in the way in which it 'is kindled' and manifested. It is, as has been well said, 'like a hidden force of nature', like stored-up electricity, discharging itself upon anyone who comes too near. It is 'incalculable' and 'arbitrary'. Anyone who is accustomed to think of deity only by its rational attributes must see in this 'wrath' mere caprice and wilful passion. But such a view would have been emphatically rejected by the religious men of the Old Covenant, for to them the Wrath of God, so far from being a diminution of His Godhead, appears as a natural expression of it, an element of 'holiness' itself, and a quite indispensable one. And in this they are entirely right. This ὀργή is nothing but the *tremendum* itself, apprehended and expressed by the aid of a naïve analogy from the domain of natural experience, in this case from the ordinary passional life of men. But naïve as it may be, the analogy is most disconcertingly apt and striking; so much so that it will always retain its value and for us no less than for the men of old be an inevitable way of expressing one element in the religious emotion. It cannot be doubted that, despite the protest of Schleiermacher and Ritschl, Christianity also has something to teach of the 'wrath of God'.

It will be again at once apparent that in the use of this

word we are not concerned with a genuine intellectual 'concept', but only with a sort of illustrative substitute for a concept. 'Wrath' here is the 'ideogram' of a unique emotional moment in religious experience, a moment whose singularly *daunting* and awe-inspiring character must be gravely disturbing to those persons who will recognize nothing in the divine nature but goodness, gentleness, love, and a sort of confidential intimacy, in a word, only those aspects of God which turn towards the world of men.

This ὀργή is thus quite wrongly spoken of as 'natural' wrath: rather it is an entirely non- or super-natural, i.e. numinous, quality. The rationalization process takes place when it begins to be filled in with elements derived from the moral reason: righteousness in requital, and punishment for moral transgression. But it should be noted that the idea of the wrath of God in the Bible is always a synthesis, in which the original is combined with the later meaning that has come to fill it in. Something supra-rational throbs and gleams, palpable and visible, in the 'wrath of God', prompting to a sense of 'terror' that no 'natural' anger can arouse.

Beside the 'wrath' or 'anger' of Yahweh stands the related expression 'jealousy of Yahweh'. The state of mind denoted by the phrase 'being jealous *for* Yahweh' is also a numinous state of mind, in which features of the *tremendum* pass over into the man who has experience of it.

2. *The element of 'Overpoweringness' ('majestas')*

We have been attempting to unfold the implications of that aspect of the *mysterium tremendum* indicated by the adjective, and the result so far may be summarized in two words, constituting, as before, what may be called an 'ideogram', rather than a concept proper, viz. 'absolute unapproachability'.

It will be felt at once that there is yet a further element which must be added, that, namely, of 'might', 'power', 'absolute overpoweringness'. We will take to represent this the term *majestas*, majesty—the more readily because anyone with a feeling for language must detect a last faint trace of the numinous still clinging to the word. The *tremendum* may then be rendered more adequately *tremenda majestas*, or 'aweful majesty'. This second element of majesty may continue to be vividly preserved, where the first, that of unapproachability, recedes and dies away, as may be seen, for example, in mysticism. It is especially in relation to this element of majesty or absolute overpoweringness that the creature-consciousness, of which we have already spoken, comes upon the scene, as a sort of shadow or subjective reflection of it. Thus, in contrast to 'the overpowering' of which we are conscious as an object over against the self, there is the feeling of one's own submergence, of being but 'dust and ashes' and nothingness. And this forms the numinous raw material for the feeling of religious humility.[1]

Here we must revert once again to Schleiermacher's expression for what we call 'creature-feeling', viz. the 'feeling of dependence'. We found fault with this phrase before on the ground that Schleiermacher thereby takes as basis and point of departure what is merely a secondary effect; that he sets out to teach a consciousness of the religious *object* only by way of an inference from the shadow it casts upon *self*-consciousness. We have now a further criticism to bring against it, and it is this. By 'feeling of dependence' Schleiermacher means consciousness of *being conditioned* (as effect by cause), and so he develops the implications of this logically enough in his sections upon Creation and Preservation. On the side of the deity the correlate to 'dependence' would thus be 'causality', i.e. God's character as all-causing and all-conditioning. But a sense of this does not enter at all into that immediate and first-hand religious emotion which we have in the moment of worship, and which we can recover in a measure for analysis; it belongs on the contrary decidedly to the *rational* side of the idea of God; its implications admit of precise conceptual determination; and it springs from quite a distinct source. The difference between the 'feeling of dependence' of Schleiermacher and that which finds typical utterance in the words of Abraham already cited might be expressed as that between the consciousness of *createdness*[2] and

[1] Cf. R. R. Marett, 'The Birth of Humility', in *The Threshold of Religion*, 2nd ed., 1914. [Tr.]   [2] *Geschaffenheit.*

the consciousness of *creaturehood*.[1] In the one case you have the creature as the work of the divine creative act; in the other, impotence and general nothingness as against overpowering might, dust and ashes as against 'majesty'. In the one case you have the fact of having been created; in the other, the status of the creature. And as soon as speculative thought has come to concern itself with this latter type of consciousness—as soon as it has come to analyse this 'majesty' —we are introduced to a set of ideas quite different from those of creation or preservation. We come upon the ideas, first, of the annihilation of self, and then, as its complement, of the transcendent as the sole and entire reality. These are the characteristic notes of mysticism in all its forms, however otherwise various in content. For one of the chiefest and most general features of mysticism is just this *self-depreciation* (so plainly parallel to the case of Abraham), the estimation of the self, of the personal 'I', as something not perfectly or essentially real, or even as mere nullity, a self-depreciation which comes to demand its own fulfilment in practice in rejecting the delusion of selfhood, and so makes for the annihilation of the self. And on the other hand mysticism leads to a valuation of the transcendent object of its reference as that which through plenitude of being stands supreme and absolute, so that the finite self contrasted with it becomes conscious even in its nullity that 'I am naught, Thou art all'. There is no thought in this of any causal relation between God, the creator, and the self, the creature. The point from which speculation starts is not a 'consciousness of absolute dependence'—of myself as result and effect of a divine cause —for that would in point of fact lead to insistence upon the reality of the self; it starts from a consciousness of the absolute superiority or supremacy of a power other than myself, and it is only as it falls back upon ontological terms to achieve its end—terms generally borrowed from natural science—that that element of the *tremendum*, originally apprehended as 'plenitude of power', becomes transmuted into 'plenitude of being'.

This leads again to the mention of mysticism. No mere

[1] *Geschöpflichkeit.*

inquiry into the genesis of a thing can throw any light upon its essential nature, and it is hence immaterial to us how mysticism historically arose. But essentially mysticism is the stressing to a very high degree, indeed the overstressing, of the non-rational or supra-rational elements in religion; and it is only intelligible when so understood. The various phases and factors of the non-rational may receive varying emphasis, and the type of mysticism will differ according as some or others fall into the background. What we have been analysing, however, is a feature that recurs in all forms of mysticism everywhere, and it is nothing but the 'creature-consciousness' stressed to the utmost and to excess, the expression meaning, if we may repeat the contrast already made, not 'feeling of our createdness' but 'feeling of our creaturehood', that is, the consciousness of the littleness of every creature in face of that which is above all creatures.

A characteristic common to all types of mysticism is the *Identification*, in different degrees of completeness, of the personal self with the transcendent Reality. This identification has a source of its own, with which we are not here concerned, and springs from 'moments' of religious experience which would require separate treatment. 'Identification' alone, however, is not enough for mysticism; it must be Identification with the Something that is at once absolutely supreme in power and reality and wholly non-rational. And it is among the mystics that we most encounter this element of religious consciousness. Récéjac has noticed this in his *Essai sur les fondements de la connaissance mystique* (Paris, 1897). He writes (p. 90):

Le mysticisme commence par la crainte, par le sentiment d'une *domination* universelle, *invincible*, et devient plus tard un désir d'union avec ce qui domine ainsi.

And some very clear examples of this taken from the religious experience of the present day are to be found in W. James (*op. cit.*, p. 66):

The perfect stillness of the night was thrilled by a more solemn silence. The darkness held a presence that was all the more felt because it was not seen. I could not any more have doubted that

He was there than that I was. Indeed, I felt myself to be, if possible, the less real of the two.

This example is particularly instructive as to the relation of mysticism to the 'feelings of identification', for the experience here recounted was on the point of passing into it.[1]

3. *The Element of 'Energy' or Urgency*

There is, finally, a third element comprised in those of *tremendum* and *majestas*, awefulness and majesty, and this I venture to call the 'urgency' or 'energy' of the numinous object. It is particularly vividly perceptible in the ὀργή or 'wrath'; and it everywhere clothes itself in symbolical expressions—vitality, passion, emotional temper, will, force, movement,[2] excitement, activity, impetus. These features are typical and recur again and again from the daemonic level up to the idea of the 'living' God. We have here the factor that has everywhere more than any other prompted the fiercest opposition to the 'philosophic' God of mere rational speculation, who can be put into a definition. And for their part the philosophers have condemned these expressions of the energy of the numen, whenever they are brought on to the scene, as sheer anthropomorphism. In so far as their opponents have for the most part themselves failed to recognize that the terms they have borrowed from the sphere of human conative and affective life have merely value as analogies, the philosophers are right to condemn them. But they are wrong, in so far as, this error notwithstanding, these terms stood for a genuine aspect of the divine nature—its non-rational aspect—a due consciousness of which served to protect religion itself from being 'rationalized' away.

For wherever men have been contending for the 'living' God or for voluntarism, there, we may be sure, have been non-rationalists fighting rationalists and rationalism. It was so with Luther in his controversy with Erasmus; and Luther's *omnipotentia Dei* in his *De Servo Arbitrio* is nothing but the

---

[1] Compare too the experience on p. 70: '. . . What I felt on these occasions was a temporary loss of my own identity'.

[2] The 'mobilitas Dei' of Lactantius.

union of 'majesty'—in the sense of absolute supremacy—
with this 'energy', in the sense of a force that knows not stint
nor stay, which is urgent, active, compelling, and alive. In
mysticism, too, this element of 'energy' is a very living and
vigorous factor, at any rate in the 'voluntaristic' mysticism,
the mysticism of love, where it is very forcibly seen in that
'consuming fire' of love whose burning strength the mystic
can hardly bear, but begs that the heat that has scorched him
may be mitigated, lest he be himself destroyed by it. And in
this urgency and pressure the mystic's 'love' claims a perceptible kinship with the ὀργή itself, the scorching and consuming wrath of God; it is the same 'energy', only differently
directed. 'Love', says one of the mystics, 'is nothing else than
quenched wrath.'

The element of 'energy' reappears in Fichte's speculations
on the Absolute as the gigantic, never-resting, active world-
stress, and in Schopenhauer's daemonic 'Will'. At the same
time both these writers are guilty of the same error that is
already found in myth; they transfer 'natural' attributes,
which ought only to be used as 'ideograms' for what is itself
properly beyond utterance, to the non-rational as real quali-
fications of it, and they mistake symbolic expressions of
feelings for adequate concepts upon which a 'scientific'
structure of knowledge may be based.

In Goethe, as we shall see later, the same element of energy
is emphasized in a quite unique way in his strange descriptions of the experience he calls 'daemonic'.

CHAPTER V

THE ANALYSIS OF 'MYSTERIUM'

Ein begriffener Gott ist kein Gott.
'A God comprehended is no God.' (TERSTEEGEN.)

W E gave to the object to which the numinous consciousness is directed the name *mysterium tremendum*, and we then set ourselves first to determine the meaning of the adjective *tremendum*—which we found to be itself only justified by analogy—because it is more easily analysed than the substantive idea *mysterium*. We have now to turn to this, and try, as best we may, by hint and suggestion, to get to a clearer apprehension of what it implies.

4. *The 'Wholly Other'*

It might be thought that the adjective itself gives an explanation of the substantive; but this is not so. It is not merely analytical; it is a synthetic attribute to it; i.e. *tremendum* adds something not necessarily inherent in *mysterium*. It is true that the reactions in consciousness that correspond to the one readily and spontaneously overflow into those that correspond to the other; in fact, anyone sensitive to the use of words would commonly feel that the idea of 'mystery' (*mysterium*) is so closely bound up with its synthetic qualifying attribute 'awful' (*tremendum*) that one can hardly say the former without catching an echo of the latter, 'mystery' almost of itself becoming 'aweful mystery' to us. But the passage from the one idea to the other need not by any means be always so easy. The elements of meaning implied in 'awefulness' and 'mysteriousness' are in themselves definitely different. The latter may so far preponderate in the religious consciousness, may stand out so vividly, that in comparison with it the former almost sinks out of sight; a case which again could be clearly exemplified from some forms of mysticism. Occasionally, on the other hand, the reverse happens, and the *tremendum* may in turn occupy the mind without the *mysterium*.

This latter, then, needs special consideration on its own

account. We need an expression for the mental reaction peculiar to it; and here, too, only one word seems appropriate, though, as it is strictly applicable only to a 'natural' state of mind, it has here meaning only by analogy: it is the word 'stupor'. *Stupor* is plainly a different thing from *tremor*; it signifies blank wonder, an astonishment that strikes us dumb, amazement absolute.[1] Taken, indeed, in its purely natural sense, *mysterium* would first mean merely a secret or a mystery in the sense of that which is alien to us, uncomprehended and unexplained; and so far *mysterium* is itself merely an ideo-gram, an analogical notion taken from the natural sphere, illustrating, but incapable of exhaustively rendering, our real meaning. Taken in the religious sense, that which is 'mysterious' is—to give it perhaps the most striking expres-sion—the 'wholly other' (θάτερον, *anyad*, *alienum*), that which is quite beyond the sphere of the usual, the intelligible, and the familiar, which therefore falls quite outside the limits of the 'canny', and is contrasted with it, filling the mind with blank wonder and astonishment.

This is already to be observed on the lowest and earliest level of the religion of primitive man, where the numinous consciousness is but an inchoate stirring of the feelings. What is really characteristic of this stage is *not*—as the theory of Animism would have us believe—that men are here con-cerned with curious entities, called 'souls' or 'spirits', which happen to be invisible. Representations of spirits and similar conceptions are rather one and all early modes of 'rationaliz-ing' a precedent experience, to which they are subsidiary. They are attempts in some way or other, it little matters how, to guess the riddle it propounds, and their effect is at the same time always to weaken and deaden the experience itself. They are the source from which springs, not religion, but the

[1] Compare also *obstupefacere*. Still more exact equivalents are the Greek θάμβος and θαμβεῖν. The sound θ a μ β (*thamb*) excellently depicts this state of mind of blank, staring wonder. And the difference between the moments of *stupor* and *tremor* is very finely suggested by the passage, Mark x. 32 (cf. *infra*, p. 158). On the other hand, what was said above of the facility and rapidity with which the two moments merge and blend is also markedly true of θάμβος, which then becomes a classical term for the (ennobled) awe of the numinous in general. So Mark xvi. 5 is rightly translated by Luther 'und sie entsetzten sich', and by the English Authorized Version 'and they were affrighted'.

rationalization of religion, which often ends by constructing such a massive structure of theory and such a plausible fabric of interpretation, that the 'mystery' is frankly excluded.[1] Both imaginative 'myth', when developed into a system, and intellectualist Scholasticism, when worked out to its completion, are methods by which the fundamental fact of religious experience is, as it were, simply rolled out so thin and flat as to be finally eliminated altogether.

Even on the lowest level of religious development the essential characteristic is therefore to be sought elsewhere than in the appearance of 'spirit' representations. It lies rather, we repeat, in a peculiar 'moment' of consciousness, to wit, the *stupor* before something 'wholly other', whether such an other be named 'spirit' or 'daemon' or 'deva', or be left without any name. Nor does it make any difference in this respect whether, to interpret and preserve their apprehension of this 'other', men coin original imagery of their own or adapt imaginations drawn from the world of legend, the fabrications of fancy apart from and prior to any stirrings of daemonic dread.

In accordance with laws of which we shall have to speak again later, this feeling or consciousness of the 'wholly other' will attach itself to, or sometimes be indirectly aroused by means of, objects which are already puzzling upon the 'natural' plane, or are of a surprising or astounding character; such as extraordinary phenomena or astonishing occurrences or things in inanimate nature, in the animal world, or among men. But here once more we are dealing with a case of association between things specifically different—the 'numinous' and the 'natural' moments of consciousness—and not merely with the gradual enhancement of one of them—the 'natural'—till it becomes the other. As in the case of 'natural fear' and 'daemonic dread' already considered, so here the transition from natural to daemonic amazement is not a mere matter of degree. But it is only with the latter that the complementary expression *mysterium* perfectly harmonizes, as will

---

[1] A spirit or soul that has been conceived and comprehended no longer prompts to 'shuddering', as is proved by Spiritualism. But it thereby ceases to be of interest for the psychology of religion.

be felt perhaps more clearly in the case of the adjectival form 'mysterious'. No one says, strictly and in earnest, of a piece of clockwork that is beyond his grasp, or of a science that he cannot understand: 'That is "mysterious" to me.'

It might be objected that the mysterious is something which is and remains absolutely and invariably beyond our understanding, whereas that which merely eludes our understanding for a time but is perfectly intelligible in principle should be called, not a 'mystery', but merely a 'problem'. But this is by no means an adequate account of the matter. The truly 'mysterious' object is beyond our apprehension and comprehension, not only because our knowledge has certain irremovable limits, but because in it we come upon something inherently 'wholly other', whose kind and character are incommensurable with our own, and before which we therefore recoil in a wonder that strikes us chill and numb.[1]

This may be made still clearer by a consideration of that degraded offshoot and travesty of the genuine 'numinous' dread or awe, the fear of ghosts. Let us try to analyse this experience. We have already specified the peculiar feeling-element of 'dread' aroused by the ghost as that of 'grue', grisly horror.[2] Now this 'grue' obviously contributes something to the attraction which ghost-stories exercise, in so far, namely, as the relaxation of tension ensuing upon our release from it relieves the mind in a pleasant and agreeable way. So far, however, it is not really the ghost itself that gives us pleasure, but the fact that we are rid of it. But obviously this is quite insufficient to explain the ensnaring attraction of the ghost-story. The ghost's real attraction rather consists in this, that of itself and in an uncommon degree it entices the imagination, awakening strong interest and curiosity; it is

---

[1] In *Confessions*, ii. 9. 1, Augustine very strikingly suggests this stiffening, benumbing element of the 'wholly other' and its contrast to the rational aspect of the numen; the *dissimile* and the *simile*:

'Quid est illud, quod interlucet mihi et percutit cor meum sine laesione? Et inhorresco et inardesco. *Inhorresco*, in quantum *dissimilis* ei sum. Inardesco, in quantum *similis* ei sum.'

('What is that which gleams through me and smites my heart without wounding it? I am both a-shudder and a-glow. A-shudder, in so far as I am unlike it, a-glow in so far as I am like it.')

[2] *gruseln, gräsen.*

the weird thing itself that allures the fancy. But it does this, not because it is 'something long and white' (as someone once defined a ghost), nor yet through any of the positive and conceptual attributes which fancies about ghosts have invented, but because it is a thing that 'doesn't really exist at all', the 'wholly other', something which has no place in our scheme of reality but belongs to an absolutely different one, and which at the same time arouses an irrepressible interest in the mind.

But that which is perceptibly true in the fear of ghosts, which is, after all, only a caricature of the genuine thing, is in a far stronger sense true of the 'daemonic' experience itself, of which the fear of ghosts is a mere off-shoot. And while, following this main line of development, this element in the numinous consciousness, the feeling of the 'wholly other', is heightened and clarified, its higher modes of manifestation come into being, which set the numinous object in contrast not only to everything wonted and familiar (i.e. in the end, to nature in general), thereby turning it into the 'supernatural', but finally to the world itself, and thereby exalt it to the 'supramundane', that which is above the whole world-order.

In mysticism we have in the 'beyond' (ἐπέκεινα) again the strongest stressing and over-stressing of those non-rational elements which are already inherent in all religion. Mysticism continues to its extreme point this contrasting of the numinous object (the numen), as the 'wholly other', with ordinary experience. Not content with contrasting it with all that is of nature or this world, mysticism concludes by contrasting it with Being itself and all that 'is', and finally actually calls it 'that which is nothing'. By this 'nothing' is meant not only that of which nothing can be predicated, but that which is absolutely and intrinsically other than and opposite of everything that is and can be thought. But while exaggerating to the point of paradox this *negation* and contrast—the only means open to conceptual thought to apprehend the *mysterium*—mysticism at the same time retains the *positive quality* of the 'wholly other' as a very living factor in its over-brimming religious emotion.

But what is true of the strange 'nothingness' of our mystics holds good equally of the *sūnyam* and the *sūnyatā*, the 'void' and 'emptiness' of the Buddhist mystics. This aspiration for the 'void' and for becoming void, no less than the aspiration of our western mystics for 'nothing' and for becoming nothing, must seem a kind of lunacy to anyone who has no inner sympathy for the esoteric language and ideograms of mysticism, and lacks the matrix from which these come necessarily to birth. To such an one Buddhism itself will be simply a morbid sort of pessimism. But in fact the 'void' of the eastern, like the 'nothing' of the western, mystic is a numinous ideogram of the 'wholly other'.

These terms 'supernatural' and 'transcendent'[1] give the appearance of positive attributes, and, as applied to the mysterious, they appear to divest the *mysterium* of its originally negative meaning and to turn it into an affirmation. On the side of conceptual thought this is nothing more than appearance, for it is obvious that the two terms in question are merely negative and exclusive attributes with reference to 'nature' and the world or cosmos respectively. But on the side of the feeling-content it is otherwise; that *is* in very truth positive in the highest degree, though here too, as before, it cannot be rendered explicit in conceptual terms. It is through this positive feeling-content that the concepts of the 'transcendent' and 'supernatural' become forthwith designations for a unique 'wholly other' reality and quality, something of whose special character we can *feel*, without being able to give it clear conceptual expression.

[1] Literally, supramundane: *überweltlich.*

CHAPTER VI

5. THE ELEMENT OF FASCINATION

THE qualitative *content* of the numinous experience, to which 'the mysterious' stands as *form*, is in one of its aspects the element of daunting 'awefulness' and 'majesty', which has already been dealt with in detail; but it is clear that it has at the same time another aspect, in which it shows itself as something uniquely attractive and *fascinating*.

These two qualities, the daunting and the fascinating, now combine in a strange harmony of contrasts, and the resultant dual character of the numinous consciousness, to which the entire religious development bears witness, at any rate from the level of the 'daemonic dread' onwards, is at once the strangest and most noteworthy phenomenon in the whole history of religion. The daemonic-divine object may appear to the mind an object of horror and dread, but at the same time it is no less something that allures with a potent charm, and the creature, who trembles before it, utterly cowed and cast down, has always at the same time the impulse to turn to it, nay even to make it somehow his own. The 'mystery' is for him not merely something to be wondered at but something that entrances him; and beside that in it which bewilders and confounds, he feels a something that captivates and transports him with a strange ravishment, rising often enough to the pitch of dizzy intoxication; it is the Dionysiac-element in the numen.

The ideas and concepts which are the parallels or 'schemata' on the rational side of this non-rational element of 'fascination' are love, mercy, pity, comfort; these are all 'natural' elements of the common psychical life, only they are here thought as absolute and in completeness. But important as these are for the experience of religious bliss or felicity, they do not by any means exhaust it. It is just the same as with the opposite experience of religious infelicity—the experience of the ὀργή or 'wrath' of God:—both alike contain fundamentally non-rational elements. Bliss or beatitude is more, far more, than the mere natural feeling of being comforted, of reliance, of the joy of love, however these may be heightened and enhanced. Just as 'wrath', taken in a purely rational or a purely ethical sense, does not exhaust that profound element of *awefulness* which is locked in the mystery of deity, so neither does 'graciousness' exhaust the profound element of *wonderfulness* and rapture which lies in the mysterious beatific experience of deity. The term 'grace' may indeed be taken as its aptest designation, but then only in the sense in which it is really applied in the language of the mystics, and in which not only the 'gracious intent' but 'something more' is meant by the word. This 'something more' has its antecedent phases very far back in the history of religions.

It may well be possible, it is even probable, that in the first stage of its development the religious consciousness started with only one of its poles—the 'daunting' aspect of the numen —and so at first took shape only as 'daemonic dread'. But if this did not point to something beyond itself, if it were not but one 'moment' of a completer experience, pressing up gradually into consciousness, then no transition would be possible to the feelings of positive self-surrender to the numen. The only type of worship that could result from this 'dread' alone would be that of ἀπαιτεῖσθαι and ἀποτρέπειν, taking the form of expiation and propitiation, the averting or the appeasement of the 'wrath' of the numen. It can never explain how it is that 'the numinous' is the object of search and desire and yearning, and that too for its own sake and not only for the sake of the aid and backing that men expect from it in the natural sphere. It can never explain how this takes place, not only in the forms of 'rational' religious worship, but in those queer 'sacramental' observances and rituals and procedures of communion in which the human being seeks to get the numen into his possession.

Religious practice may manifest itself in those normal and easily intelligible forms which occupy so prominent a place in the history of religion, such forms as propitiation, petition, sacrifice, thanksgiving, &c. But besides these there is a series of strange proceedings which are constantly attracting greater and greater attention, and in which it is claimed that we may recognize, besides mere religion in general, the particular roots of mysticism. I refer to those numerous curious modes of behaviour and fantastic forms of mediation, by means of which the primitive religious man attempts to master 'the mysterious', and to fill himself and even to identify himself with it. These modes of behaviour fall apart into two classes. On the one hand the 'magical' identification of the self with the numen proceeds by means of various transactions, at once magical and devotional in character—by formula, ordination, adjuration, consecration, exorcism, &c.: on the other hand are the 'shamanistic' ways of procedure, possession, indwelling, self-fulfilment in exaltation and ecstasy. All these have, indeed, their starting-points simply in magic, and their intention at first was certainly simply to appropriate the prodigious force of the numen for the natural ends of man. But the process does not rest there. Possession of and by the numen becomes an end in itself; it begins to be sought for its own sake; and the wildest and most artificial methods of asceticism are put into practice to attain it. In a word, the *vita religiosa* begins; and to remain in these strange and bizarre states of numinous possession becomes a good in itself, even a way of salvation, wholly different from the profane goods pursued by means of magic. Here, too, commences the process of development by which the experience is matured and purified, till finally it reaches its consummation in the sublimest and purest states of the 'life within the Spirit' and in the noblest mysticism. Widely various as these states are in themselves, yet they have this element in common, that in them the *mysterium* is experienced in its essential, positive, and specific character, as something that bestows upon man a beatitude beyond compare, but one whose real nature he can neither proclaim in speech nor conceive in thought, but may know only by a direct and living experience. It is a bliss which embraces all those blessings that are indicated or suggested in positive fashion by any 'doctrine of salvation', and it quickens all of them through and through; but these do not exhaust it. Rather by its all-pervading, penetrating glow it makes of these very blessings more than the intellect can conceive in them or affirm of

D

them. It gives the peace that passes understanding, and of which the tongue can only stammer brokenly. Only from afar, by metaphors and analogies, do we come to apprehend what it is in itself, and even so our notion is but inadequate and confused.

'Eye hath not seen, nor ear heard, neither have entered into the heart of man, the things which God hath prepared for them that love him.' Who does not feel the exalted sound of these words and the 'Dionysiac' element of transport and fervour in them? It is instructive that in such phrases as these, in which consciousness would fain put its highest consummation into words, 'all images fall away' and the mind turns from them to grasp expressions that are purely negative. And it is still more instructive that in reading and hearing such words their merely negative character simply is not noticed; that we can let whole chains of such negations enrapture, even intoxicate us, and that entire hymns—and deeply impressive hymns—have been composed, in which there is really nothing positive at all! All this teaches us the independence of the positive content of this experience from the implications of its overt conceptual expression, and how it can be firmly grasped, thoroughly understood, and profoundly appreciated, purely in, with, and from the feeling itself.

Mere love, mere trust, for all the glory and happiness they bring, do not explain to us that moment of rapture that breathes in our tenderest and most heart-felt hymns of salvation, as also in such eschatological hymns of longing as that Rhyme of St. Bernard in which the very verses seem to dance.

> Urbs Sion unica, mansio mystica, condita coelo,
> Nunc tibi gaudeo, nunc tibi lugeo, tristor, anhelo,
> Te, quia corpore non queo, pectore saepe penetro;
> Sed caro terrea, terraque carnea, mox cado retro.
> Nemo retexere, nemoque promere sustinet ore,
> Quo tua moenia, quo capitolia plena nitore.
> Id queo dicere, quo modo tangere pollice coelum,
> Ut mare currere, sicut in aere figere telum.
> Opprimit omne cor ille tuus decor, O Sion, O Pax.
> Urbs sine tempore, nulla potest fore laus tibi mendax.

O nova mansio, te pia concio, gens pia munit,
Provehit, excitat, auget, identitat, efficit, unit.[1]

This is where the living 'something more' of the *fascinans*, the element of fascination, is to be found. It lives no less in those tense extollings of the blessing of salvation, which recur in all religions of salvation, and stand in such remarkable contrast to the relatively meagre and frequently childish import of that which is revealed in them by concept or by image. Everywhere salvation is something whose meaning is often very little apparent, is even wholly obscure, to the 'natural' man; on the contrary, *so far as he understands it*, he tends to find it highly tedious and uninteresting, sometimes downright distasteful and repugnant to his nature, as he would, for instance, find the beatific vision of God in our own doctrine of salvation, or the *henōsis* of 'God all in all' among the mystics. 'So far as he understands', be it noted; but then he does not understand it in the least. Because he lacks the inward teaching of the Spirit, he must needs confound what is offered him as an expression for the experience of salvation —a mere ideogram of what is felt, whose import it hints at by analogy—with 'natural' concepts, as though it were itself just such an one. And so he 'wanders ever farther from the goal'.

It is not only in the religious feeling of longing that the moment of fascination is a living factor. It is already alive and present in the moment of 'solemnity', both in the gathered concentration and humble submergence of private devotion, when the mind is exalted to the holy, and in the common worship of the congregation, where this is practised with earnestness and deep sincerity, as, it is to be feared, is with us a thing rather desired than realized. It is this and nothing else that in the solemn moment can fill the soul so full and

[1] 'O Sion, thou city sole and single, mystic mansion hidden away in the heavens, now I rejoice in thee, now I moan for thee and mourn and yearn for thee; thee often I pass through in the heart, as I cannot in the body, but being but earthly flesh and fleshly earth soon I fall back. None can disclose or utter in speech what plenary radiance fills thy walls and thy citadels. I can as little tell of it as I can touch the skies with my finger, or run upon the sea or make a dart stand still in the air. This thy splendour overwhelms every heart, O Sion, O Peace! O timeless City, no praise can belie thee. O new dwelling-place, thee the concourse and people of the faithful erects and exalts, inspires and increases, joins to itself, and makes complete and one.'

keep it so inexpressibly tranquil. Schleiermacher's assertion[1] is perhaps true of it, as of the numinous consciousness in general, viz. that it cannot really occur alone on its own account, or except combined and penetrated with rational elements. But, if this be admitted, it is upon other grounds than those adduced by Schleiermacher; while, on the other hand, it may occupy a more or less predominant place and lead to states of calm ($\dot{\eta}\sigma\upsilon\chi\acute{\iota}a$) as well as of transport, in which it *almost* of itself wholly fills the soul. But in all the manifold forms in which it is aroused in us, whether in eschatological promise of the coming kingdom of God and the transcendent bliss of Paradise, or in the guise of an entry into that beatific reality that is 'above the world'; whether it come first in expectancy or pre-intimation or in a present experience ('When I but *have* Thee, I ask no question of heaven and earth'); in all these forms, outwardly diverse but inwardly akin, it appears as a strange and mighty propulsion towards an ideal good known only to religion and in its nature fundamentally non-rational, which the mind knows of in yearning and presentiment, recognizing it for what it is behind the obscure and inadequate symbols which are its only expression. And this shows that above and beyond our rational being lies hidden the ultimate and highest part of our nature, which can find no satisfaction in the mere allaying of the needs of our sensuous, psychical, or intellectual impulses and cravings. The mystics called it the basis or ground of the soul.

We saw that in the case of the element of the mysterious the 'wholly other' led on to the supernatural and transcendent and that above these appeared the 'beyond' ($\dot{\epsilon}\pi\acute{\epsilon}\kappa\epsilon\iota\nu a$) of mysticism, through the non-rational side of religion being raised to its highest power and stressed to excess. It is the same in the case of the element of 'fascination'; here, too, is possible a transition into mysticism. At its highest point of stress the fascinating becomes the 'overabounding', 'exuberant',[2] the mystical 'moment' which exactly corresponds upon this line to the $\dot{\epsilon}\pi\acute{\epsilon}\kappa\epsilon\iota\nu a$ upon the other line of approach, and which is to be understood accordingly. But while this feeling of the 'over-abounding' is specially characteristic of mysti-

[1] *Glaubenslehre*, § 5.   [2] *das Überschwengliche*.

cism, a trace of it survives in all truly felt states of religious beatitude, however restrained and kept within measure by other factors. This is seen most clearly from the psychology of those great experiences—of grace, conversion, second birth—in which the religious experience appears in its pure intrinsic nature and in heightened activity, so as to be more clearly grasped than in the less typical form of piety instilled by education. The hard core of such experiences in their Christian form consists of the redemption from guilt and bondage to sin, and we shall have presently to see that this also does not occur without a participation of non-rational elements. But leaving this out of account, what we have here to point out is the unutterableness of what has been yet genuinely experienced, and how such an experience may pass into blissful excitement, rapture, and exaltation verging often on the bizarre and the abnormal.[1] This is vouched for by the autobiographical testimony of the 'converted' from St. Paul onward. William James has collected a great number of these, without, however, himself noticing the non-rational element that thrills in them.

Thus, one writes

. . . For the moment nothing but an ineffable joy and exaltation remained. It is impossible fully to describe the experience. It was like the effect of some great orchestra, when all the separate notes have melted into one swelling harmony, that leaves the listener conscious of nothing save that his soul is being wafted upwards and almost bursting with its own emotion. (*Varieties of Religious Experience*, p. 66.)

And another:

. . . The more I seek words to express this intimate intercourse, the more I feel the impossibility of describing the thing by any of our usual images. (Ibid., p. 68.)

---

[1] This may be found fatal to the attempt to construct a 'religion within the limits of pure reason', or 'of humanity'; but, none the less, the matter is as we have described it, as far as concerns the psychological inquiry into religion, which asks, not what it is within the aforementioned limits, but what it is in its own essential nature. And for that matter this proceeding of constructing a 'humanity' prior to and apart from the most central and potent of human capacities is like nothing so much as the attempt to frame a standard idea of the human body after having previously cut off the head.

And almost with the precision of dogma, a third (Jonathan Edwards) indicates the qualitative difference of the experience of beatitude from other 'rational' joy:

> The conceptions which the saints have of the loveliness of God and that kind of delight which they experience in it are quite peculiar and entirely different from anything which a natural man can possess or of which he can form any proper notion. (Ibid., p. 229.)

Cf. also pp. 192, 225; and the testimony of Jacob Boehme given on p. 417. Also this of Boehme:

> But I can neither write nor tell of what sort of Exaltation the triumphing in the Spirit is. It can be compared with nought, but that when in the midst of death life is born, and it is like the resurrection of the dead.

With the mystics these experiences pass up wholly into the 'over-abounding'. 'O that I could tell you what the heart feels, how it burns and is consumed inwardly! Only, I find no words to express it. I can but say: Might but one little drop of what I feel fall into Hell, Hell would be transformed into a Paradise.' So says St. Catherine of Genoa; and all the multitude of her spiritual kindred testify to the same effect.

What we Christians know as the experiences of grace and the second birth have their parallels also in the religions of high spiritual rank beyond the borders of Christianity. Such are the breaking out of the saving 'Bodhi', the opening of the 'heavenly eye', the *Jñāna*, by *Išvaras prasāda*, which is victorious over the darkness of nescience and shines out in an experience with which no other can be measured. And in all these the entirely non-rational and specific element in the beatific experience is immediately noticeable. The qualitative character of it varies widely in all these cases, and is again in them all very different from its parallels in Christianity; still in all it is very similar in intensity, and in all it is a 'salvation' and an absolute 'fascination', which in contrast to all that admits of 'natural' expression or comparison is deeply imbued with the 'over-abounding' ('exuberant') nature of the numen.

And this is also entirely true of the rapture of Nirvana,

which is only in appearance a cold and negative state. It is only conceptually that 'Nirvana' is a negation; it is felt in consciousness as in the strongest degree positive; it exercises a 'fascination' by which its votaries are as much carried away as are the Hindu or the Christian by the corresponding objects of their worship. I recall vividly a conversation I had with a Buddhist monk. He had been putting before me methodically and pertinaciously the arguments for the Buddhist 'theology of negation', the doctrine of Anātman and 'entire emptiness'. When he had made an end, I asked him, what then Nirvana itself is; and after a long pause came at last the single answer, low and restrained: 'Bliss—unspeakable'. And the hushed restraint of that answer, the solemnity of his voice, demeanour, and gesture, made more clear what was meant than the words themselves.

And so we maintain, on the one hand, following the *via eminentiae et causalitatis*, that the divine is indeed the highest, strongest, best, loveliest, and dearest that man can think of; but we assert on the other, following the *via negationis*, that God is not *merely* the ground and superlative of all that can be thought; He is in Himself a subject on His own account and in Himself.

*   *   *   *   *

In the adjective δεινός the Greek language possesses a word peculiarly difficult to translate, and standing for an idea peculiarly difficult to grasp in all its strange variations. And if we ask whence this difficulty arises, the answer is plain; it is because δεινός is simply the numinous (mostly of course at a lower level, in an arrested form, attenuated by rhetorical or poetic usage). Consequently δεινός is the equivalent of *dirus* and *tremendus*. It may mean evil or imposing, potent and strange, queer and marvellous, horrifying and fascinating, divine and daemonic, and a source of 'energy'. Sophocles means to awaken the feeling of 'numinous awe' through the whole gamut of its phases at the contemplation of man, the creature of marvel, in the choric song of the *Antigone*:

πολλὰ τὰ δεινά, κοὐδὲν ἀνθρώπου δεινότερον πέλει.

This line defies translation, just because our language has no term that can isolate distinctly and gather into one word the total numinous impression a thing may make on the mind. The nearest that German can get to it is in the expression *das Ungeheuere* (monstrous), while in English 'weird' is perhaps the closest rendering possible. The mood and attitude represented in the foregoing verse might then be fairly well rendered by such a translation as:

Much there is that is weird; but nought is weirder than man.

The German *ungeheuer* is not by derivation simply 'huge', in quantity or quality;—this, its common meaning, is in fact a rationalizing interpretation of the real idea; it is that which is not *geheuer*, i.e. approximately, the *uncanny*—in a word, the numinous. And it is just this element of the uncanny in man that Sophocles has in mind. If this, its fundamental meaning, be really and thoroughly felt in consciousness, then the word could be taken as a fairly exact expression for the numinous in its aspects of mystery, awefulness, majesty, augustness, and 'energy'; nay, even the aspect of fascination is dimly felt in it.

The variations of meaning in the German word *ungeheuer* can be well illustrated from Goethe.[1] He, too, uses the word first to denote the huge in size—what is too vast for our faculty of space-perception, such as the immeasurable vault of the night sky. In other passages the word retains its original non-rational colour more markedly; it comes to mean the uncanny, the fearful, the dauntingly 'other' and incomprehensible, that which arouses in us *stupor* and θάμβος; and finally, in the wonderful words of Faust which I have put at the beginning of this book, it becomes an almost exact synonym for our 'numinous' under all its aspects.

> Das Schaudern ist der Menschheit bestes Teil.
> Wie auch die Welt ihm das Gefühl verteuere,
> Ergriffen fühlt er tief das Ungeheuere.[2]

[1] Cf. *Wilhelm Meisters Wanderjahre*, Bk. I, ch. 10; *Wahlverwandtschaften*, 2. 15; *Dichtung und Wahrheit*, 2. 9: 4. 20.

[2] Awe is the best of man: howe'er the world's
Misprizing of the feeling would prevent us,
Deeply we feel, once gripped, the weird Portentous.
(GOETHE, *Faust*, Second Part, Act 1, Sc. v.)

CHAPTER VII

ANALOGIES AND ASSOCIATED FEELINGS

IN order to give an adequate account of this second aspect of the numinous, we were led to add to its original designation as *mysterium tremendum* that it at the same time exercises a supreme 'fascination'. And this its dual character, as at once an object of boundless awe and boundless wonder, quelling and yet entrancing the soul, constitutes the proper *positive* content of the *mysterium* as it manifests itself in conscious feeling. No attempt of ours to describe this harmony of contrasts in the import of the *mysterium* can really succeed; but it may perhaps be adumbrated, as it were from a distance, by taking an analogy from a region belonging not to religion but to aesthetics. In the category and feeling of the *sublime* we have a counterpart to it, though it is true it is but a pale reflexion, and moreover involves difficulties of analysis all its own. The analogies between the consciousness of the sublime and of the numinous may be easily grasped.[1] To begin with, 'the sublime', like 'the numinous', is in Kantian language an idea or concept 'that cannot be unfolded' or explicated (*unauswickelbar*). Certainly we can tabulate some general 'rational' signs that uniformly recur as soon as we call an object sublime; as, for instance, that it must approach, or threaten to overpass, the bounds of our understanding by some 'dynamic' or 'mathematic' greatness, by potent manifestations of force or magnitude in spatial extent. But these are obviously only conditions of, not the essence of, the impression of sublimity. A thing does not become sublime merely by being great. The concept itself remains unexplicated; it has in it something mysterious, and in this it is like that of the numinous. A second point of resemblance is

---

[1] We are often prone to resort to this familiar feeling-content to fill out the negative concept 'transcendent', explaining frankly God's 'transcendence' by His 'sublimity'. As a figurative analogical description this is perfectly allowable, but it would be an error if we meant it literally and in earnest. Religious feelings are not the same as aesthetic feelings, and 'the sublime' is as definitely an aesthetic term as 'the beautiful', however widely different may be the facts denoted by the words.

that the sublime exhibits the same peculiar dual character as the numinous; it is at once daunting, and yet again singularly attracting, in its impress upon the mind. It humbles and at the same time exalts us, circumscribes and extends us beyond ourselves, on the one hand releasing in us a feeling analogous to fear, and on the other rejoicing us. So the idea of the sublime is closely similar to that of the numinous, and is well adapted to excite it and to be excited by it, while each tends to pass over into the other.

The Law of the Association of Feelings

As these expressions 'excite' and 'pass over' will later assume importance, and as the latter in particular is hedged about with misconceptions which are prominent in the modern doctrines of Evolution and give rise to quite erroneous conclusions, we will enter at once upon a closer consideration of them.

It is a well-known and fundamental psychological law that ideas 'attract' one another, and that one will excite another and call it into consciousness, if it resembles it. An entirely similar law holds good with regard to feelings. A feeling, no less than an idea, can arouse its like in the mind; and the presence of the one in my consciousness may be the occasion for my entertaining the other at the same time. Further, just as in the case of ideas the law of reproduction by similarity leads to a mistaken substitution of ideas, so that I come to entertain an idea x, when y would have been the appropriate one, so we may be led to a corresponding substitution of feelings, and I may react with a feeling x to an impression to which the feeling y would normally correspond. Finally, I can pass from one feeling to another by an imperceptibly gradual transition, the one feeling x dying away little by little, while the other, y, excited together with it, increases and strengthens in a corresponding degree. But it is important here to recognize the true account of the phenomenon. What passes over—undergoes transition—is not the feeling itself. It is not that the actual feeling gradually changes in quality or 'evolves', i.e. transmutes itself into a quite different one, but rather that I pass over or make the transition from one feeling to another as my circumstances change, by the gradual decrease of the one and increase of the other. A transition of the actual feeling into another would be a real 'transmutation', and would be a psychological counterpart to the alchemist's production of gold by the transmutation of metals.

And yet it is this transmutation that is assumed by the modern 'Evolutionism'—more properly to be called 'Transmutationism'—by the introduction of the equivocal phrase, 'gradually evolve' (i.e. from a thing of a certain quality to something qualitatively different), or the no less equivocal words 'Epigenesis', 'Heterogony',[1] and their like. In this way, they would have us believe, the feeling, e.g. of moral obligation, 'evolves' or develops. At first, so it is said, all that exists is the simple constraint of uniform custom, as seen in the community of the clan. Then, out of that, it is said, 'arises' the idea of a universally obligatory 'ought'. How the idea can do so is not disclosed. Now such a theory misses the fact that in moral obligation we have something *qualitatively* quite different from constraint by custom. The finer and more penetrating psychological analysis that can apprehend differences in quality is rudely ignored and in consequence the whole problem is misconceived. Or, if something of the essential difference is felt, it is covered up and glozed over by the phrase 'gradually evolve', and the one thing is made to turn into the other *par la durée*, much as milk grows sour from standing. But 'ought' is a primary and unique meaning, as little derivable from another as blue from bitter, and there are not 'transmutations' in the psychological any more than in the physical world. The idea 'ought' is only 'evolvable' out of the spirit of man itself, and then in the sense of being 'arousable', because it is already potentially implanted in him. Were it not so, no 'evolution' could effect an introduction for it.

The evolutionists may be quite correct in reconstructing the kind of historical process that took place, viz. the gradual

---

[1] Neither Heterogony nor Epigenesis is genuine Evolution. They are rather just what the biologists call *generatio equivoca*, and therefore mere formation of an aggregate by addition and accumulation.

and successive entry upon the scene of different 'moments' of feeling-consciousness in historical sequence, and the order of entry itself may have been correctly discovered. But the explanation of this process is quite different from that which they intend; it is, namely, the law of the excitation and arousing of feelings and ideas according to the measure of their resemblance. There is in point of fact a very strong analogy between constraint by custom and constraint by moral obligation, as both are constraints upon conduct. Consequently the former can *arouse* the latter in the mind if it —the latter—was already potentially planted there; the feeling of 'ought' may start into consciousness at the presence of the other feeling, and the man may gradually effect a transition to it from that other. But what we are concerned with is the *replacement* of the one by the other, and not the *transmutation* of the one into the other.

Now it is just the same with the feeling of the numinous as with that of moral obligation. It too is not to be derived from any other feeling, and is in this sense 'unevolvable'. It is a content of feeling that is qualitatively *sui generis*, yet at the same time one that has numerous analogies with others, and therefore it and they may reciprocally excite or stimulate one another and cause one another to appear in the mind. Instead of framing 'epigenetic' and other fabrications of the course the evolution of religion has taken, it is our task to inquire into these 'stimuli' or 'excitations', these elements that cause the numinous feeling to appear in consciousness, to intimate by virtue of what analogies they came to be able to do so, and so to discover the series or chain of these stimuli by whose operation the numinous feeling was awakened in us.

Such a power of stimulation characterizes the feeling of the sublime, in accordance with the law we found, and through the analogies it bears to the numinous feeling. But this is indubitably a stimulus that only makes its appearance late in the excitation-series, and it is probable that the feeling of the sublime is itself first aroused and disengaged by the precedent religious feeling—not from itself, but from the rational spirit of man and its *a priori* capacity.

Schematization

The 'association of ideas' does not simply cause the idea *y* to reappear in consciousness with the given idea *x* occasionally only, it also sets up under certain circumstances lasting combinations and connexions between the two. And this is no less true of the association of feelings. Accordingly we see religious feeling in permanent connexion with other feelings which are conjoined to it in accordance with this principle of association. It is, indeed, more accurate to say 'conjoined' than really 'connected', for such mere conjunctions or chance connexions according to laws of purely external analogy are to be distinguished from necessary connexions according to principles of true inward affinity and cohesion. An instance of a connexion of this latter kind—an example, indeed, of an inner *a priori* principle—is (following the theory of Kant) the connexion of the category of causality with its temporal 'schema', the temporal sequence of two successive events, which by being brought into connexion with the category of causality is *known* and recognized as a causal relation of the two. In this case analogy between the two—the category and the schema—has also a place, but it is not chance external resemblance but essential correspondence, and the fact that the two belong together is here a necessity of our reason. On the basis of such a necessity the temporal sequence 'schematizes' the category.

Now the relation of the rational to the non-rational element in the idea of the holy or sacred is just such a one of 'schematization', and the non-rational numinous fact, schematized by the rational concepts we have suggested above, yields us the complex category of 'holy' itself, richly charged and complete and in its fullest meaning. And that the schematism is a genuine one, and not a mere combination of analogies, may be distinctly seen from the fact that it does not fall to pieces, and cannot be cut out as the development of the consciousness of religious truth proceeds onwards and upwards, but is only recognized with greater definiteness and certainty. And it is for the same reason inherently probable that there is more, too, in the combination of 'the holy' with 'the sublime' than a mere association of feelings; and perhaps we may say that, while as a matter of historical genesis such an association was the means whereby this combination was awakened in the mind and the occasion for it, yet the inward and lasting character of the connexion in all the higher religions does prove that 'the sublime' too is an authentic 'schema' of 'the holy'.

The intimate interpenetration of the non-rational with the rational elements of the religious consciousness, like the interweaving of warp and woof in a fabric, may be elucidated by taking another familiar case, in which a universal human feeling, that of personal affection, is similarly interpenetrated by a likewise thoroughly non-rational and separate element, namely, the sex instinct. It goes without saying that this latter lies just on the opposite side of 'reason' to the numinous consciousness; for, while this is 'above all reason', the sex impulse is below it, an element in our instinctive life. 'The numinous' infuses the rational from above, 'the sexual' presses up from beneath, quite wholesomely and normally out of the nature which the human being shares with the general animal world, into the higher realm of the specifically 'humane'. But though the two things I am comparing are thus manifestly opposite extremes, they have a closely corresponding relation to that which lies between them, viz. the reason. For the quite special domain of the 'erotic' is only brought into existence as the reproductive instinct passes up out of the merely instinctive life, penetrates the higher humane life of mind and feeling, and infuses wishes, cravings, and longings in personal liking, friendship, and love, in song and poetry and imaginative creation in general. Whatever falls within the sphere of the erotic is therefore always a composite product, made up of two factors: the one something that occurs also in the general sphere of human behaviour as such, as friendship and liking, the feeling of companionship, the mood of poetic inspiration or joyful exaltation, and the like; and the other an infusion of a quite special kind, which is not to be classed with these, and of which no one can have any inkling, let alone understand it, who has not learnt from the actual inward experience of *erōs* or love. Another point in which the 'erotic' is analogous to the 'holy' is in having in the main no means of linguistic expression but terms drawn from other fields of mental life, which only cease to be 'innocuous' (i.e. only become genuinely 'erotic' terms) when it is realized that the lover, like the orator, bard, or singer, expresses himself not so much by the actual words he uses as by the accent, tone, and imitative gesture which reinforce them.

The phrase 'he loves me' is verbally identical, whether it is said by a child of its father or by a girl of her lover. But in the second case a 'love' is meant which is at the same time 'something more' (viz. *sexual* love), and something more not only in quantity but in quality. So, too, the phrase 'We ought to fear, love, and trust him'[1] is verbally identical, whether it refers to the relation of child to father or to that of man to God. But again in the second case these ideas are infused with a meaning of which none but the religious-minded man can have any comprehension or indeed any inkling, whose presence makes, e.g. the 'fear of God' 'something more' than any fear of a man, qualitatively, not merely quantitatively, though retaining the essence of the most genuine reverence felt by the child for its father. And Suso means in the same way to distinguish 'love' and 'love of God', when he says:

There was never a string so dulcet-toned but ceased to sound if stretched to a withered frame; a heart poor in love can no more understand speech rich in love than a German can an Italian.[2]

There is another kind of experience in which we may find an example of the way in which rational elements in our feeling-consciousness may be thus penetrated by quite non-rational ones, and an example even more proximate to the complex feeling of the holy than that just described—'erotic' experience;—in so far as the non-rational element is, like the numinous feeling but unlike the sexual impulse, at the same time *supra*-rational. I refer to the state of mind induced in us by a song set to music. The verbal text of the song expresses feelings that are 'natural', homesickness perhaps, or

[1] Luther's amplification of the First Commandment.
[2] Works, ed. Denifle, p. 309.

confidence in time of danger, hope for a future good, or joy in a present possession—all concrete elements in our 'natural' human lot, and capable of being described in conceptual terms. But it is otherwise with the music, purely as music. It releases a blissful rejoicing in us, and we are conscious of a glimmering, billowy agitation occupying our minds, without being able to express or explain in concepts what it really is that moves us so deeply. And to say that the music is mournful or exultant, that it incites or restrains, is merely to use signs by analogy, choosing them for their resemblance to the matter in hand out of other regions of our mental life; and at any rate we cannot say what the object or ground of this mourning or exulting may be. Music, in short, arouses in us an experience and vibrations of mood that are quite specific in kind and must simply be called 'musical'; but the rise and fall and manifold variations of this experience exhibit—though again only in part—definite, if fugitive, analogies and correspondences with our ordinary non-musical emotional states, and so can call these into consciousness and blend with them. If this happens, the specific 'music-consciousness' is thereby 'schematized' and rationalized, and the resultant complex mood is, as it were, a fabric, in which the general human feelings and emotional states constitute the warp, and the non-rational music-feelings the woof. The song in its entirety is therefore music 'rationalized'.

Now here is illustrated the contrast between the legitimate and the illegitimate processes of 'rationalization'. For, if the song may be called music 'rationalized' in the legitimate sense, in programme-music we have a musical 'rationalism' in the bad sense. Programme-music, that is to say, misinterprets and perverts the idea of music by its implication that the inner content of music is not—as in fact it is—something unique and mysterious, but just the incidental experiences—joy and grief, expansion and repression—familiar to the human heart. And in its attempt to make of musical tones a language to recount the fortunes of men programme-music abolishes the autonomy of music, and is deceived by a mere resemblance into employing as a means what is an end and substantive content in its own right. It is just the same mistake as when the 'august' aspect of the numinous is allowed to evaporate into the 'morally good', instead of merely being 'schematized' by it, or as when we let 'the holy' be identified with 'the perfectly good' will. And not only programme-music is at fault here. The 'music-drama' of Wagner, by attempting a thoroughgoing unification of the musical and the dramatic, commits the same offence against both the non-rational spirit of the former and the autonomy of either. We can only succeed in very partial and fragmentary fashion in 'schematizing' the non-rational factor in music by means of the familiar incidents of human experience. And the reason is just this, that the real content of music is not drawn from the ordinary human emotions at all, and that it is in no way merely a second language, alongside the usual one, by which these emotions find expression. Musical feeling is rather (like numinous feeling) something 'wholly other', which, while it affords analogies and here and there will run parallel to the ordinary emotions of life, cannot be made to coincide with them by a detailed point-to-point correspondence. It is, of course, from those places where the correspondence holds that the spell of a composed song arises by a blending of verbal and musical expression. But the very fact that we attribute to it a spell, an enchantment, points in itself to that 'woof' in the fabric of music of which we spoke, the woof of the unconceived and non-rational.[1]

But we must beware of confounding in any way the non-rational of music and the non-rational of the numinous itself, as Schopenhauer, for example, does. Each is something in its own right, independently of the other. We shall discuss later whether, and how far, the former may become a means of expression for the latter.

[1] This is the point of view from which to estimate both the excellent and the inadequate features of E. Hanslick's book, *Vom Musikalisch-Schönen*.

E

Chapter VIII

THE HOLY AS A CATEGORY OF VALUE

Sin and Atonement

WE have already met that strange and profound mental reaction to the numinous which we proposed to call 'creature-feeling' or creature-consciousness, with its concomitant feelings of submergence and prostration and of the diminution of the self into nothingness; bearing always in mind that these expressions do not hit with precision, but merely hint at what is really meant,[1] inasmuch as this 'diminution of the self', &c., is something very different from the littleness, weakness, or dependence of which we may become aware under other conditions than that of numinous feeling. And we had to notice that this experience marks a definite depreciation or disvaluation of the self in respect, so to speak, of its reality and very existence. We have now to put alongside of this another sort of self-disvaluation, which has long been a matter of common observation, and only needs to be suggested in order to be recognized. 'I am a man of *unclean* lips and dwell among a people of unclean lips.' 'Depart from me, for I am a *sinful* man, O Lord.' So say respectively Isaiah and Peter, when the numinous reality encounters them as a present fact of consciousness. In both cases this self-depreciating feeling-response is marked by an immediate, almost instinctive, spontaneity. It is not based on deliberation, nor does it follow any rule, but breaks, as it were, palpitant from the soul—like a direct reflex movement at the stimulation of the numinous. It does not spring from the consciousness of some committed transgression, but rather is an immediate datum given with the feeling of the numen: it proceeds to 'disvalue' together with the self the tribe to which the person belongs, and indeed, together with that, all existence in general. Now it is to-day pretty generally agreed

---

[1] Cf. Hugo of St. Victor's words: 'Sumpta sunt vocabula, ut intellegi aliquatenus posset quod comprehendi non poterat'. ('These words were chosen, that that which could not be comprehended might yet in some measure be understood.')

that, all this being the case, these outbursts of feeling are not simply, and probably at first not at all, *moral* depreciations, but belong to a quite special category of valuation and appraisement. The feeling is beyond question not that of the transgression of the moral law, however evident it may be that such a transgression, where it has occurred, will involve it as a consequence: it is the feeling of absolute 'profaneness'.

But what is this? Again something which the 'natural' man cannot, as such, know or even imagine. He, only, who is 'in the Spirit' knows and feels what this 'profaneness' is; but to such an one it comes with piercing acuteness, and is accompanied by the most uncompromising judgement of self-depreciation, a judgement passed, not upon his character, because of individual 'profane' actions of his, but upon his own very existence as creature before that which is supreme above all creatures. And at the same moment he passes upon the numen a judgement of *appreciation* of a unique kind by the category diametrically contrary to 'the profane', the category 'holy', which is proper to the numen alone, but to it in an absolute degree; he says: '*Tu solus sanctus*'. This '*sanctus*' is not merely 'perfect' or 'beautiful' or 'sublime' or 'good', though, being like these concepts also a *value*, objective and ultimate, it has a definite, perceptible analogy with them. It is the positive *numinous* value or worth, and to it corresponds on the side of the creature a numinous *disvalue* or 'unworth'.

In every highly-developed religion the appreciation of moral obligation and duty, ranking as a claim of the deity upon man, has been developed side by side with the religious feeling itself. None the less a profoundly humble and heartfelt recognition of 'the holy' may occur in particular experiences without being always or definitely charged or infused with the sense of moral demands. The 'holy' will then be recognized as that which commands our respect, as that whose real value is to be acknowledged inwardly. It is not that the awe of holiness is itself simply 'fear' in face of what is absolutely overpowering, before which there is no alternative to blind, awe-struck obedience. '*Tu solus sanctus*' is rather a paean of *praise*, which, so far from being merely a faltering confession of the divine supremacy, recognizes and extols a value, precious beyond all conceiving. The object of such praise is not simply absolute might, making its claims and compelling their fulfilment, but a might that has at the same time the supremest *right* to make the highest claim to service, and receives praise because it is in an absolute sense worthy to be praised. 'Thou art *worthy* to receive praise and honour and power' (Rev. iv. 11).

When once it has been grasped that *qādôsh* or *sanctus* is not originally a *moral* category at all, the most obvious rendering of the words is 'transcendent' ('supramundane', *überweltlich*). The one-sided character of this rendering to which we had to take exception has been supplemented by the more detailed exposition of the numinous and its implications. But its most essential defect remains to be noted: 'transcendent' is a purely ontological attribute and not an attribute of *value*; it denotes a character that can, if need be, abash us, but cannot inspire us with *respect*. It might once again, therefore, be an advantage to introduce another term to underline this side of the numinous, and the words *augustus* and σεμνός suggest themselves for the purpose. *Augustus*, 'august', no less than σεμνός, is really appropriate only to numinous objects—to rulers only as offspring or descendants of gods. Then, while σεβαστός indicates the *being* of the numen, σεμνός or *augustus* would refer rather to its supreme worth or *value*, its illustriousness. There will, then, in fact be two values to distinguish in the numen; its 'fascination' (*fascinans*) will be that element in it whereby it is of *subjective* value (= beatitude) to man; but it is 'august' (*augustum*) in so far as it is recognized as possessing in itself *objective* value that claims our homage.

Mere 'unlawfulness' only becomes 'sin', 'impiety', 'sacrilege', when the character of *numinous unworthiness* or *disvalue* goes on to be transferred to and centred in *moral* delinquency. And only when the mind feels it as 'sin' does the transgression of law become a matter of such dreadful gravity for the conscience, a catastrophe that leads it to despair of its own power. The meaning of 'sin' is not understood by the 'natural', nor even by the merely moral, man; and the theory of certain dogmatists, that the demand of morality as such urged man on to an inner collapse and then obliged him to look round for some deliverance, is palpably incorrect. There are serious-minded men of sincere moral endeavour who cannot understand what such a 'deliverance' or 'redemption' may be, and dismiss it with a shrug of the shoulders. They are aware that they are erring and imperfect men, but they know and put into practice the methods of self-discipline, and so labour onward upon their way with sturdy resolution. The morally robust older rationalism was lacking neither in a sincere and respectful recognition of the moral law nor in honest endeavour to conform to it. It knew well and sternly condemned what was 'wrong', and the aim of its exhortations and instruction was that men should realize better and take more in earnest the facts of moral right and wrong. But no 'downfall' or 'collapse' and no 'need of redemption' came within its scheme, because the objection brought against it by its opponents was in fact just; rationalism lacked understanding of what 'sin' is.[1] Mere morality is not the soil from which grows either the need of 'redemption' and deliverance or the need for that other unique good which is likewise altogether and specifically numinous in character, 'covering', and 'atonement'. There would perhaps be less disputing as to the warrant and value of these latter in Christian doctrine if dogmatic theology itself had not transferred them from their mystical sphere into that of rational ethics and attenuated them into moral concepts. They were thus taken from a sphere where they have an authentic and necessary place to one where their validity is most disputable.

[1] Cf. the testimony of Theodore Parker—certainly a man of far from crude mental development—as to his own experience, given by W. James, *Varieties*, p. 81:

'They (sc. the heathen of classical antiquity) were conscious of wrath, of cruelty, avarice, drunkenness, lust, sloth, cowardice, and other actual vices, and struggled and got rid of the deformities; but they were not conscious of "enmity against God" and didn't sit down and whine and groan against nonexistent evil. I have done wrong things enough in my life, and do them now: I miss the mark, draw bow, and try again. But . . . I know there is much "health in me"; and in my body, even now, there dwelleth many a good thing, spite of consumption and Saint Paul.'

If there is nothing crude about such a statement, it is at any rate *superficial*. The depths of the non-rational consciousness must be stirred to find with Anselm 'quanti ponderis sit peccatum'.

We meet the 'moment' of 'covering' in specially clear form in the religion of Yahweh, in its rites and the emotion they excite; but it is contained also, though more obscurely, in many other religions. It comprises, first, a manifestation of the numinous awe, viz. the feeling that the 'profane' creature cannot forthwith approach the numen, but has need of a covering or shield against the ὀργή of the numen. Such a 'covering' is then a 'consecration', i.e. a procedure that renders the approacher himself 'numinous', frees him from his 'profane' being, and fits him for intercourse with the numen. The means of 'consecration', however—'means of grace' in the proper sense—are derived from, or conferred and appointed by, the numen itself, which bestows something of its own quality to make man capable of communion with it. And this act is something very different from the 'annulment of mistrust', the phrase in which Ritschl seeks to rationalize these relations between God and man.

'Atonement', following our view, is a 'sheltering' or 'covering', but a profounder form of it. It springs directly from the idea of numinous value or worth and numinous disvalue or unworth as soon as these have been developed. Mere awe, mere need of shelter from the *tremendum*, has here been elevated to the feeling that man in his 'profaneness' is not *worthy* to stand in the presence of the holy one, and that his own entire personal unworthiness might defile even holiness itself. This is obviously the case in the vision of the call of Isaiah; and the same note recurs, less emphatically but quite unmistakably, in the story of the centurion of Capernaum (Luke vii. 1–10), and his words: 'I am not worthy that thou shouldest enter under my roof'. Here we have both the light thrill of awe before the *tremendum* of the numen and also, and more especially, the feeling of this unique disvalue or unworth of the profane confronted by the numen, which suggests to the man that even holiness itself may be tainted and tarnished by his presence.

Here, then, comes in the felt necessity and longing for 'atonement', and all the more strongly when the close presence of the numen, intercourse with it, and enduring possession of it, becomes an object of craving, is even desired as the *sum-*

mum bonum. It amounts to a longing to transcend this sunder-
ing unworthiness, given with the self's existence as 'creature'
and profane natural being. It is an element in the religious
consciousness, which, so far from vanishing in the measure
in which religion is deepened and heightened, grows on the
contrary continually stronger and more marked. Belonging,
as it does, wholly to the non-rational side of religion, it may
remain latent while, in the course of religious evolution, the
rational side at first unfolds and assumes vigorous and definite
form; it may retire for a time behind other elements and
apparently die away, but only to return more powerfully and
insistently than before. And again it may grow to be the sole,
one-sided, exclusive interest, a cry that drowns all other notes,
so that the religious consciousness is distorted and disfigured;
as may readily happen where through long periods of time
the rational aspects of religion have been fostered unduly and
at the cost of the non-rational.

The special character of this consciousness of need for
atonement may perhaps be brought home more clearly by an
analogy from our 'natural' emotional life; but at the same
time it is important that the religious feeling we are considering should itself be kept distinct from its analogue, as the
two are frequently confounded. The analogy is with the
feeling arising from moral transgression. There, too, we
practise a kind of self-depreciation which is clear and familiar
and perfectly intelligible to us, when we esteem ourselves
guilty of a bad action and the action itself as morally evil.
The evil of the action *weighs upon us* and deprives us of our
self-respect. We *accuse* ourselves and *remorse* sets in. But
alongside this self-depreciation stands a second one, which
while it may have reference to the same action as the other
yet avails itself of definitely different categories. The same
perverse action that before weighed upon us now *pollutes* us;
we do not accuse ourselves, we are defiled in our own eyes.
And the characteristic form of emotional reaction is no
longer remorse but *loathing*. The man feels a need, to express
which he has recourse to images of *washing* and cleansing.
The two kinds of self-depreciation proceed on parallel lines
and may relate to the same action; but none the less it is

obvious that they are, inwardly and in their essence, deter-
minately different. Now the second of them has a plain
analogy with the need for 'atonement', and so can fairly be
drawn upon for its elucidation; while at the same time it is
yet nothing more than an analogy from another sphere, viz.
that of morality.

No religion has brought the mystery of the need for atonement or expiation to so complete, so profound, or so powerful
expression as Christianity. And in this, too, it shows its
superiority over others. It is a more perfect religion and
more perfectly religion than they, in so far as what is potential
in religion in general becomes in Christianity a pure actuality.
And the distrust and suspicion which so widely obtains with
regard to this mystery is only to be explained from the general
custom—for which our theoretical cult of homiletics, liturgy,
and catechism is largely responsible—of taking into account
only the rational side of religion. Yet this atonement mystery
is a 'moment' which no Christian teaching that purports
to represent the religious experience of the Christian and
biblical tradition can afford to surrender. The teacher will
have to make explicit, by an analysis of the Christian religious experience, how the 'very numen', by imparting itself
to the worshipper, becomes itself the means of 'atonement'.
And in this regard it does not matter so very much what the
decisions of the commentators are as to what, if anything,
St. Paul or St. Peter wrote on the subject of expiation and
atonement, or whether, indeed, there is any 'scriptural
authority' for the thing at all. Were there in scripture no
word written about it, it might still be written to-day from
our own experience. But it would indeed be extraordinary if
it had not long ago been written of. For the God of the New
Testament is not less holy than the God of the Old Testament, but more holy. The interval between the creature and
Him is not diminished but made absolute; the unworthiness
of the profane in contrast to Him is not extenuated but enhanced. That God none the less admits access to Himself and
intimacy with Himself is not a mere matter of course; it is
a grace beyond our power to apprehend, a prodigious
paradox. To take this paradox out of Christianity is to make

it shallow and superficial beyond recognition. But if this is so, the intuitions concerning, and the need felt for, 'covering' and 'atonement' result immediately. And the divinely appointed means of God's self-revelation, where experienced and appraised as such—'the Word', 'the Spirit', 'the Person of Christ',—become that to which the man 'flees', in which he finds refuge, and in which he 'hides' himself, in order that, consecrated and cleansed of his 'profaneness' thereby, he may come into the presence of Holiness itself.

That these ideas are viewed with a certain distrust may be traced to two causes. One is, that what is a specifically religious element is distortingly moralized. If we start from mere morality and in relation to a God understood as being the personification of the moral order endowed with love, then all these things are wholly inapplicable and a source of genuine difficulty. But we are concerned with *religious* (not merely moral) intuitions, and it is impossible to dispute how right or wrong they are with a man whose interest is wholly in morality and not in religion, and who is therefore quite incapable of appreciating them. Whoever, on the other hand, penetrates to the unique centre of the religious experience, so that it starts awake in his own consciousness, finds that the truth of these intuitions is experienced directly, as soon as he penetrates into their depths.

The other ground of distrust is that usually in our theological systems an attempt is made to develop conceptual *theories* of these ideas, which are all pure intuitions, emotional rather than conceptual in character. They are thus made objects of speculation, and the final outcome is the quasi-mathematical 'doctrine of imputation' and its drastic ascription to the credit of the 'sinner' of the 'merit' of Christ, not to mention the learned inquiry whether this transaction involves an 'analytic' or a 'synthetic' judgement of God.

*   *   *   *   *

Let us look back once more from the point we have reached over the course our inquiry has so far taken. As the sub-title of this book suggests, we were to investigate the non-rational element in the idea of the divine. The words 'non-rational' and 'irrational' are to-day used almost at random. The non-rational is sought over the most widely different regions, and writers generally shirk the trouble of putting down precisely what they intend by the term, giving it often the most multifarious meanings or applying it with such vague generality that it admits of the most diverse interpretations. Pure fact in contrast to law, the empirical in contrast to reason, the contingent in contrast to the necessary, the psychological in contrast to transcendental fact, that which is known *a posteriori* in contrast to that which is determinable *a priori*; power, will, and arbitrary choice in contrast to reason, knowledge, and determination by value; impulse, instinct, and the obscure forces of the subconscious in contrast to insight, reflection, and intelligible plan; mystical depths and stirrings in the soul, surmise, presentiment, intuition, prophecy, and finally the 'occult' powers also; or, in general, the uneasy stress and universal fermentation of the time, with its groping after the thing never yet heard or seen in poetry or the plastic arts—all these and more may claim the names 'non-rational', 'irrational', and according to circumstances are extolled or condemned as modern 'irrationalism'. Whoever makes use of the word 'non-rational' to-day ought to say what he actually means by it. This we did in our introductory chapter. We began with the 'rational' in the idea of God and the divine, meaning by the term that in it which is clearly to be grasped by our power of conceiving, and enters the domain of familiar and definable conceptions. We went on to maintain that beneath this sphere of clarity and lucidity lies a hidden depth, inaccessible to our conceptual thought, which we in so far call the 'non-rational'.

The meaning of the two contrasted terms may be made plainer by an illustration. A deep joy may fill our minds without any clear realization upon our part of its source and the object to which it refers, though some such objective reference there must always be. But as attention is directed to it the obscure object becomes clearly identified in precise conceptual terms. Such an object cannot, then, be called, in our sense of the word, 'non-rational'. But it is quite otherwise with religious 'bliss' and its essentially numinous aspect,

the *fascinans*. Not the most concentrated attention can elucidate the object to which this state of mind refers, bringing it
out of the impenetrable obscurity of feeling into the domain
of the conceptual understanding. It remains purely a felt
experience, only to be indicated symbolically by 'ideograms'.
That is what we mean by saying it is non-rational.

And the same is true of all the moments of the numinous
experience. The consciousness of a 'wholly other' evades
precise formulation in words, and we have to employ symbolic
phrases which seem sometimes sheer paradox, that is, *ir*-
rational, not merely non-rational, in import. So with religious
awe and reverence. In ordinary fear and in moral reverence
I can indicate in conceptual terms what it is that I fear or
revere; injury, e.g., or ruin in the one case, heroism or strength
of character in the other. But the object of *religious* awe or
reverence—the *tremendum* and *augustum*, cannot be fully determined conceptually: it is non-rational, as is the beauty of a
musical composition, which no less eludes complete conceptual analysis.

Confronted by the fact of the non-rational thus interpreted
we cannot be satisfied with a mere bare statement, which
would open the door to all the vague and arbitrary phraseology of an emotionalist irrationalism. We are bound to try,
by means of the most precise and unambiguous symbolic and
figurative terms that we can find, to discriminate the different
elements of the experience so far as we can in a way that can
claim general validity.

Chapter IX

MEANS OF EXPRESSION OF THE NUMINOUS

1. *Direct Means*

IT may serve to make the essential nature of the numinous consciousness clearer if we call to mind the manner in which it expresses itself outwardly, and how it spreads and is transmitted from mind to mind. There is, of course, no 'transmission' of it in the proper sense of the word; it cannot be 'taught', it must be 'awakened' from the spirit. And this could not justly be asserted, as it often is, of religion as a whole and in general, for in religion there *is* very much that *can* be taught—that is, handed down in concepts and passed on in school instruction. What is incapable of being so handed down is this numinous basis and background to religion, which can only be induced, incited, and aroused. This is least of all possible by mere verbal phrase or external symbol; rather we must have recourse to the way all other moods and feelings are transmitted, to a penetrative imaginative sympathy with what passes in the other person's mind. More of the experience lives in reverent attitude and gesture, in tone and voice and demeanour, expressing its momentousness, and in the solemn devotional assembly of a congregation at prayer, than in all the phrases and negative nomenclature which we have found to designate it. Indeed, these never give a positive suggestion of the object to which the religious consciousness refers; they are only of assistance in so far as they profess to indicate *an* object, which they at the same time contrast with another, at once distinct from and inferior to it, e.g. 'the invisible', 'the eternal' (non-temporal), 'the supernatural', 'the transcendent'. Or they are simply ideograms for the unique content of feeling, ideograms to understand which a man must already have had the experience himself. Far the best means are actual 'holy' situations or their representation in description. If a man does not *feel* what the numinous is, when he reads the sixth chapter of Isaiah, then no 'preaching, singing, telling', in

Luther's phrase, can avail him. Little of it can usually be noticed in theory and dogma, or even in exhortation, unless it is actually *heard*. Indeed no element in religion needs so much as this the *viva vox*, transmission by living fellowship and the inspiration of personal contact.[1]

But the mere word, even when it comes as a living voice, is powerless without the 'spirit in the heart' of the hearer to move him to apprehension. And this spirit, this inborn capacity to receive and understand, is the essential thing. If that is there, very often only a very small incitement, a very remote stimulus, is needed to arouse the numinous consciousness. It is indeed astonishing to see how small a stimulus suffices—and that too coming sometimes only in clumsy and bewildered guise—to raise the spirit of itself to the strongest pitch of the most definitely religious excitement. But where the wind of the spirit blows, there the mere 'rational' terms themselves are indued with power to arouse the feeling of the 'non-rational', and become adequate to tune the mood at once to the right tone. Here 'schematization' starts at once and needs no prompting. He who 'in the spirit' reads the written word lives in the numinous, though he may have neither notion of it nor name for it, nay, though he may be unable to analyse any feeling of his own and so make explicit to himself the nature of that numinous strand running through the religious experience.

2. *Indirect Means*

For the rest, the methods by which the numinous feeling is presented and evoked are indirect; i.e. they consist in those means by which we express kindred and similar feelings belonging to the 'natural' sphere. We have already become acquainted with these feelings, and we shall recognize them

[1] Suso says of the transmission of the mystical experience: 'One thing there may be known; unlike as it is, when a man heareth himself a dulcet instrument of strings sweetly sounding, compared to whoso but heareth tell thereof, even so are the words which are received in the purity of grace and flow forth out of a living heart by a living mouth unlike to those same words if they are beheld upon the dead parchment. . . . For there they grow cold, I know not how, and wither away like roses that have been plucked. For the lovely melody that above all toucheth the heart is then quenched to silence; and in the waste places of the withered heart are they then received.'

at once if we consider what are the means of expression which religion has employed in all ages and in every land.

One of the most primitive of these—which is later more and more felt to be inadequate, until it is finally altogether discarded as 'unworthy'—is quite naturally the 'fearful' and horrible, and even at times the revolting and the loathsome. Inasmuch as the corresponding feelings are closely analogous to that of the *tremendum*, their outlets and means of expression may become indirect modes of expressing the specific 'numinous awe' that cannot be expressed directly. And so it comes about that the horrible and dreadful character of primitive images and pictures of gods, which seems to us to-day frequently so repellent, has even yet among naïve and primitive natures—nay, occasionally even among ourselves—the effect of arousing genuine feelings of authentic religious awe. And, vice versa, this awe operates as a supremely potent stimulus to express the element of terror in different forms of imaginative representation. The hard, stern, and somewhat grim pictures of the Madonna in ancient Byzantine art attract the worship of many Catholics more than the tender charm of the Madonnas of Raphael. This trait is most signally evident in the case of certain figures of gods in the Indian pantheon. Durgā, the 'great Mother' of Bengal, whose worship can appear steeped in an atmosphere of profoundest devotional awe, is represented in the orthodox tradition with the visage of a fiend. And this same blending of appalling frightfulness and most exalted holiness can perhaps be even more clearly studied in the eleventh book of the Bhagavad-Gītā,[1] in which Vishnu—who is yet to his votaries the very principle of goodness—displays himself to Aryuna in the true height of his divinity. Here, too, the mind has recourse for mode of expression first to the fearful and dreadful, though this is at the same time permeated with that element of 'the grand' to which we next turn.

This mode of expression, by way of 'grandeur' or 'sublimity', is found on higher levels, where it replaces mere

[1] See Appendix II. Nowhere can the non-rational element of ὀργή be better studied than in this chapter, one of the perfectly classical passages for the theory of Religion.

'terror' and 'dread'. We meet it in an unsurpassable form in the sixth chapter of Isaiah, where there is sublimity alike in the lofty throne and the sovereign figure of God, the skirts of His raiment 'filling the temple' and the solemn majesty of the attendant angels about Him. While the element of 'dread' is gradually overborne, the connexion of 'the sub-lime' and 'the holy' becomes firmly established as a legiti-mate schematization and is carried on into the highest forms of religious consciousness—a proof that there exists a hidden kinship between the numinous and the sublime which is something more than a merely accidental analogy, and to which Kant's *Critique of Judgement* bears distant witness.

So far we have been concerned with that element or factor of the numinous which was the first our analysis noted and which we proposed to name symbolically 'the aweful' (*tremendum*). We pass now to consider the means by which the second—the element of 'the mysterious' (*mysterium*)—is expressed. Here we light upon the analogical mode of mani-festation that in every religion occupies a foremost and extraordinary place, and the theory of which we are now in a position to give. I refer to *miracle*. 'Miracle is the dearest child of Faith'; if the history of religions had not already taught us the truth of Schiller's saying, we might have reached it by anticipation *a priori* from the element of 'the mysterious', as already shown. Nothing can be found in all the world of 'natural' feelings bearing so immediate an analogy—*mutatis mutandis*—to the religious consciousness of ineffable, unutter-able mystery, the 'absolute other', as the incomprehensible, unwonted, enigmatic thing, in whatever place or guise it may confront us. This will be all the more true if the un-comprehended thing is something at once *mighty* and *fearful*, for then there is a twofold analogy with the numinous—that is to say, an analogy not only with the *mysterium* aspect of it, but with the *tremendum* aspect, and the latter again in the two directions already suggested of *fearfulness* proper and *subli-mity*. This exemplifies the general truth already considered that any form of the numinous consciousness may be stirred by means of feelings analogous to it of a 'natural' kind, and then itself pass over into these, or, more properly, be replaced by them. And, in fact, this is everywhere manifest in the experience of man. Whatever has loomed upon the world of his ordinary concerns as something terrifying and baffling to the intellect; whatever among natural occurrences or events in the human, animal, or vegetable kingdoms has set him astare in wonder and astonishment—such things have ever aroused in man, and become endued with, the 'daemonic dread' and numinous feeling, so as to become 'portents', 'prodigies', and 'marvels'. Thus and only thus is it that 'the miraculous' rose. And, in the reverse direction, the feeling of the *numen* as 'the mysterious' worked as a potent stimulus on the naïve imagination, inciting it to expect miracles, to invent them, to 'experience' them, to recount them, just as before the felt awefulness of the numen became a stimulus to select or fashion inventively, as a means of religious expression, images of fear and dread. 'The mysterious' became an untiring impulse, prompting to inexhaustible invention in folk-tale and myth, saga and legend, permeating ritual and the forms of worship, and remaining till to-day to naïve minds, whether in the form of narrative or sacrament, the most powerful factor that keeps the religious consciousness alive. But here too, as in the case of the fearful and terrible, progress to a higher stage of development shows the gradual elimination of this merely external analogue to the numinous, viz. the miraculous; and so we see how, on the more enlightened levels, 'miracle' begins to fade away; how Christ is at one with Mohammed and Buddha in declining the role of mere wonder-worker; how Luther dismisses the 'outward miracles' disparagingly as 'jugglery' or 'apples and nuts for children'; and finally how the 'supernaturalism' of miracle is purged from religion as something that is only an imperfect analogue and no genuine 'schema' of the numinous.

There are other manifestations of this tendency of the feeling of the 'mysterious' to be attracted to objects and aspects of experience analogous to it in being 'uncomprehended'. It finds its most unqualified expression in the spell exercised by the only half intelligible or wholly unintelligible language of devotion, and in the unquestionably real enhancement of the awe of the worshipper which this produces.

Instances of this are—the ancient traditional expressions, still retained despite their obscurity, in our Bible and hymnals; the special emotional virtue attaching to words like 'Hallelujah', *Kyrie eleison*, 'Selah', just because they are 'wholly other' and convey no clear meaning; the Latin in the service of the Mass, felt by the Catholic to be, not a necessary evil, but something especially holy; the Sanskrit in the Buddhist Mass of China and Japan; the 'language of the gods' in the ritual of sacrifice in Homer; and many similar cases. Especially noticeable in this connexion are the half-revealed, half-concealed elements in the service of the Mass, in the Greek Church liturgy, and so many others; we can see here one factor that justifies and warrants them. And the same is true of the remaining portions of the old Mass which recur in the Lutheran ritual. Just because their design shows but little of regularity or conceptual arrangement, they preserve in themselves far more of the spirit of worship than the proposed recastings of the service put forward by the most recent practical reformers. In these we find carefully arranged schemes worked out with the balance and coherence of an essay, but nothing unaccountable, and for that very reason suggestive; nothing accidental, and for that very reason pregnant in meaning; nothing that rises from the deeps below consciousness to break the rounded unity of the wonted disposition, and thereby point to a unity of a higher order— in a word, little that is really spiritual. All the cases cited, then, derive their power of suggestion from the same source; they are all instances of the analogy to 'the mysterious' afforded by that which is not wholly understood, unwonted and at the same time venerable through age; and in the resemblance they present to the 'mysterious' they arouse it in the mind by a sort of 'anamnēsis' or reminder, and at the same time constitute its outward analogical representation.

3. *Means by which the Numinous is expressed in Art*

In the arts nearly everywhere the most effective means of representing the numinous is 'the sublime'. This is especially true of architecture, in which it would appear to have first been realized. One can hardly escape the idea that this feeling for expression must have begun to awaken far back in the remote Megalithic Age. The motive underlying the erection of those gigantic blocks of rock, hewn or unworked, single monoliths or titanic rings of stone, as at Stonehenge, may have well been originally to localize and preserve and, as it were, to store up the numen in solid presence by magic; but the change to the motive of *expression* must have been from the outset far too vividly stimulated not to occur at a very early date. In fact the bare feeling for solemn and imposing magnitude and for the pomp of sublime pose and gesture is a fairly elementary one, and we cannot doubt that this stage had been reached when the *mastabas*, obelisks and pyramids were built in Egypt. It is indeed beyond question that the builders of these temples, and of the Sphinx of Gizeh, which set the feeling of the sublime, and together with and through it that of the numinous, throbbing in the soul almost like a mechanical reflex, must themselves have been conscious of this effect and have intended it.

Further, we often say of a building, or indeed of a song, a formula, a succession of gestures or musical notes, and in particular of certain manifestations of ornamental and decorative art, symbols, and emblems, that they make a 'downright magical' impression, and we feel we can detect the special characteristic of this 'magical' note in art with fair assurance even under the most varying conditions and in the most diverse relationships. The art of China, Japan, and Tibet, whose specific character has been determined by Taoism and Buddhism, surpasses all others in the unusual richness and depth of such impressions of the 'magical', and even an inexpert observer responds to them readily. The designation 'magical' is here correct even from the historical point of view, since the origin of this language of form was properly magical representations, emblems, formularies, and contrivances. But the actual impression of 'magic' is quite independent of this historical bond of connexion with magical practices. It occurs even when nothing is known of the latter; nay, in that case it comes out most strongly and unbrokenly. Beyond dispute art has here a means of creating a unique impression—that of the magical—apart from and independent of reflection. Now the magical is nothing but a suppressed and dimmed form of the numinous, a crude form of it which great art purifies and ennobles. In great art the point is reached at which we may no longer speak of the 'magical', but rather are confronted with the numinous itself, with all its impelling motive power, transcending reason, expressed in sweeping lines and rhythm.[1] In no art, perhaps, is this more fully realized than in the great landscape painting and religious painting of China in the classical period of the T'ang and Sung dynasties. It has been said of this great art:

These works are to be classed with the profoundest and sublimest of the creations of human art. The spectator who, as it were, immerses himself in them feels behind these waters and clouds and mountains the mysterious breath of the primeval Tao, the pulse of innermost being. Many a mystery lies half-concealed and half-revealed in these pictures. They contain the knowledge of the 'nothingness' and the 'void', of the 'Tao' of heaven and earth, which is also the Tao of the human heart. And so, despite their perpetual agitation, they seem as remotely distant and as profoundly calm as though they drew secret breath at the bottom of a sea.[2]

To us of the West the Gothic appears as the most numinous of all types of art. This is due in the first place to its sublimity; but Worringer in his work, *Probleme der Gothik*, has done a real service in showing that the peculiar impressiveness of Gothic does not consist in its sublimity alone, but draws upon a strain inherited from primitive magic, of which

---

[1] This numinous–magical character is specially noticeable in the strangely impressive figures of the Buddha in early Chinese art; and here too it affects the observer independently of 'ideas', i.e. without his knowing anything about the speculative doctrines of Buddhism. Thus Sirén justly says of the great Buddha from the Lung-Men Caves (T'ang Dynasty):

'Anyone who approaches this figure will realize that it has a religious significance without knowing anything about its *motif*. . . . It matters little whether we call it a prophet or a god, because it is a complete work of art permeated by a spiritual will, which communicates itself to the beholder. . . . The religious element of such a figure is immanent; it is "a presence" or an atmosphere rather than a formulated idea. . . . It cannot be described in words, because it lies beyond intellectual definition.'

(Oswald Sirén, *Chinese Sculpture*, London, 1925, vol. i, p. 20.)

[2] From an article by Otto Fischer on Chinese landscape painting in *Das Kunstblatt*, Jan. 1920.

he tries to show the historical derivation. To Worringer, then, the impression Gothic makes is one of magic; and, whatever may be said of his historical account of the matter, it is certain that in this at least he is on the right track. Gothic *does* instil a spell that is more than the effect of sublimity. But 'magic' is too low a word: the tower of the Cathedral of Ulm is emphatically not 'magical', it is *numinous*. And the difference between the numinous and the merely magical can nowhere be felt more clearly than in the splendid plate Worringer gives in his book of this marvellous work of architecture. But when this is said, we may still keep the word 'magic' in use to denote the style and means of artistic expression by which the impression of the numinous comes into being.

But in neither the sublime nor the magical, effective as they are, has art more than an indirect means of representing the numinous. Of directer methods our Western art has only two, and they are in a noteworthy way *negative*, viz. *darkness* and *silence*. The darkness must be such as is enhanced and made all the more perceptible by contrast with some last vestige of brightness, which it is, as it were, on the point of extinguishing; hence the 'mystical' effect begins with semi-darkness. Its impression is rendered complete if the factor of the 'sublime' comes to unite with and supplement it. The semi-darkness that glimmers in vaulted halls, or beneath the branches of a lofty forest glade, strangely quickened and stirred by the mysterious play of half-lights, has always spoken eloquently to the soul, and the builders of temples, mosques, and churches have made full use of it.

Silence is what corresponds to this in the language of musical sounds. 'Yahweh is in his holy temple, let all the earth keep silence before him.' (Hab. ii. 20.) Neither we nor (probably) the prophet any longer bear in mind that this 'keeping silence' (as εὐφημεῖν in Greek), if regarded from the historical, 'genetic' standpoint, springs from the fear of using words of evil omen, which therefore prefers to be altogether speechless. It is the same with Tersteegen in his 'God is present, let all in us be silent'. With prophet and psalmist and poet we feel the necessity of silence from another and quite independent motive. It is a spontaneous reaction to the feeling of the actual *numen praesens*. Once again, what is found coming upon the scene at a higher level of evolution cannot be explained by merely interpolating links in a 'historico-genetic' chain of development; and the Psalmist and Tersteegen and even we ourselves are at least as interesting subjects for the analysis of the psychologist of religion as are the 'primitives', with their habitual practice of εὐφημία, the silence that merely avoids words of ill augury.

Besides silence and darkness oriental art knows a third direct means for producing a strongly numinous impression, to wit, *emptiness* and *empty distances*. Empty distance, remote vacancy, is, as it were, the sublime in the horizontal. The wide-stretching desert, the boundless uniformity of the steppe, have real sublimity, and even in us Westerners they set vibrating chords of the numinous along with the note of the sublime, according to the principle of the association of feelings. Chinese architecture, which is essentially an art in the laying out and grouping of buildings, makes a wise and very striking use of this fact. It does not achieve the impression of solemnity by lofty vaulted halls or imposing altitudes, but nothing could well be more solemn than the silent amplitude of the enclosed spaces, courtyards, and vestibules which it employs. The imperial tombs of the Ming emperors at Nanking and Peking are, perhaps, the strongest example of this, including, as they do, in their plan the empty distances of an entire landscape. Still more interesting is the part played by the factor of void or emptiness in Chinese painting. There it has almost become a special art to paint empty space, to make it palpable, and to develop variations upon this singular theme. Not only are there pictures upon which 'almost nothing' is painted, not only is it an essential feature of their style to make the strongest impression with the fewest strokes and the scantiest means, but there are very many pictures—especially such as are connected with contemplation—which impress the observer with the feeling that the void itself is depicted as a subject, is indeed the main subject of the picture. We can only understand this by recalling what was said above on the 'nothingness' and the 'void' of

the mystics and on the enchantment and spell exercised by
the 'negative hymns'. For 'void' is, like darkness and silence,
a negation, but a negation that does away with every 'this'
and 'here', in order that the 'wholly other' may become
actual.

Not even music, which else can give manifold expression
to all the feelings of the mind, has any positive way to express
'the holy'. Even the most consummate Mass-music can only
give utterance to the holiest, most numinous moment in the
Mass—the moment of transubstantiation—by sinking into
stillness: no mere momentary pause, but an absolute cessation of sound long enough for us to 'hear the silence' itself;
and no devotional moment in the whole Mass approximates
in impressiveness to this 'keeping silence before the Lord'. It
is instructive to submit Bach's Mass in B minor to the test in
this matter. Its most mystical portion is the 'Incarnatus' in
the 'Credo', and there the effect is due to the faint, whisper-
ing, lingering sequence in the fugue structure, dying away
pianissimo. The held breath and hushed sound of the passage,
its weird cadences, sinking away in lessened thirds, its pauses
and syncopations, and its rise and fall in astonishing semi-
tones, which render so well the sense of awe-struck wonder—
all this serves to express the *mysterium* by way of intimation,
rather than in forthright utterance. And by this means Bach
attains his aim here far better than in the 'Sanctus'. This
latter is, indeed, an incomparably successful expression of
Him, whose is 'the power and the glory', an enraptured and
triumphant choric hymn to perfect and absolute sovereignty.
But it is very far distant from the mood of the text that
accompanies the music, which is taken from Isa. vi, and
which the composer should have interpreted in accordance
with that passage as a whole. No one would gather from this
magnificent chorus that the Seraphim covered their faces
with two of their wings.[1] In this point Mendelssohn shows
very fine sensibility in his musical setting of Ps. ii at the words
(v. 11): 'Serve the Lord with fear, and rejoice with trem-

---

[1] The Jewish tradition has been, however, very well aware of the import of
the matter. In the splendid New Year's Day Hymn of Melek Elyōn the words
run: 'All the mighty ones on high *whisper low*: Yahweh is King.'

bling.' And here too the matter is expressed less in the music itself than in the way the music is restrained and repressed—one might almost say, abashed—as the Cathedral choir at Berlin so well knows how to render it. And, if a final example may be cited, the 'Popule meus' of Thomas Luiz gets as near to the heart of the matter as any music can. In this the first chorus sings the first words of the *Trisagion*: 'Hagios, ho theos, hagios ischyros, hagios athanatos', and the second chorus sings in response the Latin rendering of the words: 'Sanctus deus, sanctus fortis, sanctus immortalis', each chorus thrilling with a sort of muffled tremor. But the *Trisagion* itself, sung *pianissimo* by singers kept out of sight far at the back, is like a whisper floating down through space, and is assuredly a consummate reproduction of the scene in the vision of Isaiah.

Chapter X

THE NUMINOUS IN THE OLD TESTAMENT

WHILE the feelings of the non-rational and numinous constitute a vital factor in every form religion may take, they are pre-eminently in evidence in Semitic religion and most of all in the religion of the Bible. Here mystery lives and moves in all its potency. It is present in the ideas of the daemonic and angelic world, which, as a 'wholly other', surrounds, transcends, and permeates this world of ours; it is potent in the Biblical eschatology and the ideal of a 'kingdom of God' contrasted with the natural order, now as being future in time, now as being eternal, but always as the downright marvellous and 'other'; and finally it impresses itself on the character of Yahweh and Elohim—that God who is nevertheless the 'Heavenly Father' of Jesus and as such fulfils, not loses, His character as Yahweh.

The lower stage of numinous consciousness, viz. daemonic dread, has already been long superseded by the time we reach the Prophets and Psalmists. But there are not wanting occasional echoes of it, found especially in the earlier narrative literature. The story in Exod. iv. 24, of how Yahweh in his ὀργή met Moses by the way 'and sought to kill him', still bears this 'daemonic' character strongly, and the tale leaves us almost with the suggestion of a ghostly apparition. And from the standpoint of the more highly developed 'fear of God' one might easily get from this and similar stories the impression that this is not yet religion at all, but a sort of pre-religious, vulgar fear of demons or the like. That would, however, be a misconception; a 'vulgar fear of demons' would refer to a 'demon' in the narrower sense of the word, in which it is a synonym for devil, fiend, or goblin, and is *contrasted* with the divine. But 'demon' in this sense has not been, any more than 'ghost' or 'spectre', a point in the transition, or, if it be preferred, a link in the chain of development which religious consciousness has undergone. Both 'demon' (= fiend) and 'spectre' are, so to speak, offshoots from the true line of progress, spurious fabrications of the fancy accompanying the numinous feeling. We must carefully distinguish from such a 'demon' the δαίμων or 'daemon' in the more general sense of the word, which, if it is not yet itself a 'god', is still less an anti-god, but must be termed a 'pre-god', the numen at a lower stage, in which it is still trammelled and suppressed, but out of which the 'god' gradually grows to more and more lofty manifestations. *This* is the phase whose after-effects can be detected in these ancient stories.

It will be worth while to consider this matter further. Two things may help to an understanding of the real relation with which we are here concerned. First, we may refer back to what was said on an earlier page upon the capacity of 'the dreadful' and 'terrible' in general to attract and arouse, and also to express, the true numinous consciousness or emotion. In the second place, we may refer to the parallel case of music. A man with a pronounced musical faculty, so long as he is a mere raw tyro, may be enraptured by the sound of the bagpipes or the hurdy-gurdy, though perhaps both become intolerable to him when his musical education has been completed. But, if he then recalls the qualitative character of his earlier musical experience and compares it with his present one, he will have to admit that, in both, one and the same side of his mind is functioning, and that what has taken place in the rise of his feeling for music to a more elevated form is no transition to something different in kind, but a process which we may call 'development' or 'growth to maturity', but can hardly further specify. Were we to hear to-day the music of Confucius, it would probably be to us merely a succession of queer noises. Yet already Confucius speaks of the power of music on the mind in a way we moderns cannot better, and touches upon just those elements which we also must recognize in the experience of music. But the most striking consideration in this regard is the way in which some savage tribes are endowed with a capacity for a ready appreciation of our music, which they grasp quickly, practise assiduously, and enjoy intensely, when it is brought before them. This endowment did not first enter their minds at the moment they heard the music by a 'heterogony', 'epigenesis', or other miracle; it simply existed all the time as a natural predisposition or latent capacity. It was aroused and began to develop as soon as the proper incitement came to stimulate it, but to the end it was yet *the selfsame* disposition that had been formerly excited to such primitive and crude manifestations. This 'crude', 'primitive' form of music is often almost or wholly unrecognizable as real music by our developed musical taste, although it was the manifestation of the same impulse and the same element of our psychical nature. Now it is exactly a parallel case when the 'God-fearing' man of to-day finds it hard to detect in the narrative of Exod. iv that which is akin to his own religious experience, or misjudges it altogether. All this involves a point of view which should be taken into consideration more generally with respect to the religion of 'primitive man', though naturally great caution should be used in applying it, seeing that very mistaken conclusions can be drawn from it and there is a real danger of confounding the lower with the higher levels of development and of making too little of the interval between them. However, it is still more dangerous to exclude this point of view altogether, as is unfortunately very commonly done.[1]

Recent research has sought to discover a difference in character between Yahweh, the austere and stern, and Elohim, the familiar, patriarchal God, and there is something very illuminating in the suggestion. Söderblom's supposition[2] is that the notion of Yahweh had its point of origin in earlier 'animistic' ideas. I do not dispute the importance of such 'animistic' ideas in the religious evolutionary process; in fact, I should go even farther than Söderblom in that respect, for he would explain them as a sort of primitive 'philosophy', and therefore has to exclude them altogether from the domain of genuinely *religious* imagination. It would be perfectly compatible with my own view to hold that where ideas of an animistic character had been framed they could serve as an important link in the 'chain of stimulation' by which true numinous consciousness is aroused (namely, in so far as they

[1] In this regard Mr. Marett in particular has important and novel considerations to offer.

[2] Söderblom, *Das Werden des Gottesglaubens*, 1916, pp. 297 ff.

served to disengage and free the obscure feeling-element of 'existent being', latent in it). But what distinguishes Yahweh from El-Shaddai–Elohim is not that the former is an 'anima', but (and the distinction may be applied to differentiate all god-types) that, whereas in Yahweh the numinous preponderates over the familiar 'rational' character, in Elohim the rational aspect outweighs the numinous. 'Outweighs' is as much as we can say, for in Elohim too the numinous element is certainly present; Elohim is, for instance, the subject of the genuinely numinous narrative of the theophany in the burning bush, with the characteristic verse (Exod. iii. 6): 'And Moses hid his face; for he was afraid to look upon God.'

For the copious and diverse characteristics of the idea of God of the ancient Israelites which might be instanced here the reader is referred to works upon the history of religion.[1] The venerable religion of Moses marks the beginning of a process which from that point onward proceeds with ever increasing momentum, by which the numinous is throughout rationalized and moralized, i.e. charged with ethical import, until it becomes the 'holy' in the fullest sense of the word. The culmination of the process is found in the Prophets and in the Gospels. And it is in this that the special nobility of the religion revealed to us by the Bible is to be found, which, when the stage represented by the 'deutero-Isaiah' is reached, justifies its claim to be a universal world-religion. Here is to be found its manifest superiority over, e.g., Islam, in which Allah is mere 'numen', and is in fact precisely Yahweh in His pre-Mosaic form and upon a larger scale. But this moralizing and rationalizing process does not mean that the numinous itself has been overcome, but merely that its preponderance has been overcome. The numinous is at once the basis upon which and the setting within which the ethical and rational meaning is consummated.

The capital instance of the intimate mutual interpenetration of the numinous with the rational and moral is Isaiah. The note struck in the vision of his call is the keynote of his entire prophecy. And nothing is in this regard more signifi-

[1] They are given exhaustively in the Encyclopaedia *Die Religion in Geschichte und Gegenwart*, vol. ii, pp. 1530, 2036.

cant than the fact that it is in Isaiah that the expression 'the Holy One of Israel' first becomes established as the expression, *par excellence*, for the deity, prevailing over all others by its mysterious potency. This remains so in the writings of the 'deutero-Isaiah', who follows the tradition of the earlier Isaiah. Assuredly in deutero-Isaiah, if in any writer, we have to do with a God whose attributes are clear to conceptual thought: omnipotence, goodness, wisdom, truth; and yet all the time these are attributes of 'the Holy One', whose strange name deutero-Isaiah too repeats no less than fifteen times and always in passages where it has a special impressiveness.

Related expressions akin to the 'holiness' of Yahweh are His 'fury', His 'jealousy', His 'wrath', the 'consuming fire', and the like. The import of them all is not only the all-requiting righteousness of God, not even merely His susceptibility to strong and living emotions, but all this ever enclosed in and permeated with the 'awefulness' and the 'majesty', the 'mystery' and the 'augustness', of His non-rational divine nature.

And this holds good, also, of the expression 'the living God'. God's 'livingness' is perceptibly akin to His 'jealousy' and is manifested in and through this, as in His other 'passions' generally.[1] It is by His 'life' that this God is differentiated from all mere 'world reason', and becomes this ultimately non-rational essence, that eludes all philosophic treatment. This is the God that lives in the consciousness of all prophets and apostles of the Old and the New Dispensation alike. And all those who later championed against the 'God of

---

[1] Cf. Deut. v. 26: 'For who is there of all flesh, that hath heard the voice of the *living* God speaking out of the midst of the fire, as we have, *and lived*?' Cf. also Josh. iii. 10; 1 Sam. xvii. 26, 36; 2 Kings xix. 4; Isa. xxxvii. 4, 17; Jer. x. 10: 'He is the *living* God: . . . at His *wrath* the earth shall tremble and the nations shall not be able to abide His *indignation*'; Jer. xxiii. 36; 2 Macc. vii. 33; Matt. xxvi. 63 (the adjuration 'by the *living* God', the God of terror and dread); and Heb. x. 31: 'It is a fearful thing to fall into the hands of the *living* God.' The Old Testament idea of the terrible 'living' God reaches its completion in the ideas of the 'avenging God', of which the most ruthless expression is in the almost appalling image of the treader of the wine-press, Isa. lxiii. 3: 'I will tread them in mine anger, and trample them in my fury; and their blood shall be sprinkled upon my garments and I will stain all my raiment.' The dreadful image recurs in the New Testament in Rev. xix. 15: 'He treadeth the wine-press of the fierceness and wrath of Almighty God.'

philosophy' the 'living God' and the God of anger and love and the emotions have unwittingly been defending the non-rational core of the Biblical conception of God from all excessive rationalization. And so far they were right. Where they were wrong and sank into anthropomorphism was in defending, not figurative 'anger' and 'emotion', but literal anger and emotion, misconceiving the numinous character of the attributes in question and holding them simply to be 'natural' attributes, taken absolutely, instead of realizing that they can only be admitted as figurative indications of something essentially non-rational by means of symbols drawn from feelings that have analogy to it.

We find the power of the numinous—in its phase of the mysterious—to excite and intensify the imagination displayed with particular vividness in Ezekiel. Here are to be classed Ezekiel's dreams and parables and fanciful delineation of God's being and sovereign state, which are, as it were, an example by anticipation of the later more spurious sort of excitement of the religious impulse to the mysterious, leading (in accordance with analogies already expounded) to the merely strange, the extraordinary, the marvellous, and the fantastic. When such an operation of the religious consciousness works itself out in accordance with a wrong analogy, the way is prepared for miracle and legend and the whole dream-world of pseudo-mysticism; and, though these are all truly enough emanations from the genuine religious experience, they are emanations broken by the opaque, dull medium through which they pass, a mere substitute for the genuine thing, and they end in a vulgar rankness of growth that over-spreads the pure feeling of the *mysterium* as it really is and chokes its direct and forthright emotional expression.

But, if Ezekiel hardly shows the numinous moment apart from an admixture of excessive fantasy and imagination, the same is not true of the Book of Job. In the 38th chapter of Job we have the element of the mysterious displayed in rare purity and completeness, and this chapter may well rank among the most remarkable in the history of religion. Job has been reasoning with his friends against Elohim, and—as far as concerns them—he has been obviously in the right.

They are compelled to be dumb before him. And then Elohim Himself appears to conduct His own defence in person. And He conducts it to such effect that Job avows himself to be overpowered, truly and rightly overpowered, not merely silenced by superior strength. Then he confesses: 'Therefore I abhor myself and *repent* in dust and ashes.' That is an admission of inward *convincement* and conviction, not of impotent collapse and submission to merely superior power. Nor is there here at all the frame of mind to which St. Paul now and then gives utterance; e.g. Rom. ix. 20: 'Shall the thing formed say to him that formed it, Why hast thou made me thus? Hath not the potter power over the clay, of the same lump to make one vessel unto honour, and another unto dishonour?' To interpret the passage in Job thus would be a misunderstanding of it. This chapter does not proclaim, as Paul does, the renunciation of, the realization of the impossibility of, a 'theodicy'; rather, it aims at putting forward a real theodicy of its own, and a better one than that of Job's friends; a theodicy able to convict even a Job, and not only to convict him, but utterly to still every inward doubt that assailed his soul. For latent in the weird experience that Job underwent in the revelation of Elohim is at once an inward relaxing of his soul's anguish and an appeasement, an appeasement which would alone and in itself perfectly suffice as the solution of the problem of the Book of Job, even without Job's rehabilitation in Chapter xlii, where recovered prosperity comes as an extra payment thrown in after quittance has been already rendered. But what is this strange 'moment' of experience that here operates at once as a vindication of God to Job and a reconciliation of Job to God?

In the words put into the mouth of Elohim nearly every note is sounded which the situation may prepare one to expect *a priori*: the summons to Job, and the demonstration of God's overwhelming power, His sublimity and greatness, and His surpassing wisdom. This last would yield forthwith a plausible and rational solution of the whole problem, if only the argument were here completed with some such sentences as: 'My ways are higher than your ways; in my deeds and my actions I have ends that you understand not'; viz. the testing or purification of the godly man, or ends that concern the whole universe as such, into which the single man must fit himself with all his sufferings. It you start from rational ideas and concepts, you absolutely *thirst* for such a conclusion to the discourse. But nothing of the kind follows: nor does the chapter intend at all to suggest such teleological reflections or solutions. In the last resort it relies on something quite different from anything that can be exhaustively rendered in rational concepts, namely, on the sheer absolute wondrousness that transcends thought, on the *mysterium*, presented in its pure, non-rational form. All the glorious examples from nature speak very plainly in this sense. The eagle, that 'dwelleth and abideth on the rock, upon the crag of the rock, and the strong place', whose 'eyes behold afar off' her prey, and whose 'young ones also suck up blood, and where the slain are, there is she'—this eagle is in truth no evidence for the *teleological* wisdom that 'prepares all cunningly and well', but is rather the creature of *strangeness* and *marvel*, in whom the wondrousness of its creator becomes apparent. And the same is true of the ostrich (xxxix. 13–18) with its *inexplicable* instincts. The ostrich is indeed, as here depicted, and 'rationally' considered, a crucial difficulty rather than an evidence of wisdom, and it affords singularly little help if we are seeking *purpose* in nature: 'which leaveth her eggs in the earth, and warmeth them in the dust, and forgetteth that the foot may crush them or that the wild beast may break them. She is hardened against her young ones as though they were not hers: her labour is in vain without fear; because God hath *deprived her of wisdom*, neither hath he imparted to her *understanding*'.

It is the same with the 'wild ass' (verse 5) and the unicorn (verse 9). These are beasts whose complete 'dysteleology' or negation of purposiveness is truly magnificently depicted; but, nevertheless, with their mysterious instincts and their inexplicable behaviour, this very negation of purpose becomes a thing of baffling significance, as in the case of the 'wild goat' (verse 1) and the hind. The 'wisdom' of the inward parts (xxxviii. 36), and the 'knowledge' of dayspring, winds, and clouds, with the mysterious ways in which they come and go, arise and vanish, shift and veer and re-form; and the wonderful Pleiades aloft in heaven, with Orion and 'Arcturus and his sons'—these serve but to emphasize the same lesson. It is conjectured that the descriptions of the hippopotamus (behemoth) and crocodile (leviathan) in xl. 15 ff. are a later interpolation. This may well be the fact; but, if so, it must be admitted that the interpolator has felt the point of the entire section extraordinarily well. He only brings to its grossest expression the thought intended by all the other examples of animals; they gave portents only, he gives us 'monsters'—but 'the monstrous' is just the 'mysterious' in a gross form. Assuredly these beasts would be the most unfortunate examples that one could hit upon if searching for evidences of the purposefulness of the divine 'wisdom'. But they, no less than all the previous examples and the whole context, tenor, and sense of the entire passage, do express in masterly fashion the downright stupendousness, the wellnigh daemonic and wholly incomprehensible character of the eternal creative power; how, incalculable and 'wholly other', it mocks at all conceiving but can yet stir the mind to its depths, fascinate and overbrim the heart. What is meant is the *mysterium* not as mysterious simply, but at the same time also as 'fascinating' and 'august'; and here, too, these latter meanings live, not in any explicit concepts, but in the tone, the enthusiasm, in the very rhythm of the entire exposition. And here is indeed the point of the whole passage, comprising alike the theodicy and the appeasement and calming of Job's soul. The *mysterium*, simply as such, would merely (as discussed above) be a part of the 'absolute inconceivability' of the numen, and that, though it might strike Job utterly dumb, could not convict him inwardly. That of which we are conscious is rather an *intrinsic value* in the incomprehensible—a value inexpressible, positive, and 'fascinating'. This is incommensurable with thoughts of rational human teleology and is not assimilated to them: it remains in all its mystery. But it is as it becomes felt in consciousness that Elohim is justified and at the same time Job's soul brought to peace.

*　　*　　*　　*　　*　　*

A very real parallel to this experience of Job is to be found in the work of a writer of our own day, which is not the less deeply impressive because it is found in the fictitious context of a novel. Max Eyth recounts in his story *Berufs-Tragik* (in the collection *Hinter Pflug und Schraubstock*) the building of the mighty bridge over the estuary of the Ennobucht. The most profound and thorough labour of the intellect, the most assiduous and devoted professional toil, had gone to the construction of the great edifice, making it in all its signifi-cance and purposefulness a marvel of human achievement. In spite of endless difficulties and gigantic obstacles, the bridge is at length finished, and stands defying wind and waves. Then there comes a raging cyclone, and building and builder are swept into the deep. Utter meaninglessness seems to triumph over richest significance, blind 'destiny' seems to stride on its way over prostrate virtue and merit. The narrator tells how he visits the scene of the tragedy and returns again.

When we got to the end of the bridge, there was hardly a breath of wind; high above, the sky showed blue-green, and with an eerie brightness. Behind us, like a great open grave, lay the Ennobucht. The Lord of life and death hovered over the waters in silent majesty. We felt His presence, as one feels one's own hand. And the old man and I knelt down before the open grave and before Him.

Why did they kneel? Why did they feel constrained to do so? One does not kneel before a cyclone or the blind forces of nature, nor even before Omnipotence merely as such. But one does kneel before the wholly uncomprehended Mystery, revealed yet unrevealed, and one's soul is stilled by feeling the way of its working, and therein its justification.

It would be possible to cite many other traces of numinous feeling in the Old Testament. But they have already been admirably put together by one who wrote sixteen hundred years ago in the same sense as we 'upon the non-rational'. This was Chrysostom. We shall be considering him later on and will not anticipate further in this place.[1]

[1] See Appendix I.

THE NUMINOUS IN THE NEW TESTAMENT

IN the Gospel of Jesus we see the consummation of that process tending to rationalize, moralize, and humanize the idea of God, which began with the earliest period of the old Hebrew tradition and became specially prominent as a living factor in the Prophets and the Psalms, continually bringing the apprehension of the numinous to a richer fulfilment by recognizing in it attributes of clear and profound value for the reason. The result was the faith in 'the fatherhood of God' in that unsurpassable form in which it is peculiar to Christianity.

But in this case, too, it would be a mistake to think that such a rationalization means that 'the numinous' is excluded or superseded. That is a misunderstanding into which we are led by the all-too-plausible delineations of 'Jesus's faith in the fatherhood of God' now prevalent, but it certainly misrepresents the attitude of the first Christian congregations. The error is only possible if we disregard in the message of Christ that which it really purports to be, first, last, and all the time, viz. 'the gospel *of the kingdom*'. As against all rationalizing attempts to tone it down into something less startling, the most recent research shows quite decisively that the 'kingdom' is just greatness and marvel absolute, the 'wholly other' 'heavenly' thing, set in contrast to the world of here and now, 'the mysterious' itself in its dual character as awe-compelling yet all-attracting, glimmering in an atmosphere of genuine 'religious awe'. As such, it sheds a colour, a mood, a tone, upon whatever stands in relation to it, upon the men who proclaim it or prepare for it, upon the life and practice that are its precondition, upon the tidings of it, upon the congregation of those who await it and attain it. All is made into a mystery—all, that is, becomes numinous. This is shown most strikingly in the name by which the company of the disciples call themselves collectively and each other individually, the numinous 'technical term' οἱ ἅγιοι, the holy ones or 'the saints'. It is manifest at once that this does not mean 'the morally perfect' people: it means the people who participate in the mystery of the final Day. Their title is the clear and unambiguous antithesis to the term 'the profane', which we have already met with. For this reason the early Christians are able later to call themselves also actually a 'priestly'—or sacerdotal—'people', that is, a group of 'consecrated' persons. But the precondition of all this was given with the gospel itself and its claim to be the preaching of the coming kingdom.

What of the Lord of this kingdom, the 'heavenly Father'? As its Lord He is not less, but far more 'holy', 'numinous', mysterious, *qādôsh*, ἅγιος, *sacer*, and *sanctus* than His kingdom. He is all these in an absolute degree, and in this aspect of His nature He represents the sublimation and the consummation of all that the old covenant had grasped by way of 'creature-consciousness', 'holy awe', and the like. Not to realize this is to turn the gospel of Jesus into a mere idyll. That these moments do not occur severally in Jesus's message in the form of special 'doctrines' is due to the circumstances already mentioned more than once. But apart from the inherent impossibility of *teaching* them, how could He have had need of 'teaching' what was simply the primary, self-evident fact to every Jew, and especially to every believer in 'the kingdom', namely, that God was 'the Holy One of Israel'? Christ had rather to teach and to proclaim what was *not* self-evident to the Jews, but His own original discovery and revelation, that this very 'Holy One' is a 'heavenly Father'. This point of view necessarily occupied the whole of His 'teaching', and all the more so because it was the point of view thrust sharply into the foreground by the two opposed influences of His time, against both of which the Gospel came historically as a reaction. On the one hand was Pharisaism, with its servitude to Law; on the other, John the Baptist, with his harsh, ascetic interpretation of God; and, in contrast to both, the gospel of the sonhood of man and the fatherhood of God came as the easy yoke, the light burden. But though it is necessarily this new message that the parables and discourses and pronouncements of Jesus complete and fill out, it is in such a way that it always remains an

overwhelming and daring paradox, claiming our utmost homage, that He who is 'in heaven' is yet 'our Father'. That that
'heavenly' Being of marvel and mystery and awe is Himself
the eternal, benignant, gracious will: this is the resolved
contrast that first brings out the deep-felt harmony in true
Christian experience; and the harmony cannot be heard
aright by the man whose ear does not detect always sounding
in it this sublimated 'seventh'.

It is significant, and yet again so natural, that the first
petition in the prayer of the Christian fellowship is: 'Hallowed
be Thy name.' What I have already said should make the
meaning of this clear in its connexion with the Biblical meaning of the word. And we can sometimes detect, even in the
teaching of Jesus, notes still vibrating which seem to suggest
a trace of that weird awe and shuddering dread before the
mysteries of the transcendent of which we have already
spoken. Such a passage is Matt. x. 28: 'But fear him which is
able to *destroy both soul and body in hell.*'

The dark and awful ring of this saying cannot be missed,
and it is a rationalization of it merely to refer it to the Judge
and His judgement on the Last Day. The same note rings out
again clearly in the saying in Heb. x. 31: 'It is a fearful thing
to fall into the hands of the living God'; and in Heb. xii. 29:
'Our God is a consuming fire.' (Here the adaptation of
Deut. iv. 24: 'The Lord is a consuming fire' into 'Our God
is a consuming fire' gives a contrast whose effect enhances
the horror of the saying.) And when occasion demands it
the Old Testament God of 'vengeance' recurs even in the
teaching of Jesus Himself, unveiled and in His own authentic
character; as, for instance, in Matt. xxi. 41: 'He will miser-
ably destroy those wicked men.'

Finally, it is in the light of, and with the background of,
this numinous experience, with its mystery and its awe—its
mysterium tremendum—that Christ's Agony in the night of
Gethsemane must be viewed, if we are to comprehend or
realize at all in our own experience what the import of that
agony was. What is the cause of this 'sore amazement' and
'heaviness', this soul shaken to its depths, 'exceeding sorrow-
ful even unto death', and this sweat that falls to the ground

like great drops of blood? Can it be ordinary fear of death in the case of one who had had death before his eyes for weeks past and who had just celebrated with clear intent his death-feast with his disciples? No, there is more here than the fear of death; there is the awe of the creature before the *mysterium tremendum*, before the shuddering secret of the numen. And the old tales come back into our mind as strangely parallel and, as it were, prophetically significant, the tales of Yahweh who waylaid Moses by night, and of Jacob who wrestled with God 'until the breaking of the day'. 'He had power with God . . . and prevailed', with the God of 'wrath' and 'fury', with the *numen*, which yet is itself '*my Father*'. In truth even those who cannot recognize 'the Holy One of Israel' elsewhere in the God of the Gospel must at least discover Him here, if they have eyes to see at all.

I have no need to dwell upon the numinous atmosphere pervading the writings of St. Paul. 'God dwelleth in a light that none may come nigh.' The 'over-aboundingness' ('exuberance') of the idea of God and the feeling of God leads with Paul to the special terminology and experiences of mysticism.[1] But it is not confined to these: it can be seen alive through all his utterances in the feelings of exalted enthusiasm and his spiritual terminology of the *pneuma*, which are alike far removed from the merely rational side of Christian piety. His dualistic depreciation of 'the flesh', as of all that pertains to creaturehood, is that numinous self-disvaluation spoken of on pp. 49 ff. carried to its extreme. These catastrophes and sudden reversals that befall the religious consciousness, the tragedy of sin and guilt, or again the glow of beatific joy, are only possible and intelligible on the basis of numinous experience. And just as the ὀργὴ Θεοῦ with St. Paul is more than the mere reaction of righteous retribution, just as it is permeated by the 'awefulness' of the numinous, so on the other side is the 'fascination' of the

---

[1] As a provisional definition of mysticism I would suggest that, while sharing the nature of religion, it shows a preponderance of its non-rational elements and an over-stressing of them in respect to the 'over-abounding' aspect of the 'numen'. A type of religious experience acquires 'mystical colouring' if it shows an inclination to mysticism. In this sense Christianity since St. Paul and St. John is not mysticism, but religion with a mystical colouring. And this is justified.

experienced love of God, that bears the spirit beyond its boundaries into the third heaven, more than the mere consummation of the natural human feeling of a child for its parent. The ὀργὴ Θεοῦ is potently and vividly present in the grand passage in Rom. i. 18 ff., where we recognize directly the jealous, passionate Yahweh of the Old Testament, here grown to a God of the universe of fearful power, who pours out the blazing vials of His wrath over the whole world. In this passage there is an intuition, genuinely non-rational in character, the sublimity of which has an almost horrible quality: that the commission of sin is the angry God's punishment for sin. St. Paul reiterates this thought—so intolerable, if considered 'rationally'—in three separate verses. 'Wherefore God also gave them up to uncleanness through the lusts of their own hearts, to dishonour their own bodies between themselves' (Rom. i. 24); 'For this cause God gave them up unto vile affections' (i. 26); 'God gave them over to a reprobate mind, . . . being filled with all unrighteousness', &c. (i. 28, 29).

To feel the full weight and force of this intuition it is necessary to escape as far as possible from the mental atmosphere of our dogmatic interpretations and judiciously toned-down catechisms, and to try to recapture the awe that could be felt by the Jew toward the fury of Yahweh, by the Hellenistic Greek toward the horror of *heimarmenē* or Destiny, and by primitive man in general toward the *ira deorum* or anger of the gods.

There is one other point in the teaching of Paul that demands notice in this connexion—his doctrine of predestination. It is perhaps precisely the 'rationalist' who feels most directly that with the idea of predestination we are standing on downright non-rational ground. Nothing remains so alien to the rationalist as this doctrine. And from his point of view he is quite right; from the standpoint of the rational this notion of predestination is a sheer absurdity, an absolute offence. Let him acquiesce in all the paradoxes of the Trinity and Christology, predestination will yet remain perpetually to confront him as a stumbling-block.

Not, as need hardly be said, in the form in which it has

been put forward since the time of Schleiermacher, following the tradition of Leibniz and Spinoza. That is simply a capitulation to natural law and *causae secundae*, a surrender to the claim of modern psychology that all human resolves and actions are subject to the compelling force of motives, so that a man is unfree and predetermined thereby. And so, this predetermination by *nature*, having been identified with the all-embracing efficacy of God, in the end the outcome of the profound and purely religious intuition of divine pre-determination—which has no concern at all with 'laws of nature'—is the comparatively trivial 'scientific' notion of universal causal connexion. There can be no more spurious product of theological speculation, no more fundamental falsification of religious conceptions than this; and it is cer-tainly not against this that the rationalist feels an antagonism, for it is itself a piece of solid rationalism, but at the same time a complete abandonment of the real religious idea of 'predestination'.

This false 'scientific' interpretation of 'predestination' having been put aside, it may be shown that as a religious idea it springs from two sources and has two quite distinct aspects, which should be distinguished by separate names. The one is 'election', the other—striking an essentially different note—'predestination' proper.

The idea of 'election'—i.e. of having been chosen out and pre-ordained by God *unto salvation*—is an immediate and pure expression of the actual religious experience of grace. The recipient of divine grace feels and knows ever more and more surely, as he looks back on his past, that he has not grown into his present self through any achievement or effort of his own, and that, apart from his own will or power, grace was imparted to him, grasped him, impelled, and led him. And even the resolves and decisions that were most his own and most free become to him, without losing the element of free-dom, something that he *experienced* rather than *did*. Before every deed of his own he sees love the deliverer in action, seeking and selecting, and acknowledges that an eternal gracious purpose is watching over his life. But this 'pre-ordainment' is purely a preordainment unto salvation and has in itself nothing to do with the *praedestinatio ambigua*, the predetermination of all men *either* to be saved *or* to be damned. The rational and logical conclusion of course would be that, if he is elected of God but others are not, God, in appointing the elect to bliss, determines also the rejected for damnation. But this conclusion is not, and must not be, drawn, for what we are concerned with is a religious intuition which, as such, stands alone and is only warrant for itself, and which indeed is outraged by any attempt to weave it into a system or make it yield a series of inferences. In this respect Schleiermacher is quite right when he says in his *Discourses upon Religion*:[1] 'Every (*sc.* religious) intuition is a self-subsistent work . . . knowing nothing of derivation and point of connexion.'

So much for 'election'. From it must be distinguished 'predestination' proper, as it appears in St. Paul, e.g. Rom. ix. 18: 'Therefore hath he mercy on whom he will, and whom he will he hardeneth.'

It is true that the thought of 'election', prominent in St. Paul, can be detected here as well. But the reflection in v. 20 is obviously the utterance of quite a different frame of mind: 'Nay, but, O man, who art thou that repliest against God? Shall the thing formed say to him that formed it, Why hast thou made me thus?' That is a line of thought wholly out of keeping with the set of ideas centring about 'election'. And yet even less can it be derived from any abstractly theoretic 'doctrine' of the all-causing nature of God. Such a doctrine we find in Zwingli, and with him it does indeed give rise to a 'doctrine of predestination', but one that is rather the artificial product of philosophical speculation than the result of immediate religious experience. The true 'predestination', springing directly from religious intuition, has its origin beyond question in St. Paul. But in him it is easily recognized as the numinous feeling in face of the *mysterium tremendum*; and that unique phase of it that we met with above (pp. 9 ff.) in the narrative of Abraham recurs here in a signally intensified form. For the religious conception in the notion of predestination is nothing but that 'creature-con-

[1] Schleiermacher, *Reden über die Religion*, ed. R. Otto, 4th ed., pp. 37–8.

sciousness', that self-abasement and the annulment of personal strength and claims and achievements in the presence of the transcendent, as such. The numen, overpoweringly experienced, becomes the all-in-all. The creature, with his being and doing, his 'willing' and 'running' (Rom. ix. 16), his schemes and resolves, becomes nothing. The conceptual expression to indicate such a felt submergence and annihilation over against the numen is then—here impotence and there omnipotence; here the futility of one's own choice, there the will that ordains all and determines all.

It is next to be noted that 'predestination' in this sense, as identical with the absolute supremacy of the numen, has nothing whatever to do with the 'unfree will' of 'Determinism'. Rather, it finds very frequently precisely in the 'free will' of the creature the contrast which makes it stand out so prominently. 'Will what thou wilt and how thou canst; plan and choose; yet must all come about as it shall and as is determined': that is the earliest and most genuine expression of the matter. In face of the eternal power man is reduced to naught, *together with* his free choice and action. And the eternal power waxes immeasurable just because it fulfils its decrees *despite* the freedom of human will. This is the aspect of the matter designedly thrust into the foreground in many typical Mohammedan narratives which profess to display the inflexibility of the decrees of Allah. In these, men are *able* to devise and decide and reject; but, however they choose or act, Allah's eternal will is accomplished to the very day and hour that was ordained. The purport of this is precisely, *not* that God and God alone is an active cause, but rather that the activity of the creature, be it never so vigorous and free, is overborne and determined absolutely by the eternal operative purpose.[1] The thought of the deity as the absolutely sole

[1] The story told by Beidhavi, an expositor of the Koran, illustrates this: Once when Azrael, the angel of Death, came before Solomon he directed his gaze upon one of the king's companions. 'Who is that?' asked the man. 'The angel of Death,' replied Solomon. 'He seems to be looking at me,' continued the other, 'so command the wind that it bear me hence and set me down in India.' Solomon did so. Then said the angel, 'I gazed upon him for so long out of astonishment, seeing it had been commanded me to fetch his soul out of India, while he was yet with thee in Canaan.' This is a predestination which

and all-embracing active cause first occurs where the creature-feeling is intensified still further, and is at the same time combined with theoretic considerations. It then leads to mysticism; and it is only again a further consequence if the speculations about being, peculiar to and characteristic of mysticism, become then attached to the thought of God as sole cause. To the creature then is denied, not merely *efficacy* as a cause, but true *reality* and complete being, and all existence and fullness of being is ascribed to the absolute entity, who alone really *is*, while all 'being' of creatures is either a function of this absolute Being—which brings them into existence —or mere illusion. This sequence of ideas is found in particularly explicit form in the mysticism of Geulincx and the Occasionalists. 'Ubi nihil vales, ibi nihil velis.' Sometimes we hear the same mystical chord in St. Paul also, as in his mysterious saying about the final issue of all things, where 'God shall be all in all'. But the passage in Romans is different. It goes no farther than the thought of predestination itself; and predestination we have found to be nothing but the intensified 'creature-feeling' in conceptual expression, and to be altogether rooted in the numinous consciousness.

A further consideration may make it plainer that this must be so. If it be really true that the consciousness of the numinous, as 'creature-feeling', is the root of the predestination idea, then we should expect that the form of religious faith marked by an undue and exaggerated insistence on the non-rational elements in the idea of God would also lean most markedly to predestination. And such is obviously the case. No religion has such a leaning to predestination as Islam; and the special quality of Islam is just that in it, from its commencement onwards, the rational and specifically moral aspect of the idea of God was unable to acquire the firm and clear impress that it won, e.g., in Christianity or Judaism. In Allah the numinous is absolutely preponderant over everything else. So that, when Islam is criticized for giving

presupposes free will just as its foil. However freely man makes his plans, Allah has always set his countermine.

[This story is told in verse by Leigh Hunt in his poem 'The Inevitable'; cf. Oxford ed. (1922), pp. 95–6. (*Trans.*)]

a merely 'fortuitous' character to the claim of morality, as though the moral law were only valid through the chance caprice of the deity, the criticism is well justified, only 'chance' and fortuitousness have nothing to do with the matter. The explanation is rather that the numinous in Allah, nay, even his uncanny and daemonic character, out-weighs what is rational in him. And this will account for what is commonly called the 'fanatical' character of this religion. Strongly excited feeling of the numen, that runs to frenzy, untempered by the more rational elements of religious experience—that is everywhere the very essence of fanaticism.

The above interpretation of the notion of predestination gives at the same time our estimate of it. It is an attempted statement, in conceptual terms and by *analogy*, of something that at bottom is incapable of explication by concepts. Fully justified in this sense as an analogical expression, it is wholly unjustified (*summum jus* becoming *summa injuria*) if its character as analogy is missed, so that it is taken as an adequate formulation of theological theory. In that case it is disastrous and intolerable to a rational religion like Chris-tianity, in spite of the attempts that are made to render it innocuous by all the arts of evasion and mitigation.

There is another element in the thought of Paul besides his notion of predestination that is rooted in the numinous: I refer to his utter depreciation of 'the flesh'. 'The flesh' with Paul is simply the condition of the creature in general. And this is utterly disparaged and depreciated by the numinous consciousness (as we saw on pp. 9 ff., 49 ff.) in contrast to the transcendent, both in regard to its existence and its value; in respect to the first as 'dust and ashes', 'nothingness', in-sufficient, weak, transient, and perishing, and in respect to the second as the 'profane', the impure, which is unable to assume the worth of holiness or to come into its presence. We find these two same sorts of depreciation among the ideas of Paul, and the specifically Pauline feature in them is only the vigour and completeness with which he expresses them. It is a quite separate question whence Paul derives this intensity in his denunciation and depreciation of 'the flesh', whether it is original to him or stimulated by the 'dualistic' environment of thought in which he moved. As has been already said, one can determine nothing about the essential nature or the value of a thing by tracing its genesis and continuous historic derivation from other sources. And at least we may maintain that Paul might well be stimulated to this emphatic expression by many genuine cases of the numinous experience recorded in the Old Testament. There too *bāsār*, the flesh, is both the principle of being 'dust and ashes' and the principle of the 'pollution' of the creature in the presence of holiness.

In St. John, no less than in St. Paul, there is a strong strain of the numinous. The element of 'awefulness', it is true, dies away in him, as so commonly in mysticism, without ever quite vanishing, for, *pace* Ritschl, even in John 'the wrath of God abideth' (John iii. 36); but this only makes the elements of 'mystery' and 'fascination' the stronger, even in their mystical form. In John, Christianity absorbs φῶς and ζωή, 'light' and 'life', into itself from the religions at rivalry with it;[1] and justly so, for only in Christianity do they win home. But what is this 'light' and this 'life'? Not to *feel* what they are is to be made of wood, but none can express it. They are a sheer abounding overplus of the non-rational element in religion.

And the same is true even of that saying of St. John to which the 'rationalists' are so specially fond of referring: 'God is a Spirit' (John iv. 24). This was the text on account of which Hegel held Christianity to be the highest because the most truly spiritual (*geistig*) religion. But Hegel meant by 'spirit' the 'absolute reason'. St. John when he speaks of

---

[1] And thereby drains these religions of their life-blood, according to 'the right of the stronger'. And henceforth these elements belong to Christianity indissolubly as its very own. For

> Wenn starke Geisteskraft
> Die Elemente
> An sich herangerafft:
> Kein Engel trennte
> Geeinte Zwienatur
> Der innigen Beiden—

and still less can the criticism of scholars! ['When the vigour of the spirit has gathered the elements into itself, then may no angel sunder the double nature now made single of the united twain.']

πνεῦμα is not thinking of 'absolute reason' but of that which is in absolute contrast to everything of 'the world' and 'the flesh', the utterly mysterious and miraculous heavenly Being who surpasses all the understanding and reason of the 'natural' man. He is thinking of that 'Spirit' which 'bloweth where it listeth, and thou hearest the sound thereof, but canst not tell whence it cometh and whither it goeth'—the Spirit which just on that account is not confined to Zion or Gerizim, and whose worship is only for those who are themselves 'in spirit and in truth'. So that this saying, apparently wholly 'rational' in import, is itself the strongest and clearest indication of the non-rational element in the Biblical idea of God.[1]

[1] Compare with this chapter my book *Reich Gottes und Menschensohn* (*The Kingdom of God and the Son of Man*).

CHAPTER XII

THE NUMINOUS IN LUTHER

IN Catholicism the feeling of the numinous is to be found as a living factor of singular power. It is seen in Catholic forms of worship and sacramental symbolism, in the less authentic forms assumed by legend and miracle, in the paradoxes and mysteries of Catholic dogma, in the Platonic and neo-Platonic strands woven into the fabric of its religious conceptions, in the solemnity of churches and ceremonies, and especially in the intimate *rapport* of Catholic piety with mysticism. For reasons already suggested, the mysterious is much less in evidence in the official systems of doctrine, whether Catholic or Protestant. Particularly since the time when the great medieval scholastics (the *theologi moderni*, so called) replaced Plato by Aristotle and welded the latter and his method on to the doctrines of the Church, Catholic orthodoxy has been subjected to a strong rationalizing influence, to which, however, actual living religious practice and feeling never conformed or corresponded. The battle here joined between so-called 'Platonism' and 'Aristotelianism', and in general the long persistent protest against the scholastics, is itself in large part nothing but the struggle between the rational and the non-rational elements in the Christian religion. And the same antithesis is clearly operative as a factor in Luther's protest against Aristotle and the *theologi moderni*.

At that time Plato himself was known (very imperfectly) chiefly through the interpretations—and misinterpretations —of him by Augustine, Plotinus, and Dionysius the Areopagite. Yet it was a true feeling that led the contrasted attitudes of mind to choose the names of Plato and Aristotle as their battle-cries. Plato did indeed make a powerful contribution towards the rationalization of his religion, for according to his *philosophy* the deity had to become identical with the 'Idea of the Good', and consequently something wholly rational and conceivable. But the most remarkable characteristic of Plato's thought is just that he himself finds science and philosophy too narrow to comprise the whole of man's mental life. He has indeed properly no philosophy of religion; he grasps the object of religion by quite different means than those of conceptual thinking, viz. by the 'ideograms' of myth, by 'enthusiasm' or inspiration, 'erôs' or love, 'mania' or the divine frenzy. He abandons the attempt to bring the object of religion into one system of knowledge with the objects of 'science' (ἐπιστήμη), i.e. reason, and it becomes something not less but greater thereby; while at the same time it is just this that allows the sheer non-rational aspect of it to be so vividly felt in Plato, and indeed vividly expressed as well as felt. No one has enunciated more definitively than this master-thinker that God transcends all reason, in the sense that He is beyond the powers of our conceiving, not merely beyond our powers of comprehension.

'Therefore is it an *impossible* task both to discover the creator and father of this whole universe and to publish the discovery of him in words for all to understand.'[1]

Aristotle's thought is much more theological than Plato's, but his temper is far less religious; and at the same time his theology is absolutely rationalistic. And this contrast between the two is repeated among those who profess themselves 'Platonists' or 'Aristotelians'.

Another influence which orthodox doctrine underwent, from the earliest patristic period onwards, and which tended to weaken the non-rational element in religion, came from the acceptance of the ancient theory of the divine ἀπάθεια or immunity from passion. The God of Greek, and especially of Stoic, theology was constructed after the ideal of the 'wise man', who achieves this 'apathy' by the overcoming of his

[1] *Timaeus*, 28 c τὸν μὲν οὖν ποιητὴν καὶ πατέρα τοῦδε τοῦ παντὸς εὑρεῖν τε ἔργον καὶ εὑρόντα εἰς πάντας ἀδύνατον λέγειν. For the non-rational and supra-rational strain in Plato the reader is referred to von Wilamowitz-Möllendorff, *Plato*, i. 418: and especially to the splendid passage from Plato's seventh letter: 341 c: 'Concerning these things [*sc.* ultimate truth] there is not, nor will there be, any treatise written by me. For they do not at all admit of being expounded in writing, as do objects of other [scientific] studies. . . . Only after long, arduous conversance with the matter itself . . . a light suddenly breaks upon the soul as from a kindled flame, and once born keeps alive of itself. . . . Only to a few men is the exposition of these things of any profit, and they only need a slight indication of them for their discovery.'

'passions' and 'affections'; and the attempt was now made to assimilate this God to the 'living God' of Scripture. And, as intimated above, an effective if unconscious factor in this contest was the antithesis between the non-rational and the rational aspects of the deity. Lactantius, in his treatise *De Ira Dei*, illustrates particularly strikingly this fight against the God of the philosophers. He uses the same wholly rational terms, taken from man's emotional life, as do his opponents, but raises them to a higher power, so that he makes God, as it were, a gigantic mind, quick with an immense vitality. But whoever in this way contends for the 'living God' is at the same time contending unwittingly for the divine in God, that which cannot be reduced to idea, world-order, moral order, principle of being, or purposive will. And many of Lactantius' own expressions point of themselves to something beyond. Thus, quoting Plato, he says: 'Quid omnino sit Deus, non esse quaerendum: quia nec inveniri possit nec enarrari.'[1] He is in general fond of emphasizing the *incomprehensibilitas* of God: 'quem nec aestimare sensu valeat humana mens nec eloqui lingua mortalis. Sublimior enim ac maior est, quam ut possit aut cogitatione hominis aut sermone comprehendi.'[2] He is fond of the expression *maiestas Dei*, and blames the philosophers for misjudging the 'unique majesty' of God. And he feels the *tremendum* in the *maiestas* when he asserts that God 'is wroth', and demands 'awe' as a fundamental characteristic of religion when he says: 'Ita fit, ut religio et maiestas et honor *metu* constet. Metus autem non est, ubi nullus irascitur.'[3] He says that a God who cannot be angry cannot love either: and a God that knows neither love nor anger would be *immobilis* and not the 'Deus *vivus*', the *living* God of Scripture.

This ancient battle of Lactantius against the *deus philosophorum* comes to life again in the Middle Ages in Duns

---

[1] Ed. Fritzsche, p. 227: 'We ought not to ask what God is altogether; for it can neither be discovered by any nor stated in words.'

[2] Ibid., p. 116: '[God] whom the human mind has no power to appraise, nor tongue of mortals to utter. For he is too sublime and too great to be grasped in the thought or the speech of man.'

[3] 'Thus it comes that religion and majesty and honour depend upon fear. But there is no fear where none is angry.'

Scotus's battle for the God of 'willing', as opposed to the God of 'being', and for the validity of volition as an essential in religion, as opposed to cognition. And the non-rational elements which are still latent in Duns Scotus break out openly in Luther in a whole series of some of his most characteristic thoughts.

This aspect of Luther's religion was later tacitly expunged, and is to-day readily dismissed as 'not the authentic Luther', or as 'a residuum of the scholastic speculations of the nominalists'. But, if that is so, it is strange that this 'residuum of Scholasticism' exercised such a power in Luther's own mental life as it palpably did. In point of fact this is not a 'residuum' at all, but beyond all question the mysterious background of his religious life, obscure and 'uncanny', and to estimate it in all its power and profundity we need to abstract the lucid bliss and joyfulness of Luther's faith in the divine grace, and to see this faith in relation to the background of that mysterious experience on which it rests. It matters not from what source, whether 'nominalism' or the traditional teaching of his Order, his consciousness was first stirred; we have in any case in Luther the numinous consciousness at first hand, stirred and agitated through its typical 'moments', as we have come to know them. It is a corroboration that these 'moments' appear in Luther in their completed series, and so point back to the common basis that unites them all.

1. We are not here concerned with the many strands, strong at the outset, weaker later, but never altogether disappearing, that connect him with mysticism. Nor are we concerned with the surviving effects of the 'numinous' element of the Catholic worship in his doctrine of the Eucharist, which cannot be wholly derived either from his doctrine of the forgiveness of sins or from his deference to the written word of scripture. Let us rather consider Luther's *mirae speculationes* upon the 'unrevealed' in God in contrast to the *facies Dei revelata* (revealed face of God), upon the *divina maiestas* and the *omnipotentia Dei* in contrast to His *gratia*, as he treats of them in his work *De Servo Arbitrio*. The investigation as to how far Luther took over 'doctrines' from Scotus does

H

not amount to much; they stand in most intimate connexion with his own innermost religious life, of which they are a genuine first-hand utterance, and should be examined as such. Luther himself guarantees expressly that he does not teach such things merely as subjects of dispute in the schools or as philosophical deductions and corollaries, but because they are a central part of the religious experience of the Christian, who must know them in order to have faith and to have life. He rejects the cautious foresight of Erasmus's view, that such things should at least be withheld from the common people, preaching them himself in public sermons (for example, upon Exodus, in reference to the hardening of Pharaoh's heart) and writing them in his letter to the men of Antwerp. And again, just before his death, speaking of his book *De Servo Arbitrio*, in which these ideas stand clearly expressed, Luther acknowledges that nothing he wrote was so truly his own.

Is this borne out in his general teaching? His words in the *Great Catechism*, 'To have a God is nothing else than to trust Him from the heart', might seem to imply the negative. And certainly to Luther God is He who 'overbrims with pure goodness'. Yet this same Luther knows depths and abysses in the Godhead that make his heart despond, from which he flees for refuge to the 'Word', like a 'hare to his cleft in the rocks', flees, it may be, to the Sacrament or to absolution, or to the comforting official pronouncements of Dr. Pommeranus, but in general no less to every word of comfort or promise in the Psalms and the Prophets. But that before which his soul quails again and again in awe is not merely the stern Judge, demanding righteousness—for He is wholly a 'God of revelation'—but rather at the same time God in His 'unrevealedness', in the awful majesty of His very Godhead; He before whom trembles not simply the transgressor of the law, but the creature, as such, in his 'uncovered' creaturehood. Luther even ventures to designate this awe-inspiring, non-rational character of deity as 'Deus ipse, ut est in sua natura et maiestate'[1] (an assumption which would be in fact a dangerous and erroneous one; for no distinction of

---

[1] 'God Himself, as He is in his own very nature and majesty.'

the non-rational and the rational aspects of God should imply that the latter is less essential than the former).

The passages relevant in this connexion from Luther's *De Servo Arbitrio* are cited often enough: but to understand the wellnigh daemonic character of this numinous feeling the reader should particularly note the effect of the following passage from Luther's sermon on Exod. xx. The preacher leaves no means untried to bring out effectively the element of numinous horror in his text:

> Yea, for the world it seemeth as though God were a mere silly yawner, with mouth ever agape, or a cuckold, who lets another lie with his wife and feigneth that he sees it not.
> But He assaileth a man, and *hath such a delight* therein that He is of His jealousy and wrath impelled to *consume* the wicked.
> Then shall we learn how that God is a consuming fire . . . That is then the consuming, devouring fire. . . . Wilt thou sin? Then will He *devour thee up.* . . . For God is a fire, that consumeth, devoureth, rageth; verily He is your undoing, as fire consumeth a house and maketh it dust and ashes.

And in another place:

> Yea, He is more terrible and frightful than the Devil. For He dealeth with us and bringeth us to ruin with power, smiteth and hammereth us and payeth no heed to us. . . . In His majesty He is a consuming fire. . . . For therefrom can no man refrain: if he thinketh on God aright, his heart in his body is struck with terror. . . . Yea, as soon as he heareth God named, he is filled with trepidation and fear.[1]

It is the absolute numen, felt here partially in its aspect of *maiestas* and *tremendum*. And the reason I introduced these terms above to denote the one side of the numinous experience was in fact just because I recalled Luther's own expressions, and borrowed them from his *divina maiestas* and *metuenda voluntas*, which have rung in my ears from the time of my earliest study of Luther. Indeed, I grew to understand the numinous and its difference from the rational in Luther's *De Servo Arbitrio* long before I identified it in the *qādôsh* of the

---

[1] *Vide* the Erlangen edition of Luther's works, xxxvi, pp. 210 ff., 222, 231, 237; xxxv, p. 167; xlvii, p. 145; l, p. 200.

Old Testament and in the elements of 'religious awe' in the history of religion in general.

One must have beheld these gulfs and abysses in Luther to understand aright how significant it is that it is the same man who, on the other hand, endeavours to put the whole of Christianity into a confiding faith. The same contrast noted above in the religion of the Gospel and in the paradoxes of the 'faith in God the Father', recurs in the religious experience of Luther, but in unexampled intensity. That it is the *unapproachable* which becomes approachable, the *Holy One* who is pure goodness, that it is '*Majesty*' which makes itself familiar and intimate—there is the inwardness of the matter, and this finds only very dubious expression in the subsequent one-sided doctrine of the schools, where the mystical character of the 'wrath'—which is of the essence of 'holiness' infused with that of 'goodness'—is referred simply to the righteousness of God, and taken thus as righteous anger or indignation.

2. Once the numinous consciousness has been aroused, it is to be expected, seeing that it is a unity, that one of its 'moments' will be found to be bound up with the rest. In the case of Luther we find next after this element of 'wrath' the numinous manifesting itself in the set of ideas which we may fairly call those of Job. The Book of Job, as was seen above, is not so much concerned with the *awefulness* of the majesty of the numen as with its *mysteriousness*; it is concerned with the non-rational in the sense of the irrational, with sheer paradox baffling comprehension, with that which challenges the 'reasonable' and what might be reasonably expected, which goes directly against the grain of reason. To this place belong Luther's violent onslaughts upon the 'whore Reason', which must seem grotesque to anyone who has not rightly grasped the problem of the non-rational element in the idea of God. But certain set phrases, constantly recurring in Luther and very typical of him, are specially significant in this connexion, as showing the strong feeling he had for the non-rational aspect of the divine nature in general. The most interesting passages are not those in which he gives this feeling currency in the small change of popular edification, that soothes itself with the thought that God's ways are too

high for us men; but those in which he lays hold of some
startling paradox. He can indeed tell in quite a homely and
popular way 'how strange a lord our God is', and refer this
to the fact that God does not esteem or count as the world
counts, and that He disciplines us by the strange ways of His
guidance. Such expressions are of general currency; but
others—and these the more characteristic—strike a loftier
note. God is altogether 'mysteriis suis et iudiciis impervesti-
gabilis' ('beyond tracking out in His mysteries and His
judgements'), displays—as in Job—His 'vera maiestas' 'in
metuendis mirabilibus et iudiciis suis incomprehensibilibus'
('in His fearful marvels and incomprehensible judgements'),
is in His essence hidden away from all reason, knows no
measure, law, or aim, and is verified in the paradox: 'ut
ergo fidei locus sit, opus est, ut omnia, quae creduntur,
abscondantur' ('in order, therefore, that there may be a place
for faith, all the things that are believed must be hidden
away'). And his concern is not simply to note this as an
inconceivable paradox, to acknowledge it and bow before it,
but to recognize that such a paradox is essential to the nature
of God and even its distinguishing characteristic.

Si enim talis esset eius iustitia, quae humano captu posset
iudicari esse iusta, *plane non esset divina* et nihilo differret ab
humana iustitia. At cum sit Deus verus et unus, deinde totus
incomprehensibilis et inaccessibilis humana ratione, par est,
immo necessarium est, ut et iustitia sua sit incomprehensibilis.[1]

Theology gives expression to its perplexed endeavour to
find a name for the elements of the non-rational and the
mysterious in the repulsive doctrine that God is *exlex* (outside
the law), that good is good because God wills it, instead of
that God wills it because it is good, a doctrine that results in
attributing to God an absolutely fortuitous will, which would
in fact turn Him into a 'capricious despot'. These doctrines
are specially prominent in the theology of Islam, and this can

---

[1] 'For were His justice such as could be adjudged as just by the human understanding it were manifestly not divine, and would differ in nothing from human
justice. But since God is true and single, yea in His entirety incomprehensible
and inaccessible to human reason, it is right, nay it follows necessarily, that His
justice also is incomprehensible.'

be immediately understood if the two positions we maintain are sound, viz. that such doctrines are really perplexed expressions of the non-rational, numinous side of the divine nature, and that this is altogether the preponderant aspect in Islam. And we find them also in Luther in the same connexion. In this very fact, however, lies the excuse for doctrines in themselves so blasphemous and horrible: they are caricatures prompted by a deficient psychology and a mistaken choice of expressions, and not by any disregard of the absoluteness of moral values.

3. From the point of view already considered in detail it will be seen that, with such feelings as a basis, it was inevitable that the doctrine of predestination would in due course make its appearance in Luther's religion. And in his case we do not need, as we did in the case of Paul, to *postulate* the close inner connexion between this doctrine and the numinous temper, for in the *De Servo Arbitrio* it is palpably evident. The one explicitly depends upon the other, and the inward bond of union between the two is so unmistakable that this treatise of Luther's becomes a sort of psychological key to related phases of religious experience.

It is only occasionally that these purely numinous elements in Luther's religious consciousness are displayed so strongly and forcibly as in the treatise *De Servo Arbitrio*. But in his battles with '*desperatio*' and with Satan, in his constantly recurring religious catastrophes and fits of melancholy, in his wrestlings for grace, perpetually renewed, which bring him to the verge of mental disorder, in all these there are more than merely rational elements at work in his soul. Moreover, even when he is speaking solely in rational terms of judgement, punishment, and the wrath of God, we must, if we are to recapture the real Luther in these expressions, hear sounding in them the profoundly non-rational strain of 'religious awe'. For this wrath of God also has often, perhaps has always, something in it of that fury of Yahweh, that ὀργή of the numen.

4. This circumstance suggests a further point. The expressions 'unrevealed God' and '*tremenda maiestas*' manifestly repeated only those 'moments' of the numinous which we

found first in our analysis of it (p. 13), especially the *tre-mendum*, the *daunting* aspect of the numinous. What of that of 'fascination' in Luther? Is it missing altogether, to be re-placed merely by the rational attributes of trustworthiness and love and the corresponding element in the mind of the worshipper, viz. faith and trustfulness? No, beyond all question it is not. Only, the element of fascination is in Luther wholly interwoven with these rational elements and comes to utterance with them and in them. This can be felt forcibly in the boisterous, almost Dionysiac, blissfulness of his experience of God.

> Christians are a blissful people, who can rejoice at heart and sing praises, stamp and dance and leap for joy. That is well pleasing to God and doth our heart good, when we trust in God and find in Him our pride and our joyfulness. Such a gift should only kindle a fire and a light in our heart, so that we should never cease dancing and leaping for joy.
> Who will extol this enough or utter it forth? It is neither to be expressed or conceived.
> If thou feelest it truly in the heart, it will be such a great thing to thee that thou wilt rather be silent than speak aught of it.[1]

Here should be borne in mind what was remarked earlier (pp. 46 ff.) respecting the interweaving of the non-rational with the rational and the consequently deepened import of rational expressions. As the awe-inspiring character of the transcendent is comprised in the God of sternness and punish-ment and justice, so is its bliss-giving character included in the God who 'overbrims with pure goodness'. Indeed it is involved in the 'over-abounding' ('exuberant') and mystical tone of Luther's actual creed. Here, as elsewhere, there is no mistaking his connexion with mysticism.[2] Though for Luther faith begins more and more to take the place of 'knowledge' and 'love of God' (*Gottes-Minne*)—which means a marked qualitative alteration of the whole religious temper, as com-pared with that of mysticism—yet, despite the change, it remains obvious that there are definite features in 'faith', as the term is used by Luther, which justify us in classing it with

---

[1] Erlangen ed., xi. 194.   [2] See Appendix VI.

the mystical ways of response to which it is in apparent contrast, and clearly distinguish it from the *fides* taught by the
Lutheran school with its determinate, well-ordered, un-
mystical temper. 'Faith' for Luther plays the same essential
part, *mutatis mutandis*, as 'knowledge' and 'love' for the earlier
mystics: it is the unique power of the soul, the *adhaesio Dei*,
which *unites* man with God: and 'unity' is the very signature
of the mystical. So that when Luther says that faith makes
man 'one cake' (*ein Kuche*) with God or Christ, or holds him
'as a ring holds a jewel' (*sicut annulus gemmam*), he is not speaking any more figuratively than when Tauler says the same of
love. 'Faith' for Luther, as 'love' for Tauler and the mystics
generally, is a something that cannot be exhaustively comprised in rational concepts, and to designate which 'figures'
and 'images' are a necessity. To him 'faith' is the centre of
the soul—the *fundus animae* or 'basis of the soul' of the mystics
—in which the union of man with God fulfils itself. It is
at the same time an independent faculty of knowledge, a
mystical *a priori* element in the spirit of man, by which he
receives and recognizes supra-sensible truth, and in this
respect identical with the 'Holy Spirit in the heart' (*Spiritus
Sanctus in corde*). 'Faith' is further the 'mighty creative thing'
in us and the strongest of *affects*, most closely akin to the
Greek 'enthusiasm' (ἐνθουσιάζεσθαι). It even takes over all
the functions which all 'enthusiasts' from Paul onwards have
ascribed to 'the Spirit'; for it is 'faith' that 'transforms us
inwardly and brings us forth anew'. In this regard, different
as it is in its inner attitude, 'faith' is very similar to the *amor
mysticus*. And in the bliss of the 'assurance of salvation'
(*certitudo salutis*) that it arouses, and the intensity of Luther's
'childlike faith', we have in a subdued form a recurrence of
the 'childhood' feelings of Paul, which go beyond mere
comfort of the soul, appeasement of conscience, or feeling of
protectedness. All subsequent mystics from Johann Arndt
to Spener and Arnold[1] have always felt these aspects of
Luther's inner life to be congenial and akin to their own, and

---

[1] [Johann Arndt, 1555–1621; Gottfried Arnold, 1666–97; Philipp Jacob
Spener, 1635–1705: the last-named was one of the founders of 'Pietism' in
Germany. (*Trans.*)]

have carefully collected the relevant passages from his writings as a defence against the attacks of the rationalized doctrine of the Lutheran school.

For in opposition to the 'rationalizations' of the schools the non-rational elements are maintained and fostered in the western mysticism that came to its later flower both on Catholic and Protestant soil. In this, as in Christian mysticism as a whole from its first stirrings, the elements of the non-rational already detailed are easily recognizable, most prominently of all those of 'mystery', 'fascination', and 'majesty'. The element of 'awe', on the other hand, recedes and is subdued; there has never been in the West a mysticism of horror, such as we find in certain kinds of Indian mysticism, both Buddhist and Hindu—in Bhagavad-Gītā, ch. 11[1]—in some forms of the Shiva and Durgā worship, and in the horrible form of Tantrism. Yet, though the *tremendum* element in Christian mysticism is subdued, it is not entirely lacking. It remains a living factor in the *caligo* and the *altum silentium*, in the 'abyss', the 'night', the 'deserts' of the divine nature, into which the soul must descend, in the 'agony', 'abandonment', 'barrenness', *taedium*, in which it must tarry, in the shuddering and shrinking from the loss and deprivation of selfhood and the 'annihilation' of personal identity. Thus Suso writes:

In this inconceivable mountain of the supra-divine Where [the 'height of the divine Majesty transcending substance'] there is a precipitousness of which all pure spirits are sensible. Here the Soul enters a secret namelessness, a marvellous alienation. It is the bottomless abyss no creature can sound— . . . the spirit perishes there, to become all-living in the wonders of the Godhead.[2]

And he can pray:

Ah, woe is me, Thy wrathful countenance is so full of fury. Thy turning away in anger is so unendurable. Woe is me! And the words of Thy enmity are so fiery, they cleave through heart and soul.[3]

[1] See Appendix II.
[2] Suso, German writings, ed. Denifle, pp. 289 ff.
[3] Ibid., p. 353.

This note is familiar also to the later mystics. Thus St. John of the Cross says:

As this clear sight of the divine comes like a violent assault upon the soul to subdue it, the soul feels such anguish in its weakness that all power and breath leave it together, while sense and spirit as though they stood burdened beneath a dark unmeasured load suffer such agony and are oppressed by such deadly fear that the soul would choose death as a mitigation and refreshment.[1]

And again:

The fourth kind of anguish is brought into being in the soul . . . from the Majesty and Glory of God.[1]

Once more:

Therefore He destroys, crushes and overwhelms (the soul) in such a deep darkness, that it feels as though melted and in its misery destroyed by a cruel death of the spirit. Even as though it were to feel it had been swallowed by some savage beast and buried in the darkness of his belly.[1]

But in our Western mysticism the writer in whom the non-rationally 'dreadful' and even the 'daemonic' phase of the numinous remains a most living element is Jakob Böhme. For all his adoption of its motives, Böhme is in his speculation and 'theosophy' sharply distinguished from the earlier mysticism. He is at one with this (as represented, for instance, by Eckhart) in aiming at a 'construction' and an understanding of God, and from Him of the world: and, like Eckhart, he finds as a starting-point for his speculation the 'primal bottom', the supra-comprehensible and inexpressible. But this stands to him, not for Being and Above-being, but for Stress and Will; it is not good and above-good, but a supra-rational identification of good and evil in an In-different, in which is to be found the potentiality for evil as well as for good, and therewith the possibility of the dual nature of deity itself as at once goodness and love on the one hand and fury and wrath on the other.[2] If the inventions and

---

[1] St. John of the Cross, *The Ascent of Mount Carmel*.

[2] The 'ferocity' is the origin of Lucifer, in whom the mere potentiality of evil is actualized. It might be said that Lucifer is 'fury', the ὀργή, hypostatized, the *mysterium tremendum* cut loose from the other elements and intensified to *mysterium*

comparisons, with whose aid Böhme composes a sort of chemico-physical romance of God, strike us as extremely queer and bizarre, the strange intuitions of the religious feeling underlying them are yet highly significant. They are intuitions of the numinous, and are akin to those of Luther. With Böhme, as with Luther, the non-rational energy and majesty of God and his 'awefulness' appear conceptualized and symbolized as 'Will'. And with Böhme, as with Luther, this is conceived as fundamentally independent of *moral* elevation or righteousness, and as indifferent toward good or evil action. It is rather a 'ferocity', a 'fiery wrath' about something unknown; or, better still, not about anything at all, but Wrath on its own account and without reference to any object; an aspect of character which would be quite meaningless if taken literally in the sense of a real conceivable and apprehensible anger. Who is not directly conscious that it is simply the non-rational element of 'awefulness', the *tremendum*, for which 'wrath', 'fire', 'fury', are excellent ideograms?[1] If such an ideogram is taken as an adequate concept, the result is anthropomorphism, such as mythology illustrates, and the writings of Lactantius (see p. 96). And if speculation follows, based upon such concepts, the result is the pseudo-science of theosophy. For the characteristic mark of all theosophy is just this: having confounded analogical

horrendum. The roots at least of this may be found in the Bible and the early Church. The ideas of propitiation and ransom are not without reference to Satan as well as to the divine wrath. The rationalism of the myth of the 'fallen angel' does not render satisfactorily the horror of Satan and of the 'depths of Satan' (Rev. ii. 24) and the 'mystery of iniquity' (2 Thess. ii. 7). It is a horror that is in some sort numinous, and we might designate the object of it as the negatively numinous. This also holds good of other religions than that of the Bible. In all religions 'the devilish' plays its part and has its place as that which, opposed to the divine, has yet something in common with it. As such it should be the subject of a special inquiry, which must be an analysis of fundamental feelings, and something very different from a mere record of the 'evolution of the idea of the devil'.

[1] Böhme's disciple, Johann Pordage, has some feeling of this when he writes: 'So hope I then, that you will not be angered with me, if you find that I impute to God acerbity and bitterness, dread, wrath, fire, . . . and the like. For even Jakob Böhme found no other words in which to express his exalted *sensation* (*Empfindung*) of God. You must then take all those forms of speech in a high divine sense, far removed from all imperfection' (*Divine and True Metaphysic*, i. 166).

and figurative ways of expressing feeling with rational concepts, it then systematizes them, and out of them spins, like
a monstrous web, a 'science of God', which is and remains
something monstrous, whether it employs, as Eckhart, the
doctrinal terms of scholasticism; or as Böhme, the alchemical
substances and mixtures of Paracelsus; or as Hegel, the
categories of an animistic logic; or as Mrs. Besant, the
elaborate diction of Indian religion. For the history of
religion it is not on account of his theosophy that Böhme is
interesting, but because in him behind the theosophy the
consciousness of the numinous was astir and alive as an
element of genuine value: so that herein Böhme was an heir
of Luther, preserving what in Luther's own school came to
be overlooked and disregarded.

For the Lutheran school has itself not done justice to the
numinous side of the Christian idea of God. By the exclusively moral interpretation it gave to the terms, it distorted
the meaning of 'holiness' and the 'wrath' of God, and already
from the time of Johann Gerhardt and onwards Lutheranism
was returning to the doctrine of divine $\dot{a}\pi\dot{a}\theta\epsilon\iota a$ or passion-
lessness. More and more it deprived the forms of worship of
the genuinely contemplative and specifically 'devotional'
elements in them. The conceptual and doctrinal—the ideal
of orthodoxy—began to preponderate over the inexpressible,
whose only life is in the conscious mental attitude of the
devout soul. The Church became a school, and her com-
munications, in truth, found a more and more contracted
access to the mind, as Tyrrell has put it somewhere, 'through
the narrow clefts of the understanding'.

Schleiermacher was the first to attempt to overcome this
rationalism, most boldly and uncompromisingly in the
rhapsody of his *Discourses*, with less heat and more subdued
tone in his *Glaubenslehre* and his theory of the 'feeling of
absolute dependence', which in point of fact give a representation—as has been pointed out already—of the first
stirring of the feeling of the numinous. It will be a task for
contemporary Christian teaching to follow in his traces and
again to deepen the rational meaning of the Christian conception of God by permeating it with its non-rational elements.

CHAPTER XIII

THE TWO PROCESSES OF DEVELOPMENT

THIS permeation of the rational with the non-rational is to lead, then, to the deepening of our rational conception of God; it must not be the means of blurring or diminishing it. For if (as suggested at the close of the last chapter) the disregard of the numinous elements tends to impoverish religion, it is no less true that 'holiness', 'sanctity', as Christianity intends the words, cannot dispense with the rational, and especially the clear ethical elements of meaning which Protestantism more particularly emphasizes in the idea of God. To get the full meaning of the word 'holy' as we find it used in the New Testament (and religious usage has established it in the New Testament sense to the exclusion of others), we must no longer understand by 'the holy' or 'sacred' the merely numinous in general, nor even the numinous at its own highest development; we must always understand by it the numinous completely permeated and saturated with elements signifying rationality, purpose, personality, morality. It is in this combined meaning that we retain and apply the term 'holy' in our subsequent chapters. But that the course of the historical development may be clearly understood, we venture first to recapitulate our view upon this matter as explicitly as possible.

That which the primitive religious consciousness first apprehends in the form of 'daemonic dread', and which, as it further unfolds, becomes more elevated and ennobled, is in origin not something rational or moral, but something distinct, non-rational, an object to which the mind responds in a unique way with the special feeling-reflexes that have been described. And this element or 'moment' passes in itself through a process of development of its own, quite apart from the other process—which begins at an early stage—by which it is 'rationalized' and 'moralized', i.e. filled with rational and ethical meaning. Taking this non-rational process of development first, we have seen how the 'daemonic dread', after itself passing through various gradations, rises to the level of 'fear of the gods', and thence to 'fear of God'. The δαιμόνιον or daemonic power becomes the θεῖον or divine power: 'dread' becomes worship; out of a confusion of inchoate emotions and bewildered palpitations of feeling grows '*religio*', and out of 'shudder' a holy awe. The feelings of dependence upon and beatitude in the numen, from being relative, become absolute. The false analogies and fortuitous associations are gradually dispelled or frankly rejected. The numen becomes God and Deity. It is then to God and Deity, as 'numen' rendered absolute, that the attribute denoted by the terms *qādôsh*, *sanctus*, ἅγιος, holy, pertains, in the first and directest sense of the words. It is the culmination of a development which works itself out purely in the sphere of the non-rational. This development constitutes the first central fact of religious study, and it is the task of religious history and psychology to trace its course.

Next, secondary and subsidiary to this, is the task of tracing the course of the process of rationalization and moralization *on the basis of* the numinous consciousness. It nearly, if not quite, synchronizes and keeps pace with the stages of the purely numinous development, and, like that, it can be traced in its different gradations in the most widely different regions of religious history. Almost everywhere we find the numinous attracting and appropriating meanings derived from social and individual ideals of obligation, justice, and goodness. These become the 'will' of the numen, and the numen their guardian, ordainer, and author. More and more these ideas come to enter into the very essence of the numen and charge the term with ethical content. 'Holy' becomes 'good', and 'good' from that very fact in turn becomes 'holy', 'sacrosanct'; until there results a thenceforth indissoluble synthesis of the two elements, and the final outcome is thus the fuller, more complex sense of 'holy', in which it is at once *good and sacrosanct*. The greatest distinction of the religion of ancient Israel, at least from Amos onwards, is precisely the intimate coalescence of both elements. No God is like the God of Israel: for He is the absolutely Holy One (= perfectly good). And, on the other hand, no law is like Yahweh's Law, for it is not merely good, but also at the same time 'holy' (= sacrosanct).

And this process of rationalization and moralization of the numinous, as it grows ever more clear and more potent, is in fact the most essential part of what we call 'the History of Salvation' and prize as the ever-growing self-revelation of the divine. But at the same time it should be clear to us that this process of the 'moralization of the idea of God', often enough represented to us as a principal problem, setting the main line for inquiry into the history of religion, is in no wise a suppression of the numinous or its supersession by something else—which would result not in a God, but a God-substitute —but rather the completion and charging of it with a new content. That is to say, the 'moralization' process assumes the numinous and is only completed upon this as basis.

CHAPTER XIV

THE HOLY AS AN *A PRIORI* CATEGORY

PART I

IT follows from what has been said that the 'holy' in the fullest sense of the word is a combined, complex category, the combining elements being its rational and non-rational components. But in *both*—and the assertion must be strictly maintained against all sensationalism and naturalism—it is a *purely a priori* category.

The rational ideas of absoluteness, completion, necessity, and substantiality, and no less so those of the good as an objective value, objectively binding and valid, are not to be 'evolved' from any sort of sense-perception. And the notions of 'epigenesis', 'heterogony', or whatever other expression we may choose to denote our compromise and perplexity, only serve to conceal the problem, the tendency to take refuge in a Greek terminology being here, as so often, nothing but an avowal of one's own insufficiency. Rather, seeking to account for the ideas in question, we are referred away from all sense-experience back to an original and underivable capacity of the mind implanted in the 'pure reason' independently of all perception.

But in the case of the non-rational elements of our category of the Holy we are referred back to something still deeper than the 'pure reason', at least as this is usually understood, namely, to that which mysticism has rightly named the *fundus animae*, the 'bottom' or 'ground of the soul' (*Seelengrund*). The ideas of the numinous and the feelings that correspond to them are, quite as much as the rational ideas and feelings, absolutely 'pure', and the criteria which Kant suggests for the 'pure' concept and the 'pure' feeling of respect are most precisely applicable to them. In the famous opening words of the *Critique of Pure Reason* he says:

That all our knowledge begins with experience there can be no doubt. For how is it possible that the faculty of cognition should be awakened into exercise otherwise than by means of

objects which affect our senses? . . . But, though all our knowledge begins *with* experience, it by no means follows that all arises
out of experience.

And, referring to empirical knowledge, he distinguishes that
part which we receive through impressions and that which
our own faculty of cognition supplies from itself, *sense-
impressions giving merely the occasion*.

The numinous is of the latter kind. It issues from the
deepest foundation of cognitive apprehension that the soul
possesses, and, though it of course comes into being in and
amid the sensory data and empirical material of the natural
world and cannot anticipate or dispense with those, yet it does
not arise *out of* them, but only *by their means*. They are the
incitement, the stimulus, and the 'occasion' for the numinous
experience to become astir, and, in so doing, to begin—at
first with a naïve immediacy of reaction—to be interfused and
interwoven with the present world of sensuous experience,
until, becoming gradually purer, it disengages itself from this
and takes its stand in absolute contrast to it. The proof that
in the numinous we have to deal with purely *a priori* cognitive elements is to be reached by introspection and a critical
examination of reason such as Kant instituted. We find, that
is, involved in the numinous experience, beliefs and feelings
qualitatively different from anything that 'natural' sense-
perception is capable of giving us. They are themselves not
perceptions at all, but peculiar interpretations and valua-
tions, at first of perceptual data, and then—at a higher level
—of posited objects and entities, which themselves no longer
belong to the perceptual world, but are thought of as supple-
menting and transcending it. And as they are not themselves
sense-perceptions, so neither are they any sort of 'transmutation' of sense-perceptions. The only 'transmutation' possible
in respect to sense-perception is the transformation of the intuitively given concrete percept, of whatever sort, into the
corresponding concept; there is never any question of the
transformation of *one* class of percepts into a class of entities
qualitatively *other*. The facts of the numinous consciousness
point therefore—as likewise do also the 'pure concepts of the
understanding' of Kant and the ideas and value-judgements

I

of ethics or aesthetics—to a hidden substantive source, from which the religious ideas and feelings are formed, which lies in the mind independently of sense-experience; a 'pure reason' in the profoundest sense, which, because of the 'surpassingness' of its content, must be distinguished from both the pure theoretical and the pure practical reason of Kant, as something yet higher or deeper than they.

The justification of the 'evolutionist' theory of to-day stands or falls with its claim to 'explain' the phenomenon of religion. That is in truth the real task of the psychology of religion. But in order to explain we must have the data from which an explanation may be forthcoming; out of nothing nothing can be explained. Nature can only be explained by an investigation into the ultimate fundamental forces of nature and their laws: it is meaningless to propose to go farther and explain these laws themselves, for in terms of what are they to be explained? But in the domain of spirit the corresponding principle from which an explanation is derived is just the spirit itself, the reasonable spirit of man, with its predispositions, capacities, and its own inherent laws. This has to be presupposed: it cannot itself be explained. None can say how mind or spirit 'is made'—though this is in effect just what the theory of epigenesis is fain to attempt. The history of humanity begins with man, and we have to presuppose man, to take him for granted as he is, in order that from him we may understand his history. That is, we must presuppose man as a being analogous to ourselves in natural propensities and capacities. It is a hopeless business to seek to lower ourselves into the mental life of a *pithecanthropus erectus*; and, even if it were not, we should still need to start from man as he is, since we can only interpret the psychical and emotional life of animals regressively by clumsy analogies drawn from the developed human mind. To try, on the other hand, to understand and deduce the human from the sub-human or brute mind is to try to fit the lock to the key instead of vice versa; it is to seek to illuminate light by darkness. In the first appearance of conscious life on dead unconscious matter we have a simple, irreducible, inexplicable datum. But that which here appears is already a manifold of qualities, and we can only interpret it as a seed of potentiality, out of which issue continually maturer powers and capacities, as the organization of the body increases in stability and complexity. And the only way we can throw any light upon the whole region of sub-human psychical life is by interpreting it once again as a sort of 'predisposition'[1] at a second remove, i.e. a predisposition to form the predispositions or faculties of the actual developed mind, and standing in relation to this as an embryo to the full-grown organism. But we are not completely in the dark as to the meaning of this word 'predisposition'.[1] For in our own awakening and growth to mental and spiritual maturity we trace in ourselves in some sort the evolution by which the seed develops into the tree— the very opposite of 'transformation' and 'epigenesis' by successive addition.[2]

We call the source of growth a hidden 'predisposition' of the human spirit, which awakens when aroused by divers excitations. That there are 'predispositions' of this sort in individuals no one can deny who has given serious study to the history of religion. They are seen as propensities, 'predestining' the individual to religion, and they may grow spontaneously to quasi-instinctive presentiments, uneasy seeking and groping, yearning and longing, and become a religious *impulsion*, that only finds peace when it has become clear to itself and attained its goal. From them arise the states of mind of 'prevenient grace', described in masterly fashion by Suso:

Loving, tender Lord! My mind has from the days of my childhood sought something with an earnest thirst of longing, Lord,

---

[1] *Anlage.*

[2] The physical analogue to these spiritual or mental relationships is the relation of potential to kinetic energy. The assumption of such a relation in the world of mind (i.e. a relation between potential and kinetic mind) is, of course, only to be expected from one who is prepared to accept as the final cause of all mind in the world as a whole the absolute mind as 'pure actuality' whose *ellampatio* or effulgence (in Leibniz's phrase) all other mind is. For all that is potential presupposes an *actual* as the ground of its possibility, as Aristotle long ago showed. But indeed how can we afford to reject such a 'pure actuality'? It is an inconsequent proceeding to postulate actuality, as is done, for a starting-point for the physical world, as a system of stored-up energy, whose transference to kinetic energy constitutes the 'rush of worlds and wheel of systems', and yet to reject the analogous assumption in the world of mind and spirit.

and what that is have I not yet perfectly apprehended. Lord, I have now for many a year been in hot pursuit of it, and never yet have I been able to succeed, for I know not aright what it is. And yet it is something that draws my heart and my soul after it, and without which I can never attain to full repose. Lord, I was fain in the earliest days of my childhood to seek it among created things, as I saw others before me do. And the more I sought, the less I found it; and the nearer I went, the further I wandered from it. . . . Now my heart rages for it, for fain would I possess it. . . . Woe is me! . . . What is this, or how is it fashioned, that plays within me in such hidden wise?[1]

These are manifestations of a *predisposition* becoming a search and a driving *impulsion*. But here, if nowhere else, the 'fundamental biogenetic law' really does hold good, which uses the stages and phases in the growth of the individual to throw light upon the corresponding stages in the growth of his species. The *predisposition* which the human reason brought with it when the species Man entered history became long ago, not merely for individuals but for the species as a whole, a *religious impulsion*, to which incitements from without and pressure from within the mind both contributed. It begins in undirected, groping emotion, a seeking and shaping of representations, and goes on, by a continual onward striving, to generate ideas, till its nature is self-illumined and made clear by an explication of the obscure *a priori* foundation of thought itself, out of which it originated.[2] And this emotion, this searching, this generation and explication of ideas, gives the warp of the fabric of religious evolution, whose woof we are to discuss later.[3]

[1] *Works*, ed. Denifle, p. 311.

[2] The reader may compare what Kant says in his Lectures on Psychology (Leipzig ed., 1889, p. 11) of 'the treasure buried in the field of obscure ideas, constituting the deep abyss of human knowledge, which we cannot sound'. This 'deep abyss' is just the *fundus animae* that is aroused in Suso.

[3] Cf. pp. 177, 178.

ITS EARLIEST MANIFESTATIONS

ONLY upon the basis of the foregoing assumptions is it possible to understand the historical origin and further development of religion. It must be admitted that when religious evolution first begins sundry curious phenomena confront us, preliminary to religion proper and deeply affecting its subsequent course. Such are the notions of 'clean' and 'unclean', belief in and worship of the dead, belief in and worship of 'souls' or 'spirits', magic, fairy tale, and myth, homage to natural objects, whether frightful or extraordinary, noxious or advantageous, the strange idea of 'power' (*orenda* or *mana*), fetishism and totemism, worship of animal and plant, daemonism and polydaemonism. Different as these things are, they are all haunted by a common—and that a numinous—element, which is easily identifiable. They did not, perhaps, take their origin out of this common numinous element directly; they may have all exhibited a preliminary stage at which they were merely 'natural' products of the naïve, rudimentary fancies of primitive times. But these things acquire a strand of a quite special kind, which alone gives them their character as forming the vestibule of religion, brings them first to clear and explicit form, and furnishes them with the prodigious power over the minds of men which history universally proves them to possess. Let us attempt to grasp this peculiar strand, common to all these modes of thought and practice which stand upon the threshold of religion.

1. We will begin with *magic*. There has been at all times, and there still is to-day, a 'natural' magic, that is to say, modes of behaviour exhibiting some simple analogy and carried out quite unreflectively and without any basis in theory, whose object is to influence and regulate an event in accordance with the wishes of the agent. It may be noticed on any skittle-alley or bowling-green. A bowler aims and plays his bowl, wishing it to run true and hit the jack. He watches eagerly as it rolls, nodding his head, his body bent

sideways, stands balancing on one leg, jerks over violently to the other side as the critical point is reached, makes as though to push the ball on with hand or foot, gives a last jerk—and the end is reached. Its hazards past, the ball rolls safely into position. What was the man doing in this case? He was not simply imitating the course of the ball; he meant to prescribe and determine it, but this obviously without any reflection on his queer behaviour, without the belief of primitive man in 'universal animism', i.e. in the animatedness of everything, in this instance, of the ball, and without a belief in some sympathetic *rapport* between his own 'soul' power and the 'soul' of the ball. His action was merely naïvely analogical, for the attainment of a definite wish. The proceedings of 'rain-makers' were often, perhaps at first were always, just the same sort of thing; and so were the naïve charms purporting to influence the course of sun and moon, clouds, and winds. But clearly, so long as they are not more than this, these are not by any means *magic* in the proper sense. There must be in addition a new ingredient, unique in quality, the element that is usually called 'supernatural efficacy'. But this expression is a misnomer: 'supernatural' has nothing to do with the case; it is much too imposing an expression, and ascribes far too much to the naïve mind. The conception of Nature as a single connected system of events united by laws is the final and most difficult outcome of abstraction; and this conception of nature, or at least some hint of it, must have been arrived at before there could be any place for its negation, the 'supernatural'. Again, nothing is explained, as Wundt would have it, by 'spirit-power' or 'soul-power'. For, first, it is to-day universally recognized that magic is independent of a belief in spirits or souls, and probably existed before it. And, second, the point at issue is not by means of what *class* of powers the magical effect was produced—whether 'soul-powers' or others—but by means of what *quality* or *character* in the powers. And this quality can be indicated solely through the 'daemonic', a character ascribed to certain definite operations of force, be they strong or weak, extraordinary or quite trivial, the work of a soul or a 'non-soul'. The quality can be only suggested through that unique element of feeling, the feeling of 'uncanniness', of which we have already spoken, whose positive content cannot be defined conceptually, and can only be indicated by that mental response to it which we called 'shuddering'.

2. The same is true of the *worship of the dead*. It does not arise out of any theory of animism, according to which the primitive man thinks of inanimate objects, and so also of the dead, as animate and operative. Even in itself this entire theory of an ostensible attribution of 'soul' or the principle of animation to everything is a mere fabrication of the study. How much more when it is clumsily spatchcocked and welded together with 'belief in spirits or souls', which is something quite different! The dead man, in point of fact, exercises a spell upon the mind only when, and only because, he is felt as a thing of horror and 'shudder'. But alike to the naïve mind of the savage and to the blasé mind of modern civilized man this feeling comes about with such an immediate compelling force that we usually accept it as something immediately self-evident, failing altogether to remark that even the estimating something as 'horrible' or 'grisly' shows the emergence of a qualitatively separate content of feeling which the mere fact of death does not explain. Feeling-reactions to the dead, if prompted 'naturally', are pretty obviously only of two kinds: on the one hand, the experient feels disgust at the corpse's putrefaction, stench, revoltingness: on the other, he feels his own will to life disturbed and checked, the fear of death and the startled fright that directly follows on the sight of a corpse, especially if it be that of a member of one's own species. Both these sorts of feeling-response, viz. disgust and startled fright, are already found manifested among animals. I observed this in a very pronounced degree on one occasion, when, upon a lonely ride, we suddenly came upon the body of a dead horse, and Diana, my excellent mount, on recognizing her dead fellow, gave every indication of the most natural fright and disgust. But these two 'moments' of feeling do not by any means afford in themselves the materials for the 'art of making shudder' (in the words of the old folk-tale). It is something new and demands to be 'learnt' as the folk-tale rightly declares: that is, this is a feeling that is not simply

present with the other 'natural' and normal mental functions, disgust, or fright, and cannot be got from these by analysis. It is a 'dread' (or awe), qualitatively *sui generis*; and even with regard to this rudimentary stage represented by the primitive 'worship of the dead' we cannot admit that we have to do merely with a universal feeling, that has simply to be pre-supposed at the outset as a regular factor of folk psychology, a collectively engendered feeling that explains itself. On the contrary, it cannot be disputed that here too there have been persons endowed with special propensities in this direction, who possessed such feelings actually, and then, by giving expression to them, aroused them in others. Even the 'awe of the dead' and from it the 'worship of the dead' have been, as it were, 'instituted' and have had 'founders'.

3. We consider next ideas of '*souls*' and '*spirits*'. It would be possible to show, did not the subject lead us too far afield, that these were not conceived by the fanciful processes of which the animists tell us, but had a far simpler origin. But again the important point is not the origin of 'spirits' in their ideational aspect, but the qualitative element of feeling relative to them. And this does not consist in the fact that 'spirits' or 'souls' are thinner or less easily visible than the body, or quite invisible, or fashioned like air: often all this is true of them; no less often none of it is; most frequently of all it is both true and false. The essence of the 'soul' lies *not* in the imaginative or conceptual expression of it, but first and fore-most in the fact that it is a *spectre*; that it arouses 'dread' or 'awe', as described above. But again, a 'spectre' is not to be explained from 'natural' feelings, and these are equally unable to explain the further development by which these 'some-things' (and this is the only core of conceptual meaning that can really be given them), at first always very eagerly shunned, later on become beings honoured in a positive way and loved, capable of rising into heroes, *pitris*, daemons, holy or sacred ones, and gods.

4. We turn to the idea of '*power*', the *mana* of the Pacific Islands and the *orenda* of the North American Indians. It can have its antecedents in very 'natural' phenomena. To notice power in plants, stones, and natural objects in general and to

appropriate it by gaining possession of them; to eat the heart or liver of an animal or a man in order to make his power and strength one's own—this is not religion but science. Our science of medicine follows a similar prescription. If the 'power' of a calf's glands is good for goitre and imbecility, we do not know what virtue we may not hope to find in frogs' brains or Jews' livers. All depends here upon observation, and our science of medicine in this respect only differs from that of the medicine-man in being more exact and in possessing experimental methods. 'Power' does not take its place in the antechamber of religion, is not appropriated by religion in 'communion rites' and 'sacraments' (as we call them), until it too has come to include the idea of 'spell' and 'magic'.

5. Volcanoes, mountain peaks, moon, sun, and clouds are regarded by primitive man as being *alive* or *animate*, not in consequence of a naïve theory of the omnipresence of 'spirit' or 'soul'—'panthelism', so called—but as a result of precisely the same criterion that we ourselves apply when we recognize anything to be alive or animate, apart from the one live thing we can observe directly, our self; that is to say, both we and the primitive credit an object with life if, and in so far as, we think we remark in it living efficacy and agency; and whether we do so rightly or wrongly is again simply a matter of more or less exact observation. But while from this criterion the natural objects mentioned above, and of course others, may be invested with life by the naïve observer, this does *not* in itself lead to myth or religion. Purely as *animate* or living beings, these entities are far from being yet 'divine' or 'gods'; nay, they do not even become so when the man turns to them with desire and petition; for petition is something less than prayer, and trust need not have a religious character. The objects in question only become 'divine'—objects of *worship*—when the category of the numinous is applied to them, and that does not come about until, first, an attempt is made to *influence* them by numinous means, viz. by magic; and, second, their special efficacy or way of working is at the same time accepted as something numinous, viz. something magical.

6. As regards *fairy-stories*, these presuppose the 'natural' impulse to fantasy, narrative, and entertainment, and its products. But the fairy-story proper only comes into being with the element of the 'wonderful', with miracle and miraculous events and consequences, i.e. by means of an infusion of the numinous. And the same holds good in an increased degree of *myth*.

7. All the factors and elements named so far in this chapter are but, as it were, the vestibule at the threshold of the real religious feeling, an earliest stirring of the numinous consciousness, which comes upon the scene blended with associated feelings in conformity to principles of analogy which it would be easy to specify for each several case. Only with the rise of the '*daemon*' do we have a really separate beginning. The most authentic form of the 'daemon' may be seen in those strange deities of ancient Arabia, which are properly nothing but wandering demonstrative pronouns, neither 'given shape and feature by means of myth', for there is in the main no mythology attached to them at all, nor 'evolved out of nature-deities', nor grown out of 'souls' or 'spirits', but none the less felt as deities of mighty efficacy, who are the objects of very living veneration. They are pure products of the religious consciousness itself. And in their case it is very evident that they do not arise as a collective product of crowd-imagination, and that they do not therefore have their origin in 'group-' or 'folk-' psychology, but were the intuitions of persons of innate prophetic powers. For there is always the *kāhin* (the primitive form of the 'prophet') belonging to these numina, and he alone experiences a numen or divine-daemonic power at first hand. Only where and when it has been 'revealed' through such a one do the forms of worship and a common cult arise. To each numen is assigned a seer and there is none without one.

8. The notions 'clean' and 'unclean', 'pure' and 'impure', are already found in a purely natural sense, prior to their religious application. The unclean is the loathsome, that which stirs strong feelings of natural disgust. And it is just during the more primitive stages of human development that the emotion of disgust exercises such special power. Probably

these emotional reactions are a part of our natural self-protective endowment, instinctive safeguards for many important vital functions. The effect of civilization is to refine these emotions of disgust and loathing by diverting them to different objects, so that things which were loathsome to the savage cease to be so and things which were not become so. This refinement spells at the same time a weakening in the intensity of the emotion; we do not now *loathe* and feel disgust with the unbridled violence and strength of the savage. In this respect we can notice even to-day a plain distinction between our more primitive rural and our more 'refined' urban population: we townsmen feel disgust at much that is harmless to the countryman, but where the latter does feel it he is affected by the emotion more radically than we are; it is a profounder reaction in him.

We have so far been concerned with the ordinary feeling of disgust. Between this and the feeling of the 'horrible' there is a very close analogy; and from this it becomes apparent, in accordance with the law of reciprocal attraction between analogous feelings and emotions, how the 'natural' unclean or impure is bound to pass over into, and develop in, the sphere of the numinous. Once, in fact, we have in our hand the key of the problem—the analogy and the law just mentioned—we can reconstruct *a priori* the actual genetic process involved, by which the one emotion prompts the other. We indeed have ourselves a direct experience of the same thing to-day in our emotional reaction to the sight of flowing blood, in which it would be hard to say whether the element of 'disgust' or 'horror' is the stronger.

Later, then, when the more maturely developed elements of 'awe' came upon the scene and went to shape the more elevated ideas of the daemonic and the divine, *sacer* and *sanctus*, things could become 'unclean' or 'impure' in the numinous sense without any substratum of 'natural' impurity to serve as point of departure. And we can learn something of the relation of feeling-analogy involved from the fact that in the reverse direction the feeling of the *numinously* impure calls up easily by association the 'natural' emotion of disgust (i.e. the feeling of the 'naturally' impure), so that things become disgustful or loathsome which intrinsically were not objects of disgust at all, but of numinous horror. In fact such secondary and derived feelings of disgust can maintain themselves independently long after the original numinous awe which they once evoked has died away. Certain *social* feelings of loathing, such as those of caste, can be explained in this way: they had once a purely daemonic root, but long after that has died out they still survive in their secondary, acquired character as feelings of disgust.

9. If the examples numbered 1 to 8 may be termed 'pre-religion', this is not in the sense that religion and the possibility of religion are explicable by their means: rather, they are themselves only made possible and can only be explained from a religious basic element, viz. the feeling of the numinous. This is a primal element of our psychical nature that needs to be grasped purely in its uniqueness and cannot itself be explained from anything else. Like all other primal psychical elements, it *emerges* in due course in the developing life of human mind and spirit and is thenceforward simply present. Of course it can only emerge if and when certain conditions are fulfilled, conditions involving a proper development of the bodily organs and the other powers of mental and emotional life in general, a due growth in suggestibility and spontaneity and responsiveness to external impressions and internal experiences. But such conditions are no more than conditions; they are not its causes or constituent elements. To recognize this is not to relegate the whole matter to the domain of mystery and supernaturalism, but simply to maintain that the same thing holds good of this which holds good of all other primal elements of our mental or spiritual life. Pleasure or pain, love or hate, all faculties of sense-perception, such as susceptibility to light and sound, consciousness of space and time, and subsequently all higher capacities of the mind, all duly emerge, sooner or later, in the course of development. That they do so in conformity to laws and under definite conditions is indisputable, but each is none the less a new, original, underivable fact, and they are only to be 'explained' on the assumption of a rich potentiality of spirit or mind, which underlies the course of their develop-

ment and realizes itself more and more abundantly in them in proportion as the conditions of organic and cerebral evolution are more fully realized. And what is true of all these other elements of our mental life is also true of the feeling of the numinous.

10. The purest case, however, of the spontaneous stirring of numinous emotion would seem to be that mentioned in No. 7 (the feeling of daemons), which is of quite special significance for the evolution of religion. This is because here the 'religious' emotion does not from the first get diverted (following the 'stimulation' of emotional associations) to earthly things, wrongly taken as numinous: but either it remains a pure feeling, as in 'panic' terror (in the literal sense of the word), or itself invents, or, better, discovers, the numinous object by rendering explicit the obscure germinal ideas latent in itself. Even this latter case is not altogether beyond the reach of introspective analysis, which, moreover, can throw some light upon the transition from mere feeling to its 'explication' and to the positing of the numinous object. At least there is none of us who has any living capacity for emotion but must have known at some time or at some place what it is to feel really 'uncanny', to have a feeling of 'eerieness'. And more exact psychological analysis will notice the following points in such a state of mind. First, there is the point of which we have already spoken, its separate and underivable, irreducible, qualitative character. Second, there is the very curious circumstance that the external features occasioning this state of mind are often quite slight, indeed so scanty that hardly any account can be given of them, so disproportionate are they to the strength of the emotional impression itself. Indeed the clutching force and violence of the emotion so far exceeds any impressiveness contributed by the circumstances of time and place that one can often scarcely speak of an 'impression' at all, but at most of an encounter, serving as cue or occasion for the felt experience. This experience of eerie shuddering and awe breaks out rather from depths of the soul which the circumstantial, external impression cannot sound, and the force with which it breaks out is so disproportionate to the mere external

stimulation that the eruption may be termed, if not entirely, at least very nearly, spontaneous. And with this we are brought to the third point which psychological analysis of the 'uncanny' experience brings to view: meanings are aroused and awakened in it of a unique and special content, though altogether obscure, latent, and germinal, which are the real ground for the emotion of awe. For, if such meanings are not there at the start in some form or other, the mental and emotional disturbance could never take place. In the fourth place, the mental state we are discussing may, on the one hand, remain pure 'feeling', pursue its course, and pass away without its obscure thought-content being rendered explicit. If in this implicit form it is summed up in a phrase, this will be merely some such exclamation as: 'How uncanny!' or 'How eerie this place is!' On the other hand, the implicit meaning may be rendered explicit. It is already a beginning of this explicative process—though still in merely negative terms— when a man says: '*It* is not quite right here'; '*It* is uncanny.' The English 'This place is haunted' shows a transition to a positive form of expression. Here we have the obscure basis of meaning and idea rising into greater clarity and beginning to make itself explicit as the notion, however vague and fleeting, of a transcendent Something, a real operative entity of a numinous kind, which later, as the development proceeds, assumes concrete form as a '*numen loci*', a daemon, an 'El', a Baal, or the like.

In Gen. xxviii. 17 Jacob says: 'How dreadful is this place! This is none other than the house of Elohim.' This verse is very instructive for the psychology of religion; it exemplifies the point that has just been made. The first sentence gives plainly the mental impression itself in all its immediacy, before reflection has permeated it, and before the meaning-content of the feeling itself has become clear or explicit. It connotes solely the *primal numinous awe*, which has been undoubtedly sufficient in itself in many cases to mark out 'holy' or 'sacred' places, and make of them spots of awful veneration, centres of a cult admitting a certain development. There is no need, that is, for the experient to pass on to resolve his mere impression of the eerie and aweful into the idea of a 'numen', a divine power, dwelling in the 'aweful' place, still less need the *numen* become a *nomen*, a named power, or the '*nomen*' become something more than a mere pronoun. Worship is possible without this further explicative process. But Jacob's second statement gives this process of explication and interpretation; it is no longer simply an expression of the actual experience.

The German expression *Es spukt hier* (literally, it haunts here) is also instructive. It has properly no true subject, or at least it makes no assertion as to what the *es*, the 'it', is which 'haunts'; in itself it contains no suggestion of the concrete representations of 'ghost', 'phantom', 'spectre', or 'spirit' common to our popular mythology. Rather is the statement simply the pure expression of the emotion of 'eeriness' or 'uncanniness' itself, when just on the point of detaching and disengaging from itself a first vaguely intimated idea of a numinous something, an entity from beyond the borders of 'natural' experience. It is to be regretted that the German language possesses no general word less vulgar than 'spuken', no word which, instead of pointing us aside, as this word does, to the domain of superstition and the impure offshoots of the numinous consciousness, should retain its fundamental meaning in an unperverted form.[1] But even so we can feel by an effort of imaginative introjection how akin the debased feeling of haunting, given by this word, is to those primary numinous experiences by which long ago seers had experience of 'aweful', 'holy', numen-possessed places, discovering thereby the starting-points for local cults and the birth-places of the 'El' worshipped there. The echo of such primeval experiences lingers in Gen. xxviii. 17 (Jacob at Bethel) and Exod. iii (the burning bush). The places here set apart by Moses and Jacob are genuine 'haunted places', at which '*es spukt*', places about which 'there is something eerie'. Only,

---

[1] The expression *es geistet hier* may serve, but it has an artificial sound. The English 'to haunt' is a nobler expression than the German *spuken*. We might legitimately translate Hab. ii. 20: 'Yahweh haunts His holy Temple.' Such a 'haunting' is frequently the meaning of the Hebrew *shākan*. And we get a fuller and truer rendering of Ps. xxvi. 8: 'the place where Thine honour dwelleth' by translating it: 'the places haunted by Thy majesty'. The *Shekīnah* is properly the *haunting presence* of Yahweh in the Temple at Jerusalem.

the feeling of being haunted has in these cases not the im-
poverished and debased sense of our modern eerie feeling of
being haunted by ghosts and spectres; it comprises all the
rich potentialities and possibilities of development inherent
in the true primal numinous emotion. Nor can we doubt that
even to-day the finer awe that may steal over us in the stillness and half-gloom of our own present-day sanctuaries has
ultimate kinship not only with that of which Schiller writes
in his verses:

> Und in Poseidons Fichtenhain
> Tritt er mit frommem Schauder ein,[1]

but also with genuine 'ghostly' emotions. The faint shiver
that may accompany such states of mind is not unrelated to
the feeling of 'creeping flesh', whose numinous character we
have already considered (p. 16). In its efforts to derive
'daemon' and 'god' forcibly from 'souls' and 'spirits', animism
is looking the wrong way. It would be, at any rate, on the
right path if it maintained that they are haunting apparitions.

This is partially proved by certain ancient, still extant
terms, which long ago had reference to the original awe of
the haunting spirit (in the good sense), and later grew to
become designations both of the lowest and the highest forms
of 'awe'. Such a term is the enigmatical word *asura* in
Sanskrit. *Asura* is the 'aweful' or 'dreadful' in the sense in
which Jacob used the word, the eerie or uncanny. Later, in
Indian religion, it is used as the technical expression for the
lower forms of the spectral, ghostly, and daemonic. But at
the same time it is from primeval times a title of the sublimest of all the gods of the Rig-Veda, the weirdly exalted
Varuna. And in the Persian expression *Ahura-mazda* it becomes the name of the one and only eternal godhead itself.
The same thing is true of the term *adbhuta*. You experience an
adbhuta when you are 'in an empty house', says an old definition.[2] It is the experience of our 'shuddering'. But, on the

---

[1] Schiller, *Die Kraniche des Ibykus* (The Cranes of Ibykus):

> 'And to Poseidon's grove of pine
> With awe devout he enters in.'

[2] *A-dbhuta* means literally the inapprehensible, inexpressible. But in the first
instance it is exactly our *mysterium stupendum*, whereas *asura* is the *tremendum*.

other hand, *adbhuta* is also the name for the supreme transcendent marvel and its attractive spell, the element of 'fascination', even for the eternal Brahman himself and his salvation, the *Adbhutam* that passes beyond the reach of speech.[1]

11. Finally, it is only upon our assumption of an *a priori* basis of ideas and feelings that an explanation is forthcoming for the interesting phenomena to which Andrew Lang[2] rightly drew attention. These do not, of course, support the hypothesis of a 'primitive monotheism', that offspring of missionary apologetic, which, eager to save the second chapter of Genesis, yet feels the shame of a modern at the walking of Yahweh 'in the garden in the cool of the day'. But they do point to facts which remain downright riddles, if we start from any naturalistic foundation of religion—whether animism, pantheism, or another—and must in that case be got out of the way by the most violent hypotheses. The essence of the matter is this, that elements and strands are to be found in numerous mythologies and the stories of savage tribes, which reach altogether beyond the point they have otherwise attained in religious rites and usages. Notions of 'high gods' are adumbrated, with whom the savage has often hardly any relations in practice, if any at all, and in whom he yet acknowledges, almost in spite of himself, a value superior to that of all other mythological images, a value which may well accord with the divine in the highest sense.

Sometimes, but by no means always, we can discern that these anticipations of a higher religious experience are the outcome of a past growth of myth. What is characteristic and at the same time so puzzling is the elevation with which they stand out from the surrounding more primitive religious life amid which they are found. Indeed, in cases where missions have introduced the preaching of Christian theism, these apprehended, exalted divinities are readily and frequently

---

[1] *Adbhuta* (and *āścarya*) would be an accurate rendering in Sanskrit for our 'numinous', were it not that the word, like the German *wunderbar* and the English 'awful', has long ago become trite and shallow from the 'profane'—non-religious—uses to which it has been so perpetually put.

[2] *Myth, Ritual, and Religion*, 1899; *The Making of Religion*, 1902; *Magic and Religion*, 1901. Cf. also P. W. Schmidt, *Grundlinien einer Vergleichung der Religionen und Mythologien der austronesischen Völker*, Vienna, 1910.

K

identified with God and reinforce the preaching of the missionary. And converts often come to admit that, though they had not honoured God, they had had knowledge of Him. It is, of course, true that this sort of fact can sometimes be explained as due to traditional influences, protracted from an earlier time, when the tribe in question was in contact with a higher theistic religion: the very names given to these higher beings sometimes prove as much. But even in this form the phenomenon is a very singular one. Why should 'savages', set in other respects in an utterly alien milieu of barbaric superstition, accept and, what is more, retain these notions, unless their own savage minds were so predisposed to them that, so far from being able to let them go, they were obliged to take at least an interest in them as a tradition and very frequently to acknowledge their authority by the felt witness of their own consciences? But, though the theory of a surviving tradition is sometimes applicable, there are many of these cases in which it is impossible to apply it without doing violence to the facts. In these we have clearly to do with anticipations and presentiments rather than survivals. Assuming the continual pressure and operation of an inward reasonable disposition to form certain ideas, these anticipations are not only no matter for surprise; they are as naturally to be expected as are the achievements of gipsy musicians, who, set otherwise in a milieu of the most primitive culture, yet respond to the pressure of a strong, innate, musical disposition. Without such an assumption the facts would remain as an insoluble puzzle.

Naturalistic psychologists, in this as in other cases, ignore a fact which might be thought at least to have a psychological interest, and which they could notice in themselves by careful introspection, namely, the *self-attestation* of religious ideas in one's own mind. This is, to be sure, more certain in the case of the naïve than in that of the more blasé mind; but many people would identify it in their own consciousness if they would only recall deliberately and impartially their hours of preparation for the ceremony of Confirmation. But what the mind 'attests' it can also under favourable circumstances evince and elicit from itself in premonitory stirring and felt surmise. The upholders of the theory of 'primitive mono-theism', on the other hand, show no less serious disregard of this central fact than the naturalistic psychologists. For if the phenomena we have been considering were based simply and solely on historical traditions and dim memories of a 'primeval revelation', as on such a theory they must be, this self-attestation from within would be just as much excluded as before.[1]

[1] Compare with this chapter my recently published book *Das Gefühl des Überweltlichen*, especially Chapter VI: 'Das Werden eines Gottes'.

CHAPTER XVI

THE 'CRUDER' PHASES

IT is not only the more developed forms of religious experience that must be counted underivable and *a priori*. The
same holds good throughout and is no less true of the primitive, 'crude', and rudimentary emotions of 'daemonic dread'
which, as we have seen, stand at the threshold of religious
evolution. *Religion is itself present at its commencement*: religion,
nothing else, is at work in these early stages of mythic and
daemonic experience. Let us consider the circumstances in
which alone the primitive and crude character of these
consists.

(*a*) First, it is due to the merely gradual emergence and
successive awakening of the several 'moments' of the numinous. The numinous only unfolds its full content by slow
degrees, as one by one the series of requisite stimuli or incitements becomes operative. But where any whole is as yet
incompletely presented its earlier and partial constituent
moments or elements, aroused in isolation, have naturally
something bizarre, unintelligible, and even grotesque about
them. This is especially true of that religious moment which
would appear to have been in every case the first to be
aroused in the human mind, viz. daemonic dread. Considered
alone and *per se*, it necessarily and naturally looks more like
the opposite of religion than religion itself. If it is singled out
from the elements which form its context, it appears rather
to resemble a dreadful form of auto-suggestion, a sort of
psychological nightmare of the tribal mind, than to have
anything to do with religion; and the supernatural beings
with whom men at this early stage profess relations appear as
phantoms, projected by a morbid, undeveloped imagination
afflicted by a sort of persecution-phobia. One can understand how it is that not a few inquirers could seriously
imagine that 'religion' began with devil-worship, and that at
bottom the devil is more ancient than God.

To this serial and gradual awakening of the different
aspects and moments of the numinous is also to be ascribed

the difficulty of classifying religions by genus and species. Every one who undertakes the task produces a different classification. For the facts to be classified are for the most part not at all related as the distinct species of one and the same genus; they are not alternative, determinate forms into which the whole—'religion'—may be analysed, but constituent elements, out of which it is to be 'synthesized' or built up. It is as though a whale should begin to show itself above the water part by part, and as though people should then attempt to classify the arched back, the end of the tail, and the head spouting water, by genus and species, instead of seeking for such a real understanding of these phenomena as would recognize each of them in its place and proper connexion with the rest as a part and member of *one* whole body, which must itself have been grasped in its entirety before its parts could be properly apprehended.

(*b*) In the second place, the 'primitiveness' of the cruder phases is due to the abrupt, capricious, and desultory character which marks the earliest form of numinous emotion; and, in consequence, to its indistinctness, which causes it to be merged and confounded with 'natural' feelings.

(*c*) It is due, next, to the fact that the valuation prompted by the moment of numinous consciousness (e.g. the 'daemonic dread' phase) is attached in the first place, and very naturally, to objects, occurrences, and entities falling within the workaday world of primitive experience, which prompt or give occasion to the stirring of numinous emotion by analogy and then divert it to themselves. This circumstance is more than anything else the root of what has been called nature-worship and the deification of natural objects. Only gradually, under pressure from the numinous feeling itself, are such connexions subsequently 'spiritualized' or ultimately altogether rejected, and not till then does the obscure content of the feeling, with its reference to absolute transcendent reality, come to light in all its integrity and self-subsistence.

(*d*) A fourth factor contributing to the crudity of primitive 'religion' is the uncontrolled, enthusiastic form, making for wild fanaticism, in which the numinous feeling storms the savage mind, appearing as religious mania, possession by the numen, intoxication, and frenzy.

(*e*) Again, a quite essential factor is the wrong schematizations it undergoes, when interpreted in terms of some experience analogous, perhaps, but not really appertaining to it. Examples of this have already been given (e.g. pp. 122–4).

(*f*) Finally, and most important, there is the deficient rationalization and moralization of the experience, for it is only gradually that the numinous feeling becomes charged with progressively rational, moral, and cultural significance.

These considerations account for the primitive and savage character of the numinous consciousness at its outset. But it must be repeated that in its content even the first stirring of 'daemonic dread' is a purely *a priori* element. In this respect it may be compared from first to last with the aesthetic judgement and the category of the beautiful. Utterly different as my mental experiences are when I recognize an object as 'beautiful' or as 'horrible', yet both cases agree in this, that I ascribe to the object an attribute that professes to interpret it, which I do not and cannot get from sense-experience, but which I rather ascribe to it by a spontaneous judgement of my own. Intuitively I apprehend in the object only its sensuous qualities and its spatial form, nothing more. That the *meaning* I call 'beautiful' fits the object, i.e. that these sense-data *mean* 'beautiful', or even that there *is* any such meaning at all—these are facts which sensory elements can in no wise supply or tell me. I must have an obscure conception of 'the beautiful itself', and, in addition, a principle of subsumption, by which I attribute it to the object, else even the simplest experience of a beautiful thing is rendered impossible. And this analogy may be pursued farther. Joy in the beautiful, however analogous to mere pleasure in the agreeable, is yet distinguishable from it by a plain difference in quality, and cannot be derived from anything other than itself; and just such is the relation of the specific religious awe to mere natural fear.

The 'crude' stage is transcended as the numen reveals 'itself' (i.e. becomes manifest to mind and feeling) ever more strongly and fully. An essential factor in this is the process by which it is filled out and charged with rational elements, whereby it passes at the same time into the region of the conceivable and comprehensible. Yet all the time all the elements of non-rational 'inconceivability' are retained on the side of the numinous and intensified as the revelation proceeds. 'Revelation' does not mean a *mere* passing over into the intelligible and comprehensible. Something may be profoundly and intimately known in feeling for the bliss it brings or the agitation it produces, and yet the understanding may find no concept for it. To *know* and to *understand conceptually* are two different things, are often even mutually exclusive and contrasted. The mysterious obscurity of the numen is by no means tantamount to unknowableness. Assuredly the *'deus absconditus et incomprehensibilis'* was for Luther no *'deus ignotus'*. And so, too, St. Paul 'knows' the peace, which yet 'passeth understanding'.

CHAPTER XVII

THE HOLY AS AN *A PRIORI* CATEGORY

Part II

WE conclude, then, that not only the rational but also the non-rational elements of the complex category of 'holiness' are *a priori* elements and each in the same degree. Religion is not in vassalage either to morality or teleology, *ethos* or *telos*, and does not draw its life from postulates; and its non-rational content has, no less than its rational, its own independent roots in the hidden depths of the spirit itself.

But the same *a priori* character belongs, in the third place, to the *connexion* of the rational and the non-rational elements in religion, their inward and necessary union. The histories of religion recount indeed, as though it were something axiomatic, the gradual interpenetration of the two, the process by which 'the divine' is charged and filled out with ethical meaning. And this process is, in fact, *felt* as something axiomatic, something whose inner necessity we feel to be self-evident. But then this inward self-evidence is a problem in itself; we are forced to assume an obscure, *a priori* knowledge of the necessity of this synthesis, combining rational and non-rational. For it is not by any means a *logical* necessity. How should it be logically inferred from the still 'crude', half-daemonic character of a moon-god or a sun-god or a numen attached to some locality, that he is a guardian and guarantor of the oath and of honourable dealing, of hospitality, of the sanctity of marriage, and of duties to tribe and clan? How should it be inferred that he is a god who decrees happiness and misery, participates in the concerns of the tribe, provides for its well-being, and directs the course of destiny and history? Whence comes this most surprising of all the facts in the history of religion, that beings, obviously born originally of horror and terror, become *gods*—beings to whom men pray, to whom they confide their sorrow or their happiness, in whom they behold the origin and the sanction of morality, law, and the whole canon of justice? And how does all this come about in such a way that, when once such ideas have been aroused, it is understood at once as the plainest and most evident of axioms, that so it must be?

Socrates, in Plato's *Republic*, ii. 382 E, says: 'God, then, is single and true in deed and word, and neither changes himself nor deceives others. . . .' And Adeimantos answers him: 'So too is it apparent to me, now that you say it.' The most interesting point in this passage is not the elevation and purity of the conception of God, nor yet the lofty rationalization and moralization of it here enunciated, but, on the side of Socrates, the apparently 'dogmatic' tone of his pronouncement—for he does not spend the least pains in demonstrating it—and, on the side of Adeimantos, the ingenuous surprise and, at the same time, the confident assurance with which he admits a truth novel to him. And his assent is such as implies convincement; he does not simply believe Socrates; he sees clearly for himself the truth of his words. Now this is the criterion of all *a priori* knowledge, namely, that, so soon as an assertion has been clearly expressed and understood, knowledge of its truth comes into the mind with the certitude of first-hand insight. And what passed here between Socrates and Adeimantos has been repeated a thousand times in the history of religions. Amos, also, says something new when he proclaims Yahweh as the God of inflexible, universal, and absolute righteousness, and yet this is a novelty that he neither proves nor justifies by an appeal to authorities. He appeals to *a priori* judgements, viz. to the religious conscience itself, and this in truth bears witness to his message.

Luther, again, recognizes and maintains such an *a priori* knowledge of the divine nature. His rage against the 'whore Reason' leads him, to be sure, usually to utterances in the opposite sense, such as the following:

It is a knowledge *a posteriori*, in that we look at God from without, at His works and His government, as one looketh at a castle or house from without and thereby feeleth (*spüret*) the lord or householder thereof. But *a priori* from within hath no wisdom of men yet availed to discover what and of what manner of being is God as He is in Himself or in His inmost essence, nor can any man know nor say aught thereof, but they to whom it has been revealed by the Holy Ghost.

Here Luther overlooks the fact that a man must 'feel' or detect the 'householder' *a priori* or not at all. But in other passages he himself allows the general human reason to possess many true cognitions of what 'God is in Himself or in His inmost essence'. Compare the following:

Atque ipsamet ratio naturalis cogitur eam concedere *proprio suo iudicio convicta*, etiamsi nulla esset scriptura. Omnes enim homines inveniunt hanc sententiam in cordibus suis scriptam et *agnoscunt* eam ac probatam, licet inviti, cum *audiant* eam tractari: primo, Deum esse omnipotentem . . . deinde, ipsum omnia nosse et praescire, neque errare neque falli posse. . . . Istis duobus corde et sensu concessis. . . .[1]

The interesting words of this statement are: *proprio suo iudicio convicta*, for they make the distinction between *cognitions* and mere 'innate ideas' or supernaturally instilled notions, both of which latter may produce 'thoughts', but not convictions '*ex proprio iudicio*'. Note also the words: 'cum *audiant* eam tractari', which exactly correspond to the experience of Plato's Adeimantos, already quoted.[2]

[1] Luther, Weimar ed., xviii. 719: 'And the natural reason itself is forced even were there no holy scripture, to grant it (*sc.* this assertion), *convinced by its own judgement.* For all men, *as soon as they hear it treated of,* find this belief written in their hearts, and acknowledge it as proved, even unwillingly: first, that God is omnipotent, . . . then, that He has knowledge and foreknowledge of all things and can neither err nor be deceived. . . . Since these two things are admitted by heart and feeling. . . .'

[2] The most interesting features in Luther in this connexion, however, are the passages upon 'Faith', in which Faith is described as a unique cognitive faculty for the apprehension of divine truth, and as such is contrasted with the 'natural' capacities of the Understanding, as elsewhere the 'Spirit' is contrasted. 'Faith' is here like the 'Synteresis' in the theory of knowledge of the mystics, the 'inward teacher' (*magister internus*) of Augustine, and the 'inward light' of the Quakers, which are all of them of course 'above reason', but yet an *a priori* element in ourselves. A particularly striking passage is the following from Luther's *Table-Talk* (Wei. v. 5820):

'Omnium hominum mentibus impressa est divinitus notitia Dei. Quod sit Deus, omnes homines sine ulla artium et disciplinarum cognitione sola natura duce sciunt, et omnium hominum mentibus hoc divinitus impressum est. Nulla umquam fuit tam fera gens et immanis, quae non crediderit, esse divinitatem quandam, quae omnia creavit. Itaque Paulus inquit: Invisibilia Dei a creatura mundi per ea, quae facta sunt, intellecta conspiciuntur,

It is the same experience which missionaries have so often undergone. Once enunciated and understood, the ideas of the unity and goodness of the divine nature often take a surprisingly short time to become firmly fixed in the hearer's mind, if he show any susceptibility for religious feeling. Frequently, thereupon, the hearer adapts the religious tradition that has hitherto been his to the new meaning he has learned. Or, where resistance is offered to the new teaching, it is yet often noticeably in the face of pressure the other way from the man's own conscience. Such experiences have been made known to me by missionaries among the Tibetans and among African negroes, and it would be interesting to make a collection of them, both in regard to the general question of the *a priori* factors in religion, and especially as throwing light upon the *a priori* knowledge of the essential interdependence of the rational and the non-rational elements in the idea of God. For this the history of religion is itself an almost unanimous witness. Incomplete and defective as the process of moralizing the 'numina' may often have been throughout

sempiterna eius virtus et divinitas. Quare omnes ethnici sciverunt esse Deum, quantumvis fuerunt Epicurei, quantumvis contenderunt, non esse Deum. Non in eo, quod negant esse Deum, simul confessi sunt esse Deum? Nemo enim negare id potest, quod nescit. Quare, etsi quidam per omnem vitam in maximis versati sunt flagitiis et sceleribus et non aliter omnino vixerunt, ac si nullus esset Deus, tamen nunquam conscientiam animis potuerunt eicere testantem et affirmantem, quod sit Deus. Et quamvis illa conscientia pravis et perversis opinionibus ad tempus oppressa fuit, redit tamen et convincit eos in extremae vitae spiritu.'

'The knowledge of God is impressed upon the mind of every man by God. Under the sole guidance of nature all men know that God is—without any acquaintance with the arts or sciences; and this is divinely imprinted upon all men's minds. There has never been a people so wild and savage that it did not believe that there is some divine power that created all things. And thus it is that Paul says: "the invisible things of God from the creation of the world are clearly seen, being understood by the things that are made, even His eternal power and Godhead." Wherefore all the Gentiles knew that there is a God, however much they were Epicureans, however much they maintained that there is no God. Did they not confess God's being in that very denial of Him? For no one can deny that of which he has no knowledge. Wherefore, although men have all their lives long been occupied in the greatest sins and crimes and have lived just as though there were no God, yet they have never been able to cast forth from their minds the conscience that testifies and affirms that God is. And although that conscience has been overborne for a time by evil and perverse opinions, yet it comes back to convict them in their life's final breath.'

the wide regions of primitive religious life, everywhere there are traces of it to be found. And wherever religion, escaping from its first crudity of manifestation, has risen to a higher type, this process of synthesis has in all cases set in and continued more and more positively. And this is all the more remarkable when one considers at what widely different dates the imaginative creation of the figures of gods had its rise in different cases, and under what diverse conditions of race, natural endowment, and social and political structure its evolution proceeded. All this points to the existence of *a priori* factors universally and necessarily latent in the human spirit: those, in fact, which we can find directly in our own religious consciousness, when we, too, like Adeimantos, naïvely and spontaneously concur with Socrates' saying, as with an axiom whose truth we have seen for ourselves: 'God is single, and true in deed and word.'

As the rational elements, following *a priori* principles, come together in the historical evolution of religions with the nonrational, they serve to 'schematize' these. This is true, not only in general of the relation of the rational aspect of 'the holy', taken as a whole, to its non-rational, taken as a whole, but also in detail of the several constituent elements of the two aspects. The *tremendum*, the daunting and repelling moment of the numinous, is schematized by means of the rational ideas of justice, moral will, and the exclusion of what is opposed to morality; and schematized thus, it becomes the holy 'wrath of God', which Scripture and Christian preaching alike proclaim. The *fascinans*, the attracting and alluring moment of the numinous, is schematized by means of the ideas of goodness, mercy, love, and, so schematized, becomes all that we mean by Grace, that term so rich in import, which unites with the holy wrath in a single 'harmony of contrasts', and like it is, from the numinous strain in it, tinged with mysticism. The 'moment' *mysteriosum* is schematized by the *absoluteness* of all rational attributes applied to the Deity. Probably the correspondence here implied—between 'the mysterious' and the *absoluteness* of all rational attributes —will not appear at first sight so immediately evident as in the two foregoing cases, wrath and grace. None the less it is a very exact correspondence. God's rational attributes can be distinguished from like attributes applied to the created spirit by being not relative, as those are, but absolute. Human love is relative, admitting of degrees, and it is the same with human knowledge and human goodness. God's love and knowledge and goodness, on the other hand, and all else that can be asserted of Him in conceptual terms, are formally absolute. The *content* of the attributes is the same; it is an *element of form* which marks them apart as attributes of God. But such an element of form is also the 'mysterious' as such: it is, as we saw on p. 31, the formal aspect of the 'wholly other'. But to this plain correspondence of the two things, 'the mysterious' and the absoluteness of rational attributes, a further one must be added. Our understanding can only compass the relative. That which is in contrast absolute, though it may in a sense be *thought*, cannot be *thought home, thought out*; it is within the reach of our conceiving, but it is beyond the grasp of our comprehension. Now, though this does not make what is 'absolute' itself genuinely 'mysterious', as this term was expounded on pp. 27–8, it does make it a genuine *schema* of 'the mysterious'. The absolute exceeds our power to comprehend; the mysterious wholly eludes it. The absolute is that which surpasses the limits of our understanding, not through its actual qualitative character, for that is familiar to us, but through its formal character. The mysterious, on the other hand, is that which lies altogether outside what can be thought, and is, alike in form, quality, and essence, the utterly and 'wholly other'. We see, then, that in the case of the moment of 'mystery', as well as those of 'awefulness' and 'fascination', there is an exact correspondence between the non-rational element and its rational *schema*, and one that admits of development.

By the continual living activity of its non-rational elements a religion is guarded from passing into 'rationalism'. By being steeped in and saturated with rational elements it is guarded from sinking into fanaticism or mere mysticality, or at least from persisting in these, and is qualified to become a religion for all civilized humanity. The degree in which both rational and non-rational elements are jointly present, united in healthy and lovely harmony, affords a criterion to measure the relative rank of religions—and one, too, that is specifically religious. Applying this criterion, we find that Christianity, in this as in other respects, stands out in complete superiority over all its sister religions. The lucid edifice of its clear and pure conceptions, feelings, and experiences is built up on a foundation that goes far deeper than the rational. Yet the non-rational is only the basis, the setting, the woof in the fabric, ever preserving for Christianity its mystical depth, giving religion thereby the deep undertones and heavy shadows of mysticism, without letting it develop into a mere rank growth of mysticality. And thus Christianity, in the healthily proportioned union of its elements, assumes an absolutely classical form and dignity, which is only the more vividly attested in consciousness as we proceed honestly and without prejudice to set it in its place in the comparative study of religions. Then we shall recognize that in Christianity an element of man's spiritual life, which yet has its analogies in other fields, has for the first time come to maturity in a supreme and unparalleled way.

CHAPTER XVIII

THE MANIFESTATIONS OF THE 'HOLY' AND THE FACULTY OF 'DIVINATION'

IT is one thing merely to believe in a reality beyond the senses and another to have experience of it also; it is one thing to have ideas of 'the holy' and another to become consciously aware of it as an operative reality, intervening actively in the phenomenal world. Now it is a fundamental conviction of all religions, of religion as such, we may say, that this latter is possible as well as the former. Religion is convinced not only that the holy and sacred reality is attested by the inward voice of conscience and the religious conscious-ness, the 'still, small voice' of the Spirit in the heart, by feeling, presentiment, and longing, but also that it may be directly encountered in particular occurrences and events, self-revealed in persons and displayed in actions, in a word, that beside the inner revelation from the Spirit there is an outward revelation of the divine nature. Religious language gives the name of 'sign' to such demonstrative actions and manifesta-tions, in which holiness stands palpably self-revealed. From the time of the most primitive religions everything has counted as a sign that was able to arouse in man the sense of the holy, to excite the feeling of apprehended sanctity, and stimulate it into open activity. Of this kind were those factors and circumstances of which we have already spoken—the thing terrible, sublime, overpowering, or astounding, and in an especial degree the uncomprehended, mysterious thing, which become the 'portent' and 'miracle'. But, as we saw, all these were not 'signs' in the true sense, but opportunities, circumstances, prompting the religious feeling to awake of itself; and the factor promoting this result was found to lie in an element common to them all, but merely analogous with 'the holy'. The interpretation of them as actual appearances of the holy itself in its own nature meant, we saw, a confound-ing of the category of holiness with something only outwardly resembling it: it was not a genuine '*anamnesis*', a genuine recognition of the holy in its own authentic nature, made manifest in appearance. And therefore we find that such false recognitions of the holy are later rejected and wholly or partly extruded as inadequate or simply unworthy, so soon as a higher level of development and a purer religious judgement have been reached. There is a precisely parallel process in another department of judgement, that of aesthetic taste. While the taste is still crude, a feeling or fore-feeling of the beautiful begins to stir, which must come from an obscure *a priori* conception of beauty already present, else it could not occur at all. The man of crude taste, not being capable of a clear 'recognition' of authentic beauty, falls into confusion and *misapplies* this obscure, dim conception of the beautiful, judging things to be beautiful which are in fact not beautiful at all. Here, as in the case of the judgement of holiness, the principle underlying the erroneous judgement of beauty is one of faint analogy. Certain elements in the thing wrongly judged to be beautiful have a closer or remoter analogy to real beauty. And later here, too, when his taste has been educated, the man rejects with strong aversion the quasi-beautiful but not really beautiful thing and becomes qualified to see and to judge rightly, i.e. to recognize as beautiful the outward object in which the 'beauty' of which he has an inward notion and standard really 'appears'.

Let us call the faculty, of whatever sort it may be, of *genuinely* cognizing and recognizing the holy in its appearances the faculty of *divination*. Does such a faculty exist, and, if so, what is its nature?

To the 'supernaturalistic' theory the matter is simple enough. Divination consists in the fact that a man encounters an occurrence that is not 'natural', in the sense of being inexplicable by the laws of nature. Since it has actually occurred, it must have had a cause; and, since it has no 'natural' cause, it must (so it is said) have a supernatural one. This theory of divination is a genuine, solidly rationalist theory, put together with rigid concepts in a strict demonstrative form and intended as such. And it claims that the capacity or faculty of divination is the *understanding*, the faculty of reflection in concept and demonstration. The transcendent is here proved as strictly as anything can be proved, logically from given premises.

It would be almost superfluous to adduce in detail in opposition to this view the argument that we have no possibility of establishing that an event did not arise from natural causes or was in conflict with the laws of nature. The religious consciousness itself rises against this desiccation and materialization of what in all religion is surely the most tender and living moment, the actual discovery of and encounter with very deity. Here, if anywhere, coercion by proof and demonstration and the mistaken application of logical and juridical processes should be excluded; here, if anywhere, should be liberty, the unconstrained recognition and inward acknowledgement that comes from deep within the soul, stirred spontaneously, apart from all conceptual theory. If not 'natural science' or 'metaphysics', at least the matured religious consciousness itself spurns such ponderously solid intellectualistic explanations. They are born of rationalism and engender it again; and, as for genuine 'divination', they not only impede it, but despise it as extravagant emotionalism, mysticality, and false romanticism. Genuine divination, in short, has nothing whatever to do with natural law and the relation or lack of relation to it of something experienced. It is not concerned at all with the way in which a phenomenon— be it event, person, or thing—came into existence, but with what it *means*, that is, with its significance as a 'sign' of the holy.

The faculty or capacity of divination appears in the language of dogma hidden beneath the fine name '*testimonium Spiritus Sancti internum*', the inner witness of the Holy Spirit —limited, in the case of dogma, to the recognition of *Scripture* as 'Holy'. And this name is the only right one, and right in a more than figurative sense, when the capacity of divination is itself grasped and appraised by divination. This is not our task here. We therefore employ a psychological rather than a religious expression as being more appropriate to the nature of our discussion.

In this sense, then, 'divination' is no new theological discovery. Schleiermacher, in his *Discourses upon Religion* (1799), Jacob Friedrich Fries, in his doctrine of *Ahndung*

L

('inkling', surmise, presage), and Schleiermacher's colleague and Fries's pupil, De Wette, have all in effect made use of it and given it a footing in theology, the last-named with special reference to the divination of the divine in history, under the name 'surmise of the divine government of the world'. I have discussed Schleiermacher's discovery at greater length in my edition of his *Discourses*,[1] and in my volume, *Kantisch-Fries'sche Religionsphilosophie und ihre Anwendung auf die Theologie*, I have given a more precise statement of the *Ahndung* theory, as it is found in Fries and De Wette. To these two works the reader is referred for a more detailed exposition of the matter, and I shall here note only very briefly the more salient features of this doctrine.

What Schleiermacher is feeling after is really the faculty or capacity of deeply absorbed *contemplation*, when confronted by the vast, living totality and reality of things as it is in nature and history. Wherever a mind is exposed in a spirit of absorbed submission to impressions of 'the universe', it becomes capable—so he lays it down—of experiencing 'intuitions' and 'feelings' (*Anschauungen* and *Gefühle*) of something that is, as it were, a sheer overplus, in addition to empirical reality. This overplus, while it cannot be apprehended by mere theoretic cognition of the world and the cosmic system in the form it assumes for science, can nevertheless be really and truly grasped and experienced in *intuition*, and is given form in single 'intuitions'. And these, in turn, assume shape in definite statements and propositions, capable of a certain groping formulation, which are not without analogy with theoretic propositions, but are to be clearly distinguished from them by their free and merely felt, not reasoned, character. In themselves they are groping intimations of meanings figuratively apprehended. They cannot be employed as 'statements of doctrine' in the strict sense, and can neither be built into a system nor used as premisses for theoretical conclusions. But, though these intuitions are limited and inadequate, they are none the less indisputably *true*, i.e. true as far as they go; and for all Schleiermacher's

[1] Schleiermacher, *Über die Religion* (Vandenhoeck & Ruprecht, Göttingen), pp. 17 ff.

aversion to the word in this connexion they must certainly be termed *cognitions*, modes of *knowing*, though, of course, not the product of reflection, but the intuitive outcome of feeling. Their import is the glimpse of an Eternal, in and beyond the temporal and penetrating it, the apprehension of a ground and meaning of things in and beyond the empirical and transcending it. They are *surmises* or *inklings* of a Reality fraught with mystery and momentousness. And it is to be noted that Schleiermacher himself sometimes avails himself of the term *ahnden* (divining, surmise) instead of his principal ones, 'intuition' and 'feeling', and expressly connects together the divination of prophecy and the knowledge of 'miracle' in the religious sense of a 'sign'.

When Schleiermacher, in expounding the nature of the experience, tries to elucidate its object by giving examples, he is for the most part led to adduce impressions of a higher τέλος, an ultimate, mysterious, cosmic purposiveness, of which we have a prescient intimation. Here he is quite in agreement with the exposition of Fries, who defines the faculty of *Ahndung* as being just a faculty of divining the 'objective teleology' of the world. And De Wette says the same thing even more unreservedly. But in Schleiermacher this rational element is none the less grounded in eternal mystery, that basis of the cosmos that goes beyond reason. This is shown in the groping, hesitant, tentative manner in which the meaning of the experience always reveals itself. And it is emphasized especially forcibly when Schleiermacher shows where in his own case this experience is to be found in the world he confronts; that it is not so much in its universal conformity to law—a rational quality, interpretable by the intellect in terms of purpose—but rather by means of what appears to us as a baffling 'exception' to law, thereby hinting at a meaning that eludes our understanding.[1]

No intellectual, dialectical dissection or justification of such intuition is possible, nor indeed should any be attempted, for the essence most peculiar to it would only be destroyed thereby. Rather it is once again to aesthetic judgements that we must look for the plainest analogy to it. And the

[1] Op. cit., p. 53.

faculty of judging (*Urteilsvermögen*), here presupposed by Schleiermacher, certainly belongs to that 'Judgement' (*Urteilskraft*), which Kant analyses in his Third Critique, and which he himself sets as 'aesthetic judgement' in antithesis to logical judgement. Only, we may not infer from this that the particular several judgements passed in this way need be judgements of 'taste' in their *content*. Kant's distinction between the 'aesthetic' and logical judgement did not mean to imply that the faculty of 'aesthetic' judgement was a judgement upon 'aesthetic' objects in the special narrow sense of the term 'aesthetic', as being concerned with the beautiful. His primary intention is simply and in general terms to separate the faculty of judgement based upon feeling of whatever sort from that of the understanding, from discursive, conceptual thought and inference; and his term 'aesthetic' is simply meant to mark as the peculiarity of the former that, in contrast to logical judgement, it is not worked out in accordance with a clear intellectual scheme, but in conformity to obscure, dim principles which must be felt and cannot be *stated* explicitly as premisses. Kant employs sometimes another expression also to denote such obscure, dim principles of judgement, based on pure feeling, viz. the phrase 'not-unfolded' or 'unexplicated concepts' (*unausgewickelte Begriffe*); and his meaning is here exactly that of the poet, when he says:

> Und wecket der dunklen Gefühle Gewalt,
> Die im Herzen wunderbar schliefen.[1]

Or again:

> Was von Menschen nicht gewusst
> Oder nicht bedacht,
> Durch das Labyrinth der Brust
> Wandelt bei der Nacht.[2]

---

[1] 'It waketh the power of feelings obscure
That in the heart wondrously slumbered.'
(SCHILLER: *Der Graf von Habsburg.*)

[2] 'What beyond our conscious knowing
Or our thought's extremest span
Threads by night the labyrinthine
Pathways of the breast of man.'
(GOETHE: *An den Mond.*)

On the other hand, those judgements that spring from pure contemplative feeling also resemble judgements of aesthetic taste in claiming, like them, objective validity, universality, and necessity. The apparently subjective and personal character of the judgement of taste, expressed in the maxim *de gustibus non disputandum*, simply amounts to this, that tastes of different degrees of culture and maturity are first compared, then so opposed one to the other that agreement is impossible. But unanimity, even in judgements of taste, grows and strengthens in the measure in which the taste matures with exercise; so that even here, despite the proverb, there is the possibility of taste being expounded and taught, the possibility of a continually improving appreciation, of convincement and conviction. And if this is true of the judgement arising from aesthetic feeling in the narrower sense, it is at least equally true of the judgement arising from 'contemplation'. Where, on the basis of a real talent in this direction, 'contemplation' grows by careful exercise in depth and inwardness, there what one man feels *can* be 'expounded' and 'brought to consciousness' in another: one man can both educate himself to a genuine and true manner of feeling and be the means of bringing others to the same point; and that is what corresponds in the domain of 'contemplation' to the part played by argument and persuasion in that of logical conviction.

Schleiermacher's exposition of his great discovery suffers from two defects. We will consider one of them here, leaving the other to the next chapter. Schleiermacher, then, naïvely and unreflectingly assumes this faculty or capacity of 'divination' to be a universal one. In point of fact it is not universal if this means that it could be presupposed necessarily in every man of religious conviction as an actual fact, though of course Schleiermacher is quite right in counting it among the general capacities of mind and spirit, and regarding it indeed as the deepest and most peculiar element in mind, and in that sense—man being defined by his intelligent mind—calling it a 'universal human' element. But what is a universal potentiality of man as such is by no means to be found in *actuality* the universal possession of every single man;

very frequently it is only disclosed as a special endowment and equipment of particular gifted individuals. And Schleiermacher gives an excellent indication of how the matter rightly lies in his very interesting exposition of the nature and function of the *Mittler* (mediator) in his first Discourse. Not Man in general (as rationalism holds), but only special 'divinatory' natures possess the faculty of divination in actuality; and it is these that receive impressions of the transcendent, not the undifferentiated aggregate of homogeneous individuals in mutual interplay, as held by modern social psychology.[1]

It is questionable whether Schleiermacher himself, in spite of his (re-)discovery of 'divination', was a really 'divinatory' nature, although in his first Discourse he maintains that he is. One of his contemporaries, to wit, Goethe, was at any rate decidedly his superior in this respect. In Goethe's life the power of divination, not latent but finding vital exercise, plays an important part, and it finds singular expression in the meaning he gives to the term 'daemonic', put with such emphasis in *Dichtung und Wahrheit*, Book 20, and in his 'talks' with Eckermann.[2] Let us briefly examine these. The most characteristic feature in his notion of the 'daemonic' is that it goes beyond all 'conceiving', surpasses 'understanding' and 'reason', and consequently is 'inapprehensible' and cannot properly be put into a statement:

The Daemonic is that which cannot be accounted for by understanding and reason. It chooses for itself obscure times of darkness. . . . In a plain, prosaic town like Berlin it would hardly find an opportunity to manifest itself. . . . In Poetry there is from first to last something daemonic, and especially in its unconscious appeal, for which all intellect and reason is insufficient, and which, therefore, has an efficacy beyond all concepts. Such is the effect in Music in the highest degree, for Music stands too

---

[1] And this is undoubtedly true as far back as the lowest levels of development, when the 'religious dread' first begins to stir in primitive form and to manifest itself in ideas. To derive these from an original group- and mass-fantasy collectively operating is itself sheer fantasy, and the results this theory helps to produce are about as queer and grotesque as any of the ideas of which it treats.

[2] Cf. Goethe's *Sämtliche Werke*, ed. Cotta, vol. xxv, pp. 124 ff.; Eckermann, *Gespräche mit Goethe*, ed. A. v. d. Linden, Part II, pp. 140 ff.

high for any understanding to reach, and an all-mastering efficacy goes forth from it, of which, however, no man is able to give an account. Religious worship cannot therefore do without music. It is one of the foremost means to work upon men with an effect of *marvel*.

'Does not the daemonic (asks Eckermann) also appear in *events*?' 'Pre-eminently so,' said Goethe, 'and assuredly in all which we cannot explain by intellect or reason. And in general it is manifested throughout nature, visible and invisible, in the most diverse ways. Many creatures in the animal kingdom are of a wholly daemonic kind, and in many we see some aspect of the daemonic operative.'

We notice here how the elements of the numinous we discovered plainly recur: the wholly non-rational, incomprehensible by concepts, the elements of mystery, fascination, awefulness, and energy. The note of the daemonic in the animal kingdom reminds us of Job and the leviathan. But in another respect Goethe's intuition falls far short of Job's intuition of the *mysterium*. By his ignoring of the warning of the book of Job and by applying to the *mysterium* the standards of the rational understanding and reason and conceptions of human purpose, the non-rational comes to involve for Goethe a contradiction between meaning and meaninglessness, sense and nonsense, that which promotes and that which frustrates human ends. Sometimes, however, he approximates it to *wisdom*, as when he says:

So there was something daemonic governing the circumstances of my acquaintance with Schiller all through. We might have met earlier or later. But that we should have met just at the time when I had my Italian tour behind me and Schiller had begun to weary of his philosophical speculations—that was a fact of great significance and fraught with success for both of us.

It even comes near the divine:

Such occurrences have often befallen me throughout my life. And one comes in such cases to believe in a higher influence (*Einwirkung*), something daemonic, to which one pays adoration, without presuming to try to explain it further.

Invariably the 'daemonic' has an import of 'energy' and

'overpoweringness', and sets its stamp upon men of vehement and overpowering personality.

'Napoleon', said I, 'seems to have been a daemonic sort of man.'

'He was so absolutely and to such a degree', said Goethe, 'that hardly any other man can be compared with him in this respect. The late Grand Duke also was a daemonic nature, full of limitless, active force and restlessness.'

'Has not Mephistopheles also "daemonic" traits?'

'No, he is much too negative a being. The daemonic manifests itself in a downright positive and active power.'

In *Dichtung und Wahrheit* (p. 126) he delineates still better the impressions such numinous persons make, and in this passage especially sets in the foreground our *tremendum* as the element alike of 'dread' and 'overpoweringness'.

This daemonic character appears in its most *dreadful* form when it stands out dominatingly in some *man*. Such are not always the most remarkable men, either in spiritual quality or natural talents, and they seldom have any goodness of heart to recommend them.[1] But an incredible force goes forth from them and they exercise an incredible power over all creatures, nay, perhaps even over the elements. And who can say how far such an influence may not extend?

But the efficacy and influence of such a 'daemonic' man, even when it is beneficent, moves to amazement rather than to admiration; it is more a tumultuous urgency than ordinary agency, and is at any rate absolutely non-rational. This is what Goethe tries to describe in the series of antitheses in *Dichtung und Wahrheit* (p. 124):

... Something that only manifested itself in contradictions and therefore could not be comprehended under any concept, still less under any one word. It was not divine, for it seemed unreasonable; not human, for it lacked understanding; not devilish, for it was beneficent; not angelic, for it often displayed malicious joy. It was like chance, for it pointed to no consequence; it resembled providence, for it indicated connexion and unity. All that hems us in seemed penetrable to it; it seemed to dispose at

[1] i.e. they are merely *'numinous'*, not *'holy'* men.

will of the inevitable elements of our being, contracting time and expanding space. Only in the impossible did it seem at home, and the possible it spurned from itself with contempt.

Although this daemonic thing can be manifested in everything corporeal and incorporeal, finding indeed most notable expression among animals, still it is pre-eminently with men that it stands in closest and most wonderful connexion, and there fashions a power which, if not opposed to the moral world order, yet intersects it in such a way that the one might be taken for the warp and the other for the woof.

There can be no clearer expression than this of the prodigiously strong impression which divination of the numinous may make upon the mind, and that obviously not on a single occasion but repeatedly, till it has become almost a matter of habit. But at the same time this 'divination' of Goethe is not one that apprehends the numinous as the prophet does. It does not rise to the elevation of the experience of Job, where the non-rational mystery is at the same time experienced and extolled as supra-rational, as of profoundest *value*, and as holiness in its own right. It is rather the fruit of a mind which, for all its depth, was not equal to such profundities as these, and to which, therefore, the non-rational counterpoint to the melody of life could only sound in confused consonance, not in its authentic harmony, indefinable but palpable. Therefore, though it is genuine divination, it is the divination of Goethe 'the pagan', as he sometimes used to call himself. Indeed, it is a divination that functions only at the level of the 'daemonic' which, as we saw, precedes religion proper, not at the level of the divine and the holy in the truest sense; and it shows very clearly how that sort of merely 'daemonic' experience of the numinous may in a highly cultivated mind only stir emotional reactions of bewilderment and bedazzlement, without giving real light or warmth to the soul. Goethe did not understand how to adjust this divination of the 'daemonic' to his own higher conception of the divine; and, when Eckermann turned the conversation to that, his answer was hesitating and evasive:

'The operative, efficacious force (said I tentatively), which we call the "daemonic", does not seem to fit in with the idea of the divine'. 'Dear boy,' said Goethe, 'what do we know of the idea of the divine, and what can our narrow conceptions presume to tell of the Supreme Being? If I called him by a hundred names, like a Turk, I should yet fall short and have said nothing in comparison to the boundlessness of his attributes.'

But, if we leave out of account the comparatively low level of Goethe's 'divination', we have yet in it a most exact example of what Schleiermacher had in mind. These are 'intuitions and feelings', if not of something divine, still of something numinous in the natural world and in history, and intuitions brought to the higher vitality by an individual with an innate 'divinatory' gift. At the same time the principles on which this divination works cannot even be suggested, for all the examples Goethe may give. What does the 'daemonic' really consist in? How does he come to be conscious of it? How does he identify it as one and the same through all the manifold and contradictory forms in which it manifests itself? These are the questions to which Goethe can suggest no answer. It is evident that in this experience he is being guided by 'mere feeling', that is, by an *a priori* principle that is not explicit and overt, but dim and obscure.

CHAPTER XIX

DIVINATION IN PRIMITIVE CHRISTIANITY

IN the last chapter we spoke of two defects in Schleier-macher's doctrine of divination. The first of these—his misleading assumption that this is a universal human faculty —has already been considered, and we have now to turn to the second. This is that, though Schleiermacher's description of divination in relation to the world of nature and history has both warmth and insight, he gives no clear detailed account, but only the scantiest hints, of what is after all its worthiest object and the object most propitious to its development, namely, the history of *religion*, especially that of the Bible and its culmination in the person of Christ Himself. His concluding 'discourse' makes emphatic and significant mention of Christianity and Christ, but Christ is here only introduced as the supreme divining *subject*, not as the *object* of divination *par excellence*. And it is the same in Schleiermacher's *Glaubenslehre*. In this, too, the significance of Christ is, essentially, intended to be fully given in the fact that he 'admits us into the power and beatitude of his consciousness of God'. Now this is a thought of high value, but it does not attain to that supreme value which Christianity imputes to Christ, of being in His own person 'holiness made manifest', that is, a person in whose being, life, and mode of living we realize of ourselves by 'intuition and feeling' the self-revealing power and presence of the Godhead. For to the Christian it is a momentous question whether or no a real divination—a direct, first-hand apprehension of holiness manifested, the 'intuition' and 'feeling' of it—can be got from the person and life of Christ; whether, in short, 'the holy' can be independently experienced in Him, making Him a real revelation of it.

In this matter we can obviously get no help from the painful and fundamentally impossible inquiries, so often started, into 'Jesus's consciousness of Himself'. They are impossible, if for no other reason, because the evidence at our disposal is neither sufficient in quantity nor appropriate to such a purpose. Jesus puts as the content of His message and all His utterances, not Himself, but the 'kingdom', its beatitude and righteousness, and, in its first and most straightforward interpretation, the 'gospel' is the 'good tidings' of the kingdom of God. What statements about Himself do occur are fragmentary and incidental. But even were this not the case, even if we could find in the gospels a detailed theory of Jesus as to His own nature, what would this prove? Religious enthusiasts have not infrequently had recourse to the most exalted modes of self-proclamation, and often enough no doubt their statements about themselves have been completely bona fide and sincere. And it is just such self-revealing statements of the prophets of all ages that are more than any others dependent for their form upon their temporal or local context, the equipment of myth or dogma with which his environment supplies the speaker. The fact that the prophet or seer or inspired teacher applies all this material to state something about himself merely demonstrates the intensity of his self-consciousness, his sense of mission, his conviction, and his claim to be believed and obeyed—all of which are to be taken for granted where a man stands forward in response to an inner call. The immediate, intuitive 'divination' of which we are speaking would indeed *not* come as a result of such statements by the prophet about himself, however complete; they can arouse a belief in his authority, but cannot bring about the peculiar experience of spontaneous insight that here is something holy made manifest. 'We have heard him ourselves and know that this is indeed the Christ' (John iv. 42).

It cannot now be doubted that such an avowal was made to him as a result of a spontaneous, original divination. This must at any rate be true of Christ's own first disciples. Otherwise it would be unintelligible how the Church could have come into existence at all. Mere proclamation, mere authoritative statement, cannot bring about these massive certainties and that impelling strength, that power to maintain and assert itself, which were necessary if the Christian community was to come into being and which can be recognized in it as its unmistakable characteristics.

Misapprehension of this is only possible if, attempting a one-sided approach to the phenomenon of the origin of the Christian Church, we try to reconstruct the facts solely by the methods of scholarship and out of the material afforded by the staled feelings and blunted sensibility of our present-day artificial civilization and complex mentality. It would be an advantage if, in addition to these methods, an attempt were made to frame a less abstract intuition of the genesis of original and genuine religious communities with the aid of living instances of the thing as it may still be found to-day. It would be necessary for this to seek places and moments at which even to-day religion shows itself alive as a naïve emotional force, with all its primal quality of impulse and instinct. This can still be studied in remote corners of the Mohammedan and Indian world. Even to-day one may come upon scenes in the streets of Mogador or Marrakesh, which have the strangest outward resemblance to those recorded by the Synoptic Gospels: 'holy men' (and very queer specimens they generally are!) now and then make their appearance, each the centre of a group of disciples, and about them the people come and go, listening to their sayings, looking at their miracles, observing how they live and what they do. Bands of adherents gather round them, more loosely or more closely united as the case may be. '*Logia*', tales, and legends form and accumulate;[1] new brotherhoods arise or, if already arisen, extend in widening circles. But the centre of it all is always the man himself, a 'holy man' in his lifetime, and what sustains the movement is always the peculiar power of his personality, the special impression he makes on the bystander. Those who should know assure us that ninety-eight per cent. of these 'holy men' are impostors; but, even so, we are left with two per cent. who are not, a surprisingly

---

[1] It is astonishing that the main problem of Gospel criticism, viz. how the collection of '*Logia*' arose, is not studied in this still-living milieu. It is even more astonishing that the *logia*-series were not long ago elucidated from the closely corresponding milieu of the 'Sayings of the Fathers' (Ἀποφθέγματα τῶν Πατέρων), from the Hadith of Muhammed, or from the Franciscan legends. And a particular striking case of the same thing is the collection of the *Logia* of Rāma-Krishna, which has grown to completion in our own day and under our very eyes.

high percentage in the case of a matter that invites and facilitates imposture as much as this does. The consideration of this remaining two per cent. should continue to throw much light on the actual fact of the genesis of a religious community. The point is that the 'holy man' or the 'prophet' is from the outset, as regards the experience of the circle of his devotees, something more than a 'mere man' (ψιλὸς ἄνθρωπος). He is the being of wonder and mystery, who somehow or other is felt to belong to the higher order of things, to the side of the numen itself. It is not that he himself teaches that he is such, but that he is experienced as such. And it is only such experiences, which, while they may be crude enough and result often enough in self-deception, must at least be profoundly and strongly felt, that can give rise to religious communities.

Such cases of contemporary religious movements afford after all a very inadequate analogy, far removed from that which occurred long ago in Palestine. Yet, if even these movements are only made possible by the fact that men actually experience, or presume that they experience, veritable holiness in the personalities of individuals, how far more true must this not be of the early Chrisitan community! That this was so is attested directly by the whole spirit and the universal conviction of the early communities as a whole, so far as we can discern it in their modest records. And certain of the slighter touches in the Synoptic portrait of Jesus confirm the fact expressly in particular cases. We may instance here the narratives already referred to of Peter's haul of fishes (Luke v. 8), and of the centurion of Capernaum (Matt. viii. 8; Luke vii. 6), which point to spontaneous responses of feeling when the holy is directly encountered in experience. Especially apt in this connexion is the passage in Mark x. 32: καὶ ἦν προάγων αὐτοὺς ὁ Ἰησοῦς· καὶ ἐθαμβοῦντο, οἱ δὲ ἀκολουθοῦντες ἐφοβοῦντο ('and Jesus went before them: and they were amazed; and as they followed, they were afraid'). This passage renders with supreme simplicity and force the immediate impression of the numinous that issued from the man Jesus, and no artistry of characterization could do it so powerfully as these few masterly and pregnant words.

The later saying in John xx. 28 (the confession of Thomas, 'My Lord and my God') may perhaps appear to us by contrast the utterance of a time too far-reaching in its formulations, and very far removed from the simplicity of the original experience of the disciples. And this passage in Mark may appeal to us all the more just because the living emotion here disdains any precise formulation at all; none the less does it contain the real roots of all later developments of Christology.

Such intimations of the numinous impression made by Jesus upon those who knew Him occur in the Gospel narrative only, as it were, incidentally to the main purpose of the narrator, who is scarcely interested in them, but absorbed rather in the record of the miraculous. In our eyes their interest is all the greater, and we can fancy how numerous similar experiences must have been of which no trace survives in the records, just because there was no miracle to be told of in connexion with them and they were simply taken for granted by the narrator as a matter of course.

To this place belong further the belief in Jesus's supremacy over the demonic world and the tendency to legend that began to take effect from the start; the fact that His own relatives take Him for a man 'possessed', an involuntary acknowledgement of the 'numinous' impression He made upon them; and in an especial degree the conviction that breaks spontaneously upon the minds of His disciples as by a sudden impact, won not from His teaching but from the very experience of Him, that He is the 'Messiah', the being who stood for the circle in which He moved as the numinous being *par excellence*. The experiential character of this belief in His Messiahship stands out clearly in Peter's first confession and Jesus's answer to it (Matt. xvi. 15–17), 'Flesh and blood have not revealed it unto thee, but my Father, which is in heaven.' Jesus himself is astonished at Peter's confession, which shows that this was not learnt on authority, but found out by Peter himself, a genuine *discovery*, arising from the impression Jesus made upon him and the testimony borne to it in the depth of the mind, where no teaching of flesh and blood, or even of 'the word', can avail, but only 'my Father in heaven' Himself and without any intermediary.

For this factor—the mind's own witness to the impression —is, it need hardly be said, an indispensable one. Without it all 'impression' is without effect, or rather no impression could occur at all. Therefore, all doctrines of the 'impression made by Christ' are inadequate if they do not pay regard to this second element, which indeed is nothing but the mental predisposition necessary for the experience of holiness, to wit, the category of the holy, potentially present in the spirit as a dim or obscure *a priori* cognition. 'Impress' or 'impression', that is, presupposes something capable of receiving impressions, and that is just what the mind is not, if in itself it is only a 'tabula rasa'. In that richer sense in which we use the word here, we do not in fact mean by 'impression' merely the 'impression' which, in the theory of the Sensationalist school, is the psychical result of sense-perception and is left behind as a psychical trace or vestige of the percept. To be 'impressed' by some one, in the sense we use the term here, means rather to cognize or recognize in him a peculiar significance and to humble oneself before it. And we maintain that this is only possible by an element of cognition, comprehension, and valuation in one's own inner consciousness, that goes out to meet the outward presented fact, i.e. by the 'spirit within'. In Schleiermacher's language the 'presentiment' goes out to meet the 'revelation' to which it belongs. Music can only be understood by the musical person; none but he receives an 'impression' of it. And to every unique kind of real impression corresponds in the same way a unique and special sort of 'congeniality', if the word may be used in this special sense of a particular disposition or aptitude, akin to the object arousing the impression. 'Nemo audit verbum, nisi spiritu intus docente.'[1] Once again let us recall the example of the beautiful. A beautiful thing can only make an impression as such, i.e. as signifying beauty, if and in so far as a man possesses in himself *a priori* the potentiality of framing a special standard of valuation, viz. aesthetic valuation. Such a disposition can only be understood as an original, obscure awareness and appreciation of the value of 'beauty' itself.

---

[1] Cf. Luther's remark that only he who is *verbo conformis* understands the Word, and cf. Augustine, *Confessions*, x. 6. 20.

Because a man has this in him, or better, because he is capable of realizing it by training, he is able to recognize beauty in the particular given beautiful object that he encounters, to feel the correspondence of this object with the hidden 'standard of value' within him. And so, and only so, will he get an 'impression'.

M

DIVINATION IN CHRISTIANITY TO-DAY

THE question whether the primitive Church did or could experience holiness in the person of Christ, which we can but answer in the affirmative, is not so important to us as the question whether we too to-day can still do so. Has the portrayal of Christ's life, His actions and achievement, as preserved and handed down by the Christian Church, the value and power of a revelation for us to-day, or do we in this matter but live upon the inheritance bequeathed us by the first community of Christians and base our faith on the authority and testimony of others? There would be no hope of answering this question, were it not that in us too that inner divining power of apprehension and interpretation which has already been considered may find a place—that witness of the spirit, only possible on the basis of a mental predisposition to recognize 'the holy' and to respond to it. If without this no understanding and no 'impression' of Christ was possible even to the first disciples, of what avail should any tradition be that requires the mediation of generations of Christian men? But if we may make this assumption of a predisposing inner 'witness of the Spirit'—as we must—the matter is very different. In that case there is no harm even in the fact that the records of Christ's life are fragmentary, that they contain manifold uncertainties, that they are intermingled with legendary and overlaid with Hellenistic elements. For the Spirit knows and recognizes what is of the Spirit.

As evidence of the way in which this inward principle—this co-witnessing spirit within us—works, prompting, interpreting, and sending out intimation and surmise, I have found the information of a keenly observant missionary from a remote field very instructive. He told me that he had found it a constant matter for fresh astonishment to see how a presentment of the Word so inadequate—which could only hint at its meaning in a difficult foreign tongue and had to work with alien conceptions—could yet at times win so surprisingly deep and inward an acceptance. And he said that here, too, the best results always were due to the responsive apprehension that came out of the hearer's heart half-way to meet the presented truth. Certainly it is only in this fact that we have a clue to the understanding of the problem of St. Paul. Persecutor of the Church as he was, the intimations he had of the being and meaning of Christ and his Gospel must have come to him piecemeal, in fragmentary hints and caricature. But the spirit from within forced upon him the acknowledgement to which he succumbed on the way to Damascus. It taught him that infinitely profound understanding of the Christ made manifest which has led a critic like Wellhausen to confess that, when all is said, no man has understood Christ himself so deeply and thoroughly as Paul.

If, now, the experience of holiness and 'the holy' in Christ is still to be possible and so afford support to our faith, one thing is evidently to be presupposed at the outset, namely, that his own most immediate and primary achievement and intention can be directly understood and appraised in our experience, so that out of this may grow the 'impression' of his holiness with a like directness. And here a difficulty seems to confront us, which has to be removed if the entire problem is not to be barred from the start. It is this: is that which we to-day think we find in the person of Christ and in Christianity at bottom at all the same as that which He really intended to achieve and that which the first community of His disciples found in Him? In other words, has Christianity really a 'principle' of its own, which, however capable of historical evolution, yet remains unchanged in essence, so that the Christianity of to-day may be measured against the faith of the first disciples and awarded a rank essentially the same?

Is Christianity at all and in a strict sense Jesus's religion? That is, is the religion we know to-day as Christianity, with its peculiar and unique content of belief and feeling, standing in all its historical greatness and supremacy when measured against other religions, with all its power to-day over the hearts and consciences of men to elevate or to excite, to launch accusation or confer benediction, to attract or to repel

—is this religion still in its essence and inner meaning the same thing as the simple, unpretentious religion and form of piety which Jesus Himself had, which He Himself aroused and 'founded' in the circle of those little, heart-stirred bands of men in that out-of-the-way corner of the world, Galilee? It must be generally agreed that it has at least changed its form and its colour very significantly since those days, and that it has been exposed to violent alterations and metamorphoses. But is there any abiding essence, any enduring 'principle' at all behind the sequence of its manifestations, susceptible of evolution and development, but remaining one and the same thoughout? Is it a case of development and evolution, or rather merely of continual transmutation, the influx of something quite different, which one man laments as a perversion, a second admires as a welcome substitution, and a third merely records as a simple historical fact?

Christianity, as it stands before us to-day in present actuality as a great 'world religion', is indubitably, so far as its claim and promise go, in the first and truest sense a religion of Redemption. Its characteristic ideas to-day are Salvation —overabounding salvation, deliverance from and conquest of the 'world' and from existence in bondage to the world, and even from creaturehood as such, the overcoming of the remoteness of and enmity to God, redemption from servitude to sin and the guilt of sin, reconciliation and atonement, and, in consequence, grace and all the doctrine of grace, the Spirit and the bestowal of the Spirit, the new birth and the new creature. These conceptions are common to Christendom, despite the manifold cleavages that divide it into different confessions, churches, and sects, and they characterize it sharply and definitely as a 'religion of redemption' *par excellence*, setting it in this respect on a level with the great religions of the East, with their sharp, dualistic antithesis of the state of liberation and bondage, nay, justifying its claim not to fall short of these in regard to the necessity of redemption and the grant of salvation, but to surpass them, both in the importance it gives to these conceptions and in the richness of meaning it finds in them. It cannot be doubted that here, in these elements, is to be found the inner 'principle' and essence of contemporary Christianity to-day, and what we have to ask is whether the wealth of mental and emotional content was in very truth the 'principle' of that plain 'religion of Jesus' long ago, whose establishment must be termed the first and most immediate achievement of Christ.

In answering this question in the affirmative, we would point to a parable which, intended to have reference to the kingdom of God, fits the principle of Christianity equally well: the parable of the grain of mustard seed and the tree that grew therefrom. This parable hints at a change and alteration, for the grown tree is something different from the seed, but an alteration that is no transformation, no transmutation or 'epigenesis', but genuine 'evolution' or development, the transition from potentiality to actuality.

The 'religion of Jesus' does not change gradually into a religion of redemption; it is in its whole design and tendency a religion of redemption from its earliest commencement, and that in the most uncompromising sense. Though it lacks the theological terms which the Church later possessed, its 'redemptive' character is manifest and unambiguous. If we try to determine as simply and concisely as possible what really characterized the message of Jesus, ignoring what was historically inessential, we are left with two central elements: (1) First, there is the proclamation of *the kingdom of God*, as no mere accessory, but the foundation of the whole Gospel. This is characteristic of His ministry from the beginning and throughout its course. (2) Second, there is the reaction against Pharisaism, and, in connexion with this, Jesus's ideal of godliness as the attitude and mind of a child when its fault has been forgiven. But both points comprise in principle everything which later became separately formulated in the specifically 'redemptive' doctrines of Christianity: Grace, Election, the Holy Ghost, and Renewal by the Spirit. These were possessed by and experienced by that first group of disciples as truly as by any later Christians, though in an implicit form. A closer consideration may make this more plain.

To speak of a 'religion of redemption' is, one may say, to be guilty of a redundancy, at any rate if we are considering the more highly developed forms of religion. For every such religion, when once it has won its autonomy and freed itself from dependent references to an ideal of merely worldly 'welfare' ($\epsilon\dot{v}\delta\alpha\iota\mu\text{ov}\acute{\iota}\alpha$), whether private or public, develops in itself unique and overabounding ideals of beatitude which may be designated by the general term 'salvation'. Such a 'salvation' is the goal to which the evolution of Indian religions has tended ever more markedly and consciously, from their beginning with the notion of deification of the Upanishad-pantheism on to the bliss-state of the Buddhist Nirvāna, which, as we have seen (pp. 38–9), is negative only in appearance. It is also the goal of the 'religions of redemption', specifically so called, which spread with such vigour over the civilized world from Egypt, Syria, and Asia Minor about the beginning of our era. Further, it is obvious to an examination sharpened by the comparative study of religions that the same tendency to 'salvation' is operative also in the vesture of eschatology that gives form to the religion of Persia. Islam, too, embodies the longing for and the experience of salvation. In this case 'salvation' is not simply in the 'hope' of the joys of Paradise: rather the most vital element in Islam is 'Islam' itself, i.e. that surrender to Allah which is not merely the dedication of the will to him, but also at the same time the entering upon the 'Allah' state of mind here and now, the object of longing and striving, a frame of mind which *is* already 'salvation', and which may possess and enrapture the man like an intoxication and can give rise to a mystic transport of bliss.

But if the idea of 'salvation' thus lies at the base of all higher religion everywhere, it is manifested quite unmistakably and in supreme fashion, both in intensity and intrinsic purity, in the 'Kingdom of Heaven' of Christianity, which is at once a tenet of faith, an object of desire, and a present experience. It is quite immaterial whether this thought in ancient Israel issued from purely political considerations, only gradually rising above the ground of mere fact, till it finally was exalted to a transcendent meaning, or whether there were from the first authentic religious motives at work to shape and develop it. All this is beside the point, inasmuch as the materials by which the religious impulse works are very frequently at first of an unspiritual, earthly nature. It is just the unresting activity and continual urgency of this impulsion, enabling it to attain to freedom and press onward and upward to ever higher levels of development—it is just this that manifests it most characteristically, and reveals best its inner essential being. And this is nothing else than the pure *impulsion* to *redemption*, and the pre-intimation and anticipation of a boded 'good', transcendent and 'wholly other', a 'salvation' comparable to those 'salvations' striven after in other religions, but supreme above them in the measure in which the Lord of the Kingdom found and possessed in the Christian experience is supreme above Brahmā, Vishnu, Ormuzd, Allah, as also above the Absolute in the form of Nirvāna, Kaivalyam, Tao, or whatever other name it may be given. So redemption is throughout the purport of the gospel even in its first and simplest form, a redemption which is both to be fulfilled by God hereafter and yet at the same time already experienced here and now. In the former aspect it comes as the assured promise of the Kingdom of God; in the latter, by the present experience of His fatherhood, instilled by the Gospel into the soul of the disciple as his most intimate possession. That the early Christians were conscious of this as something entirely novel and unheard of and exceeding all measure (a good *news*), is seen in the saying of Jesus that 'the Law and the Prophets were until John: since that time the gospel of the kingdom of God is preached' (Luke xvi. 16), in which John the Baptist, who also preached a 'Kingdom of God', is yet classed with 'the Law and the Prophets'.

But to describe this novelty most truly and concisely it would be necessary to *invent* the saying of Paul (Rom. viii. 15), did it not already stand written:

For ye have not received the spirit of bondage again to fear; but ye have received the spirit of adoption, whereby we cry, Abba, Father.

Here Paul has penetrated to the heart of the matter, breaking definitely with the older religion and seizing unerringly upon the very principle and essence of the new. And this 'principle and essence' was the same for the first fishermen by the Lake of Galilee and has remained one and the same throughout the whole history of Christianity. With it is given the new attitude to sin and guilt, to law and to freedom, and, *in principle*, 'justification', 'second birth', 'renewal', the bestowal of the Spirit, new creation, and the blissful freedom of God's children. It was inevitable that these or similar expressions and doctrines and the profound speculation to which they would give rise should make their appearance when the Word called to the Spirit responsive to it.[1]

And so Christ's first and direct work and achievement, as we can clearly understand it to-day, is the effectual bestowal of 'salvation' as future hope and present possession by arousing a faith in his God and in the Kingdom of God.

And now how can Divination, in respect to such work of Christ, awake in us also, in us who stand so remote in time from Him? How can we, too, come to experience in Him 'holiness made manifest'?

Obviously not through demonstration and proof, by applying some conceptual rule. We cannot suggest any conceptual criterion in the form: 'When the elements x and y are brought together, a revelation results.' It is just this impossibility which makes us speak of 'divination', 'intuitive apprehension'. The experience must come, not by demonstration, but by pure *contemplation*, through the mind submitting itself unreservedly to a pure 'impression' of the object. For this purpose all that was given and contained in the message and work of Jesus must be combined with the picture of His Person and life and viewed as a whole and in its context with the long and wonderful advance in the religious history of Israel and Judah that was the preparation for it, and with the interplay of diverse tributary lines of development which, even where apparently divergent, ultimately converged upon this as their single culmination. Account must be taken of the elements of 'fulfilment' which the Gospel contains, and due

---

[1] We can even comprehend thereby the later influx of 'dualistic' or 'gnostic' currents, or at least see how they became possible. A man like Marcion is an extreme 'Jesu-ist' as well as an extreme 'Paul-ist'.

heed given to the attraction and impelling force which it owed to its contrast with its Judaic environment or to parallels which it bore to this. And all the while, for the full impression to be received, regard is to be paid to the non-rational, the woof of the web, the strange setting of the whole experience, which can nowhere be felt so palpably as in the case of Jesus Christ—how His effect upon the men of his own day rises and ebbs, revealing his spiritual content, on which the salvation of the world depends, ever more and more manifestly, and revealing at the same time that mysteriously growing opposition of powers in which the problem of Job recurs a thousand-fold more urgently—where we have the suffering and the defeat not merely of a righteous person, but of all that is most vitally important for the highest interests of humanity. In fine there is that burden of non-rational, mystical significance, which hangs like a cloud over Golgotha. Whoever can thus immerse himself in contemplation and open his whole mind resolutely to a pure impression of all this combined will surely find growing in him, obedient to an inward standard that defies expression, the pure feeling of 'recognition of holiness', the 'intuition of the eternal in the temporal'. If something eternal, something holy, ever results from the blending and interpenetration of rational and non-rational, purposive and indefinable elements in the way we tried to describe, in the person of Jesus this stands as nowhere else potently and palpably apparent.

And in a very real sense we of the later day are not worse but more fortunately placed for grasping it than Jesus's own contemporaries. Realization of Him through 'surmise (*Ahndung*) of the divine government of the world'[1] depends essentially upon two factors. On the one hand there is the general view of the marvellous spiritual history of Israel as a connected whole, with its prophetic and religious development, and with Christ appearing as its culmination. And on the other hand there is the complete life-work and achievement of Christ himself in its entirety. Now in both cases a general comprehensive view is more perfectly to be attained by us to-day than in the time of Christ; for, not only is our historical

[1] An expression of De Wette. (V. p. 147.)

insight more keen, but we can also see the whole in better perspective at our greater distance. Whoever sinks in contemplation of that great connected development of the Judaic religion which we speak of as the 'Old Covenant up to Christ' must feel the stirrings of an intimation that something Eternal is there, directing and sustaining it and urging it to its consummation. The impression is simply irresistible. And whoever then goes on to consider how greatly the scene is set for the completion of the whole story and the mighty stature of the personality that is its fulfilment, His firm, unfaltering hold upon God, His unwavering, unfailing righteousness, His certitude of conviction and assurance in action so mysterious and profound, His spiritual fervour and beatitude, the struggles and trustfulness, self-surrender and suffering, and finally the conqueror's death that were His—whoever goes on to consider all this must inevitably conclude: 'That is god-like and divine; that is verily Holiness. If there is a God and if He chose to reveal Himself, He could do it no otherwise than thus.'

Such a conclusion is not the result of logical compulsion; it does not follow from clearly conceived premises; it is an immediate, underivable judgement of pure recognition, and it follows a premiss that defies exposition and springs directly from an irreducible feeling of the truth. But that, as we have seen, is just the manner in which genuine divination, in the sense of an intuition of religious significance, takes place.

Such an intuition, once granted, issues, for us no less than for the first disciples, necessarily and independently of exegesis or the authority of the early Church, in a series of further intuitions respecting the Person, the Work, and the Words of Christ, and it is the task of theology to render these explicit. Such are the intuitions gained of 'sacred history' in general, of its preparation in prophecy, and of its fulfilment in Jesus's 'Messiahship'—the Being in whom all the religious potentialities of prophet and psalmist and all the anticipatory movements and currents in the old covenant became actualized, in whom all previous development found its culmination, and the evolution of a people at once its real significance

and its goal, the completion of its course and the consummation of its allotted historical task. And there are further
intuitions which have the same origin: the intuition by which
we recognize in Christ the portrayal and presentment of God,
divining in His agony and victory, His redemptive search and
love, the very stamp and signature of God; the intuition of
his 'Sonship', by which we recognize Christ as the 'only
begotten', the called, the fully empowered with deity, as one
whose being, only made possible and intelligible of God,
repeats and reveals the divine nature in human fashion; or
the intuition of the 'new covenant', of adoption and reconciliation through Christ, of His life-work and self-surrender to
God as sacrifice and as a warrant of divine grace. And last,
not least, the intuition of the 'covering' and 'propitiating'
Mediator. For the abyss between creature and Creator,
'*profanum*' and '*sanctum*', sin and holiness, is not diminished
but increased by that deeper knowledge that comes from the
Gospel of Christ: and, as a result of the emotion spontaneously
stirred in the recognition of it, that in which 'the holy' stands
self-revealed is taken here, as in other cases, both as the refuge
from, and the means by which to approach, Holiness. And
this impulsion of the mind to see in Christ mediator and pro-
pitiator may be roused to seek expression spontaneously,
even in cases where it is not—as in Hebrew and primitive
religion—prepared for and sustained by a traditional cult
and mysticism of 'sacrifice'. That is, it is a natural religious
instinct, due to the pressure of the numinous experience and
to nothing else.

We are not, then, to deplore the fact that intuitions of this
kind find a place in the doctrines of the Christian faith: they
do so of necessity. What we must deplore is, that their free
character, as springing from 'divination', is so generally mis-
interpreted; that too commonly we dogmatize and theorize
about them, deducing them from 'necessary truths' of exegesis
or dogma (which are in fact always dubious), and so failing
to recognize them for what they are, free-floating utterances
and trial flights at expression of the numinous feeling; and
that too often we give them an emphasis which puts them
unwarrantably at the centre of our religious interest, a place

which nothing but the experience itself of God ought to occupy.

In this connexion we may draw attention to what are commonly called the 'miracles' of Christ, but which we may perhaps more aptly call, in the words of Mark xvi. 20, 'signs following' (ἐπακολουθοῦντα σημεῖα). It is not upon them primarily that the experience of 'holiness made manifest' is based; but, where there has been real 'divination', there certain traits in the portrait of Christ come to acquire a fresh significance, as confirmation of the divination rather than its ground. I refer to the signs of exalted spiritual power over nature to be detected in the portrait of Jesus. These have their parallels elsewhere in the history of religion: in the great prophets of Israel, for instance, they are shown in the form of that visionary intuition and boding foreknowledge with which the prophet was endowed for his calling. In the life of Christ they recur unmistakably as 'gifts of the Spirit', raised to a supreme power. These things are not 'miracles', for they are powers of the spirit, and so are as 'natural' as our will itself is, with its control over our body. But they clearly only come upon the scene where the spirit is itself exalted to its fullest stature and in its fullest vitality, and are most of all to be expected where the spirit is in closest and most intimate union with its eternal cause and foundation, and is thereby set free to the highest it can itself achieve.[1]

It is, in the last place, clear that it is in the Passion and death of Christ that the objects of the strongest religious intuition must be sought. If His Incarnation, His mission, and the manner of His life come to be considered as a piece of self-revelation, in which an eternal Will of Love is mirrored, before all else is this Love and Faith seen accomplished in the Passion. The Cross becomes in an absolute sense the 'mirror of the eternal Father' (*speculum aeterni Patris*); and not of the 'Father' alone—the highest rational interpretation of the holy—but of Holiness as such. For what makes Christ in a special sense the summary and climax of the course of antecedent religious evolution is pre-eminently this—that in His life, suffering, and death is repeated in classic and absolute

[1] See further Appendix VII.

form that most mystical of all the problems of the Old Covenant, the problem of *the guiltless suffering of the righteous*, which
re-echoes again and again so mysteriously from Jeremiah
and deutero-Isaiah on through Job and the Psalms. The
38th chapter of Job is a prophecy of Golgotha. And on Golgotha the solution of the problem, already adumbrated in
Job, is repeated and surpassed. It lay, as we saw, entirely in
the non-rational aspect of deity, and yet was none the less a
solution. In Job the suffering of the righteous found its significance as the classic and crucial case of the revelation, more
immediately actual and in more palpable proximity than any
other, of the transcendent mysteriousness and 'beyondness'
of God. The Cross of Christ, that monogram of the eternal
mystery, is its completion. Here rational are enfolded with
non-rational elements, the revealed commingled with the
unrevealed, the most exalted love with the most awe-inspiring
'wrath' of the numen, and therefore, in applying to the Cross
of Christ the category 'holy', Christian religious feeling has
given birth to a religious intuition profounder and more vital
than any to be found in the whole history of religion.

This is what must be borne in mind in the comparison of
religions, when we seek to decide which of them is the most
perfect. The criterion of the value of a religion as religion
cannot ultimately be found in what it has done for culture,
nor in its relation to the 'limits of the reason' or the 'limits of
humanity' (which, forsooth, are presumed capable of being
drawn in advance apart from reference to religion itself!), nor
in any of its external features. It can only be found in what
is the innermost essence of religion, the idea of holiness as
such, and in the degree of perfection with which any given
religion realizes this.

There can naturally be no defence of the worth and validity
of such religious intuitions of pure feeling that will convince
a person who is not prepared to take the religious consciousness itself for granted. Mere general argument, even moral
demonstrations, are in this case useless, are indeed for obvious
reasons impossible from the outset. On the other hand the
criticisms and confutations attempted by such a person are
unsound from the start. His weapons are far too short to

touch his adversary, for the assailant is always standing right outside the arena! But if these intuitions, these separate responses to the impress upon the spirit of the Gospel story and the central Person of it—if these intuitions are immune from rational criticism, they are equally unaffected by the fluctuating results of biblical exegesis and the laboured justifications of historical apologetics. For they are possible without these, springing, as they do, from first-hand *personal divination*.[1]

---

[1] Compare with this chapter my book *Reich Gottes und Menschensohn* (*The Kingdom of God and the Son of Man*).

CHAPTER XXI

HISTORY AND THE *A PRIORI* IN RELIGION: SUMMARY AND CONCLUSION

WE have considered 'the holy' on the one hand as an *a priori* category of mind, and on the other as manifesting itself in outward appearance. The contrast here intended is exactly the same as the common contrast of inner and outer, general and special revelation. And if we take 'reason' (*ratio*) as an inclusive term for all cognition which arises in the mind from principles native to it, in contrast to those based upon facts of history, then we may say that the distinction between holiness as an *a priori* category and holiness as revealed in outward appearance is much the same as that between 'reason' (in this wide sense) and history.

Every religion which, so far from being a mere faith in traditional authority, springs from personal assurance and inward convincement (i.e. from an inward first-hand cognition of its truth)—as Christianity does in a unique degree—must presuppose principles in the mind enabling it to be independently recognized as true.[1] But these principles must be *a priori* ones, not to be derived from 'experience' or 'history'. It has little meaning, however edifying it may sound, to say that they are inscribed upon the heart by the pencil of the Holy Spirit 'in history'. For whence comes the assurance that it was the pencil of the 'Holy Spirit' that wrote, and not that of a deceiving spirit of imposture, or of the 'tribal fantasy' of anthropology? Such an assertion is itself a presumption that it is possible to distinguish the signature of the Spirit from others, and thus that we have an *a priori* notion of what is of the Spirit independently of history.

And there is a further consideration. There is something presupposed by history as such—not only the history of mind or spirit, with which we are here concerned—which alone

---

[1] The attestation of such principles is the '*testimonium Spiritus Sancti internum*' of which we have already spoken. And this must clearly be itself immediate and self-warranted, else there would be need of another 'witness of the Holy Spirit' to attest the truth of the first, and so on *ad infinitum*.

makes it history, and that is the existence of a *quale*, something with a potentiality of its own, capable of *becoming*, in
the special sense of coming to be that to which it was predisposed and predetermined. An oak-tree can *become*, and thus
have a sort of 'history'; whereas a heap of stones cannot.
The random addition and subtraction, displacement and re-
arrangement, of elements in a mere aggregation can certainly
be followed in narrative form, but this is not in the deeper
sense an historical narrative. We only have the history of a
people in proportion as it enters upon its course equipped
with an endowment of talents and tendencies; it must already
be something if it is really to *become* anything. And biography
is a lamentable and unreal business in the case of a man who
has no real unique potentiality of his own, no special idiosyn-
crasy, and is therefore a mere point of intersection for various
fortuitous causal series, acted upon, as it were, from without.
Biography is only a real narration of a real life where, by the
interplay of stimulus and experience on the one side and predisposition and natural endowment on the other, something
individual and unique comes into being, which is therefore
neither the result of a 'mere self-unfolding' nor yet the sum
of mere traces and impressions, written from without from
moment to moment upon a *tabula rasa*. In short, to propose
a history of mind is to presuppose a mind or spirit deter-
minately qualified; to profess to give a history of religion is to
presuppose a spirit specifically qualified for religion.

There are, then, three factors in the process by which religion comes into being in history. First, the interplay of predisposition and stimulus, which in the historical development
of man's mind actualizes the potentiality in the former, and
at the same time helps to determine its form. Second, the
groping recognition, by virtue of this very disposition, of
specific portions of history as the manifestation of 'the holy',
with consequent modification of the religious experience
already attained both in its quality and degree. And third,
on the basis of the other two, the achieved fellowship with
'the holy' in knowing, feeling, and willing. Plainly, then,
religion is only the offspring of history in so far as history on
the one hand develops our disposition for knowing the holy,

and on the other is itself repeatedly the manifestation of the holy. 'Natural' religion, in contrast to historical, does not exist, and still less does 'innate' religion.[1]

A priori cognitions are not such as every one does have—such would be *innate* cognitions—but such as every one is *capable* of having. The loftier *a priori* cognitions are such as —while every one is indeed capable of having them—do not, as experience teaches us, occur spontaneously, but rather are 'awakened' through the instrumentality of other more highly endowed natures. In relation to these the universal 'predisposition' is merely a faculty of *receptivity* and a *principle of judgement and acknowledgement*, not a capacity to produce the cognitions in question for oneself independently. This latter capacity is confined to those specially 'endowed'. And this 'endowment' is the universal disposition on a higher level and at a higher power, differing from it in quality as well as in degree. The same thing is very evident in the sphere of art: what appears in the multitude as mere receptiveness, the capacity of response and judgement by trained aesthetic taste, reappears at the level of the *artist* as invention, creation, composition, the original production of genius. This difference of level and power, e.g. in musical composition, seen in the contrast between what is a mere capacity for musical experience and the actual production and revelation of music, is obviously something more than a difference of degree. It is very similar in the domain of the religious consciousness, religious production, and revelation. Here, too, most men have only the 'predisposition', in the sense of a receptiveness and susceptibility to religion and a capacity for freely recognizing and judging religious truth at first hand. The 'Spirit' is only 'universal' in the form of the '*testimonium Spiritus internum*' (and this again only '*ubi ipsi visum fuit*'). The higher stage, not to be derived from the first stage of mere receptivity, is in the sphere of religion *the prophet*. The prophet corresponds in the religious sphere to the creative artist in that of art: he is the man in whom the Spirit shows itself alike as the power to hear the 'voice within' and the power of

[1] For the distinction between 'innate' and *a priori* cf. R. Otto, *Religionsphilosophie*, p. 42.

N

divination, and in each case appears as a creative force. Yet the prophet does not represent the highest stage. We can think of a third, yet higher, beyond him, a stage of revelation as underivable from that of the prophet as was his from that of common men. We can look, beyond the prophet, to one in whom is found the Spirit in all its plenitude, and who at the same time in His person and in His performance is become most completely the object of divination, in whom Holiness is recognized apparent.

Such a one is more than Prophet. He is the Son.

APPENDIX I

CHRYSOSTOM ON THE INCONCEIVABLE IN GOD

'But that is an impertinence to say that He who is beyond the apprehension of even the higher Powers can be comprehended by us earthworms, or compassed and comprised by the weak forces of our understanding!'

This protest of Chrysostom occurs at the beginning of the third of his five discourses Περὶ Ἀκαταλήπτου (De Incomprehensibili), which were directed against the 'ἀνόμοιοι' who were perverting the Christian community of Antioch, and more especially against disciples of the Arian Aëtios, with their doctrine θεὸν οἶδα ὡς αὐτὸς ὁ θεὸς ἑαυτὸν οἶδε ('I know God as He is known to Himself'). Our histories of dogma do not generally say much, if anything, upon these sermons of Chrysostom, and their contribution to 'dog-matics' is not indeed very important. But their interest for the psychology of religion is all the greater; and this would still remain, even if they had not contained the passages bearing upon Christology, which begin at the conclusion of the fourth sermon. For we have in them the primary promptings of genuine religious feeling in its specifically numinous character, excited to a passionate intensity and directed with all the charm and eloquence of the 'Golden-mouthed' against the theoretical 'Aristotelian' God of the schools. All that is non-rational in the feeling of God is here in conflict with what is rational and capable of rationalization and threatens to break loose from it altogether.

A strange spectacle! For does not the distinguishing character of Christianity consist in just this—that God is near us, that we can possess and apprehend Him, and that man himself is His image and likeness? And yet we find this Father of the Church battling passionately, as for something that concerned the very essence of Christianity, for the view that God is the Inconceivable, the Inexpressible, that which gives denial to every notion. And this he does *not* do on speculative grounds, with the aid of the terms and phrases of any 'school' of theology; it is rather a sort of instinct in him that guides him with astonishing assurance and accuracy to track out and collect the most wonderful texts of Scripture, so that their full weight becomes felt, as his profoundly penetrating interpretation explains and applies them.

First and chiefly he takes his stand against 'Conceiving' and 'Comprehension' in general, against the idea of τὸ καταληπτόν,

and against the οἰκεῖοι λογισμοί (i.e. constructions of the understanding) which seek to delimit and circumscribe God (περιγράφειν,
περιλαμβάνειν). For his opponents had maintained that a conceptual knowledge of God is possible, definitive, and exhaustive,
by means of notions, in fact by a single notion (viz. of ἀγεννησία,
unbegottenness), in a word, that it is possible 'to know God
exactly' (μετ' ἀκριβείας εἰδέναι). 'But we,' says Chrysostom, 'in
opposition to this view, call Him τὸν ἀνέκφραστον, τὸν ἀπερινόητον
θεόν, τὸν ἀόρατον, τὸν ἀκατάληπτον, τὸν νικῶντα γλώττης δύναμιν
ἀνθρωπίνης, τὸν ὑπερβαίνοντα θνητῆς διανοίας κατάληψιν, τὸν ἀνεξιχνίαστον ἀγγέλοις, τὸν ἀθέατον τοῖς Σεραφίμ, τὸν ἀκατανόητον τοῖς
Χερουβίμ, τὸν ἀόρατον ἀρχαῖς ἐξουσίαις δυνάμεσιν, καὶ ἁπλῶς πασῇ
τῇ κτίσει.'[1] (Migne, p. 721.) 'He *insults* God who seeks to apprehend His essential being' (ὑβρίζει δὲ ὁ τὴν οὐσίαν αὐτοῦ περιερ-
γαζόμενος, 714 e), he says, and goes on to urge that God is
incomprehensible even in His works—how much more in His
own essential nature; even in His 'demeanings' (συγκαταβάσεις)
—how much more in His own transcendent majesty; even to the
Cherubim and Seraphim—how much more to mere 'humanity'
(ἀνθρωπίνη φύσις)!

The ἀκατάληπτον in this sense is for Chrysostom primarily the
'exceeding greatness' of God, which escapes our mental grasp and
compass because of the ἀσθένεια τῶν λογισμῶν, the over-short
reach of our faculty of conception. We call it 'incomprehensibility', and distinguish from it the 'inapprehensibility' which
springs, not from the 'exceeding greatness', but from the 'wholly
otherness' of God (θάτερον τοῦ θείου), from what is alien and
remote in Him, from what we have called the '*mysterium stupendum*'.
And it is instructive to see how for Chrysostom, too, this latter
sense of ἀκατάληπτον passes into the former, sometimes blending
with it, sometimes plainly distinguished as something beyond and
higher than it. We have said already that we have the experience
of the 'wholly other', where we come upon something which not
merely overtops our every concept, but astounds us by its absolute
and utter difference from our whole nature. Chrysostom similarly
contrasts the ἀνθρωπίνη φύσις with the θεῖα φύσις as being incommensurable with it, and therefore incapable of understanding it,
and his words refer not only to the narrowness and meagreness

[1] 'We call Him the inexpressible, the unthinkable God, the invisible, the
inapprehensible; who quells the power of human speech and transcends the
grasp of mortal thought; inaccessible to the angels, unbeheld of the Seraphim,
unimagined of the Cherubim, invisible to principalities and authorities and
powers, and, in a word, to all creation.'

of our understanding, but just to this sheer difference in quality of the 'wholly other'.

This sort of apostrophe is common with him: Ἄνθρωπος ὢν θεὸν πολυπραγμονεῖς; ἀρκεῖ γὰρ τὰ ὀνόματα ψιλὰ τῆς ἀνοίας δεῖξαι τὴν ὑπερβολήν· ἄνθρωπος γῆ καὶ σποδὸς ὑπάρχων, σὰρξ καὶ αἷμα, χόρτος καὶ ἄνθος χόρτου, σκιὰ καὶ καπνὸς καὶ ματαιότης (712).[1] And the same note sounds even more clearly in an exposition of Rom. ix. 20, 21 (715). As little as the clay can master or comprehend the potter because of its essential difference from him, even so little can man comprehend God. 'Or rather, far less, for man—the potter— is in the end himself but clay. But the difference between the being of God and the being of man is of such a kind that no word can express it and no thought appraise it.' His position is put more unmistakably still in the following passage:

'He dwells, says St. Paul, in an unapproachable light.[2] Observe here the exactitude of St. Paul's expression. . . . For he says not merely in an incomprehensible, but (what conveys far more) in an altogether "unapproachable light". We say "inconceivable" and "incomprehensible" of something which, though it eludes conception, does not elude all inquiry and questioning. "Unapproachable", on the other hand, means something which in principle excludes the very possibility of inquiry, which is quite inaccessible by conceptual investigation. A sea into which divers may plunge, but which they cannot fathom, would represent the merely "incomprehensible" (ἀκατάληπτον). It would only represent the "unapproachable" (ἀπρόσιτον) if it remained in principle beyond search and beyond discovery.' (p. 721.) And so too in the fourth discourse (upon Eph. iii. 8) (p. 729): Τί ἔστιν ἀνεξιχνίαστον ; μὴ δυνάμενον ζητηθῆναι, οὐ μόνον δὲ μὴ δυνάμενον εὑρεθῆναι, ἀλλ' οὐδὲ ἀνιχνευθῆναι. ('What is "unsearchable"? To be beyond searching, that is, to be such as excludes not discovery only but also tracing.')

And this line of thought draws him imperceptibly farther. The bounds of the 'incomprehensible' are extended, and the whole numinous consciousness is set astir in it, one element in the feeling prompting to the others. The *mysterium stupendum* passes directly over into *mysterium tremendum* and *maiestas*, so that we might entitle the Discourses, instead of *De Incomprehensibili*, *De Numine ac Numinoso*.

[1] 'Dost thou, a man, presume to busy thyself with God? Nay, the bare names (of man) suffice to show the extent of this folly; man that is *earth* and *dust, flesh* and *blood*, *grass* and the *flower of grass*, *shadow* and *smoke* and *vanity*.'
[2] 1 Tim. vi. 16 φῶς οἰκῶν ἀπρόσιτον. R.V. 'unapproachable'.

Specially noticeable in this connexion is the passage in which Chrysostom brings clearly out the psychological distinction between numinous and merely rational *wonder*. He cites that truly significant text from Ps. cxxxix. 14, which runs in the Septuagint: 'I praise Thee: for that Thou madest Thyself fearfully wondrous',[1] and then gives a subtle analysis of the feelings there expressed.

'What does "fearfully" mean here? Many things move us to wonder in which there is nothing "fearful"—the beauty of a colonnade, for example; the beauty of pictures, or bodily loveliness. Again, we wonder at the greatness of the sea and its measureless expanse, but terror and "fear" only seize upon us when we gaze down into its *depths*. So, too, here the Psalmist. When he gazes down into the immeasurable, yawning (ἀχανές) Depth[2] of the divine Wisdom, dizziness comes upon him and he recoils in terrified wonder and cries: . . . "Thy knowledge is too wonderful for me; it is high, above my power (I am too weak for it: LXX)."' The 'dizziness' and the unique feeling of the uncanny, which we have called *stupor* and *tremor*, are here clearly noted by Chrysostom. And he rightly cites also the profoundly numinous exclamation of St. Paul (Rom. xi. 33): 'Dizzy before the unfathomable main and gazing down into its yawning depths, he recoils precipitately and cries aloud: "O the depth of the riches both of the wisdom and knowledge of God. . . ."' (Migne, p. 705.)

The passage on page 733 should be read in close connexion with this. Nowhere has the awe and even the eerie shuddering and amazement at the supernatural been more vividly and truly recaptured in feeling, and nowhere has it been portrayed with a more gripping and constraining power. *Expertus loquitur!* This is the voice not of the Platonist or Neoplatonist; it is the voice of antiquity itself, typified in one who had found in Paganism and Judaism and Christianity alike those primal and elemental experiences out of which all religion has arisen and without which no religion is worthy of the name, and who had made them his very own in all the force of growth—sometimes rank and violent enough—which originally characterized them. Chrysostom describes thus the experience of Dan. x. 5–8, and the state of ecstasy into which Daniel falls in his encounter with the Unseen: 'For just as happens when the charioteer looses hold of the reins in terror, so that the horses bolt and the chariot overturns, . . . so

[1] Ἐξομολογήσομαί σοι ὅτι φοβερῶς ἐθαυμαστώθης.
[2] Reading βάθος for the undoubtedly erroneous πέλαγος.

it befell the Prophet. His affrighted soul could not bear the sight of the Angel made manifest, could not endure the supernatural light, and was overwhelmed. It strove to break free from the bonds of the flesh as from a harness . . . and he lay there in a swoon.' Very similar is the comment on the vision of Ezekiel. Chrysostom realizes that the awe in these experiences does not find its origin in any self-depreciation of an ethical or rational sort (e.g. from an uneasy conscience or the like), but that they are the natural reactions of the creature, of the ἀσθένεια φύσεως face to face with transcendent, unearthly reality, as such. 'I cite to you the case of the holy Daniel, the friend of God, who, because of his wisdom and righteousness, might well have been justly confident, just in order that no one may suppose, if I show even him to you weakening, collapsing, powerless, and overwhelmed before the presence of the Angel, that this befalls him because of his sins and his evil conscience, but that this example may throw a clear light on the impotence of our nature.'

Naturally the passage in Gen. xviii. 27 has not escaped him; still less the scene in Isa. vi. 'But let us now leave St. Paul and the prophets and ascend into Heaven to see if haply any one there knows what God's essential being is. . . . What do we hear from the Angels? Do they inquire and reason meticulously among themselves about God's nature? By no means. What do they do? They praise Him. They fall down and worship Him with a great trembling (μετὰ πολλῆς τῆς φρίκης, p. 707). They turn their eyes away, and can themselves not endure the vouchsafed revelation of God.' Again: 'Tell me, wherefore do they cover their faces and hide them with their wings? Why, but that they cannot endure the dazzling radiance and its rays that pour from the Throne?' Nor does he ignore the *loci classici* of the *tremenda maiestas*, viz. Ps. civ. 32 and Job ix. 6 sqq.: 'He looketh on the earth and it trembleth: he toucheth the hills and they smoke.' Ps. cxiv. 3: 'The sea saw and fled: Jordan was driven back.' 'πᾶσα ἡ κτίσις σαλεύεται, δέδοικε, τρέμει.' And he concludes his commentary upon all this with the remark: (I will conclude, for) 'thought grows weary, not from the extent of what I have spoken but from the trembling it brings. For the soul that concerns itself in these contemplations trembles and is appalled (ἔκαμεν ἡμῖν ἡ διάνοια, οὐ τῷ πλήθει ἀλλὰ τῇ φρίκῃ τῶν εἰρημένων. τρέμει γὰρ καὶ ἐκπέπληκται ἡ ψυχὴ ἐπὶ πολὺ ταῖς ἄνω ἐνδιατρίβουσα θεωρίαις)' (p. 725).

Chrysostom, then, is combating the arrogance and overweening presumptuousness of the human understanding and of the creature in general in imagining that any escape is possible from the in-comprehensible, supreme, transcendent, and 'wholly other' nature of God. And it is because he wishes to shatter this human complacency, to overawe and overwhelm, that he portrays these aspects of the numinous. But he does not leave out the others or fail to note the paradox, that this 'incomprehensible' is at the same time a *'fascinans'* and an intimate and essential possession of the human soul. Blank amazement is to him at the same time enraptured adoration; speechlessness in the presence of the in-apprehensible passes over—and only an understanding of the 'harmony of contrasts' can show how—into a humble gratitude that it *is* so, that it is 'fearfully wonderful'. He cites again Ps. cxxxix. 14, and interprets it thus: 'See here the nobility of this servant of God (David). "I thank Thee" (εὐχαριστῶ σοι), he says in effect, "for that I have a Lord who is beyond comprehen-sion." ' Tersteegen means the same when he uses the words 'A comprehended God is no God' to express praise; as does Goethe, in the words of the archangels' hymn in *Faust*:

Ihr Anblick gibt den Engeln Stärke,
Weil keiner sie ergründen mag.[1]

And so with Chrysostom: this ἀκατάληπτον is ἐκείνη μακαρία οὐσία —a favourite and recurring expression of his. And we feel that this 'Being' is 'incomprehensible' *because* it is 'blessed', and 'blessed' *because* it is 'incomprehensible'. In the very passion with which he battles for the unimaginable God, who makes His worshipper weak and dizzy with awe, there yet glows—unuttered and unexpressed—an enthusiastic sense of the soul having been carried away in rapture and taken up into the being of God.

The ἀκατάληπτον involves a denial of conceptual designations, and hence come the negative attributes of deity, which Chryso-stom frequently employs, singly or in series—a *negativa theologia* in little. But this 'negative theology' does not mean that faith and feeling are dissipated and reduced to nothing; on the contrary, it contains within it the loftiest spirit of devotion, and it is out of such 'negative' attributes that Chrysostom fashions the most solemn confessions and prayers. He thereby shows once more that feeling and experience reach far beyond conceiving, and that a concep-tion negative in form may often become the symbol (what we have called an 'ideogram') for a content of meaning which, if

[1] 'Its (*sc.* the Sun's) aspect gives the angels strength *because* none may fathom it.' [The usual reading is *wenn*, 'though', for *weil*, 'because'. *Trans.*]

absolutely unutterable, is none the less in the highest degree positive. And the example of Chrysostom at the same time shows that a 'negative theology' can and indeed must arise, not only from the 'infusion of Hellenistic speculation and nature mysticism', but from purely and genuinely religious roots, namely, the experience of the numinous.

The insistence upon the 'inconceivable and incomprehensible' in God did not cease to be a point of honour in Christian theology with Chrysostom. The forms this protest took did indeed vary: it appears as the assertion at one time that God stands above the reach of all possible predication whatever, and so is Nothingness and the 'Silent Desert'; at another, that He is ἀνώνυμος, πανώνυμος, ὁμώνυμος; at another, that He can indeed be made the subject of predication, but only in so far as all attributes are mere 'nomina ex parte intellectus nostri'; or again, the sternest form of all, it reproduces the line of thought of Job, as can be seen now and then in Luther in his notion of the deus absconditus—the thought, namely, that God Himself is not only above every human grasp, but in antagonism to it.[1]

All these doctrines are preserving a heritage passionately won against the opposition of ancient errors. They do so, certainly, at the cost of a one-sided emphasis, for the meaning Christians attach to the word 'God' is indubitably also a profoundly rational one, the basis indeed of all reason. Yet this is bound up with a still profounder meaning, which, as we have seen, is beyond and above all conception.

With the discourse of Chrysostom we may compare Gregory of Nyssa, Contra Eunomium (Migne, Patr. Gr. xlv). What stirs Chrysostom passionately as a matter of the first moment is indeed only of secondary importance in Gregory, incidental to his dogmatic inquiries. But even so he, too, can write (p. 601): εἰ δέ τις ἀπαιτοίη τῆς θείας οὐσίας ἑρμηνείαν τινὰ καὶ ὑπογραφὴν καὶ ἐξήγησιν, ἀμαθεῖς εἶναι τῆς τοιαύτης σοφίας οὐκ ἀρνησόμεθα . . . ὅτι οὐκ ἔστι τὸ ἀόριστον κατὰ τὴν φύσιν ἐπινοίᾳ τινὶ ῥημάτων διαληφθῆναι. ἐπεὶ οὖν κρεῖττόν ἐστι καὶ ὑψηλότερον τῆς ὀνομαστικῆς σημασίας τὸ Θεῖον [numen says the Latin translator] σιωπῇ τιμᾶν τὰ ὑπὲρ λόγον τε καὶ διάνοιαν μεμαθήκαμεν. ('But if one asks for an interpretation or description or explanation of the divine nature we shall not deny that in such a science as this we are

[1] Compare also Luther's Short Form of the Ten Commandments, the Creed, and the Lord's Prayer (1520): 'I venture to put my trust in the one God alone, the invisible and incomprehensible, who hath created Heaven and Earth and is alone above all creatures.'

unlearned. . . . For there is no way of comprehending the indefinable as it is by a scheme of words. For the Divine is too noble and too lofty to be indicated by a name: and we have learned to honour by silence that which transcends reason and thought.')

But another, long before Chrysostom—the 'heretic' Marcion—writing in a different situation, not within but on the fringe of the Church, had experienced the inconceivable aspect of the numinous and extolled it in words of an almost intoxicated fervour: 'O it is a marvel beyond marvels, enravishment, power, and wonder, that one can say naught about the Gospel, and think naught about it and compare it to nothing.'

It is remarkable to see how the several moments of the numinous in experience are constantly compounded and blended afresh so as to produce quite special and peculiar types of religion. In Marcion the original moment *tremendum* is silenced before the consoling power of the Gospel, in fulfilment of the word 'Perfect love casts out fear'. But there remains strongly and profoundly felt the 'wholly other', the ineffable and inconceivable, in his 'strange God', and in the first words of his treatise, whose 'violent ferment' (in Harnack's phrase) reveals the element of 'fascination'. The sense of the 'august' lives in the 'feeling of distance' in face of the 'strange God', and in that, too, we detect a light thrill that is the awe of the *tremendum* reawakened and returning in a nobler form.[1]

Appendix II

THE NUMINOUS IN POETRY, HYMN, AND LITURGY

Example of 'numinous' poetry

From *Bhagavad-Gītā*, Chapter XI (Barnett's translation slightly altered)

In the *Bhagavad-Gītā*, Krishna, the embodiment of Vishnu—Vishnu himself in human form—instructs Aryuna in the deepest mysteries of his religion. Aryuna then desires to behold God himself in his own form, and his petition is granted. And now in Chapter XI there follows a theophany of terrific grandeur, which seeks to give a feeling of the unapproachable essence of the Divine before which the creature trembles and falls, by embodying the

---

[1] See Harnack, *Marcion* (1921), p. 138.

human and 'natural' means of terror, majesty, and sublimity. Aryuna stands in his war-chariot, about to enter the carnage of the battle against his brother Yudhishthira's enemies. Krishna is his charioteer. Aryuna tells him his request. 'Show to me thy changeless Self, Sovran of the Rule.' Krishna-Vishnu answers him:

7. Behold now, O Wearer of the Hair-Knot, the whole universe, moving and unmoving, solely lodged in this my body, and all else that thou art fain to see.

8. But for that thou canst not see Me with this thine own eye. I give thee a divine eye; behold my sovran Rule.

9. Thus speaking, Hari (i.e. Vishnu), the great Lord of the Rule, then showed to Pritha's son his sovran form supreme,

10. of many mouths and eyes, of many divine ornaments, with uplifted weapons many and divine;

11. wearing divine flower-chaplets and robes, with anointment of divine perfumes, compound of all marvels, the boundless god facing all ways.

12. If the light of a thousand suns should of a sudden rise in the heavens, it would be like to the light of that mighty being. . . .

14. Thereupon the Wealth-Winner (i.e. Aryuna), smitten with amazement, with hair standing on end, bowed his head, and with clasped hands spake to the God. . . .

17. 'I behold Thee bearing diadem, mace, and disc, massed in radiance, on all sides glistening, hardly discernible, shining round about as gleaming fire and sun, immeasurable. . . .

20. For this mid-space between heaven and earth and all the quarters of the sky are filled with Thee alone. Seeing this Thy fearful and wonderful form, O great-hearted one, the threefold world quakes.

21. These hosts of Suras come unto Thee; some, affrighted, praise with clasped hands. With cries of "Hail!" the hosts of Great Saints and Adepts sing to Thee hymns of abounding praise.

22. All the Spirits and Divine Powers that live in heaven and earth, in clouds and winds, in air and water, Daemons, Manes, Asuras, Saints, and Adepts, all gaze on Thee in amazement.

23. Looking upon Thy mighty form of many mouths and eyes, of many arms and thighs and feet, of many bellies, and grim with many teeth, O mighty-armed one, the worlds and I quake.

24. For as I behold Thee touching the heavens, glittering, many-hued, with yawning mouths, with wide eyes agleam, my inward soul trembles, and I find not constancy nor peace, O Vishnu.

25. Seeing Thy mouths grim with teeth, like to the fire of the last day, I recognize not the quarters of the heavens, and take no joy; Lord of Gods, home of the universe, be gracious!

26. These sons of Dhritarashtra all, with the hosts of kings, Bhishma, Drona, and the Charioteer's son yonder, and likewise the chief of our warriors,

27. hasting enter into Thy mouths grim with fangs and terrible; some, caught between the teeth, appear with crushed heads.

28. As many currents of rivers flow to meet the sea, so these warriors of the world of mankind pass into Thy blazing mouths.

29. As moths with exceeding speed pass into a lighted fire to perish, so pass the worlds with exceeding speed into Thy mouths to perish.

30. Thou devourest and lickest up all the worlds around with flaming mouths; filling the whole universe with radiance, grim glow Thy splendours, O Vishnu!

31. Relate to me who Thou art in this grim form. Homage to Thee, chief of gods; be gracious! I would fain know Thee as First Being. . . .'

Thereupon Vishnu reassumes his friendly Krishna-form. Arjuna's petition to comprehend the incomprehensible is not granted him. It is forbidden to man, as Luther says, 'to soar into the height of Majesty': he must confine himself to the Word of gracious Promise. Such a word is imparted. The tremendous chapter closes with the words which expositors take as the sum and epitome of the whole Gītā:

55. 'He who does what he does for Me alone; who is given over to Me, who is devoted to Me, void of attachment, without hatred to any born being, O son of Pandu, comes to Me.'

The Numinous in Hymn and Liturgy

A comparison of two poems may indicate the difference between a merely 'rational' glorification of the Godhead and one that also prompts to a feeling of the non-rational, the numinous, in its aspect of *mysterium tremendum*. Gellert can sing of 'The Honour of God from Nature' powerfully and finely enough—

> Die Himmel rühmen des Ewigen Ehre,
> Ihr Schall pflanzt seinen Namen fort.

Here everything is bright, rational, and intimate up to the last verse:

> Ich bin Dein Schöpfer, bin Weisheit und Güte,
> Ein Gott der Ordnung und Dein Heil.
> Ich bin's! Mich liebe von ganzem Gemüte,
> Und nimm an meiner Gnade teil.

But, beautiful as this hymn is, we do not encounter there the 'honour of God' in all its fullness. Some element is missing, and what this is we feel at once when we compare with this hymn that composed at an earlier date by E. Lange, 'To the Majesty of God':

> Vor Dir erbebt der Engel Chor,
> Sie schlagen Aug' und Antlitz nieder,
> So schrecklich kommst Du ihnen vor
> Und davon schallen ihre Lieder. . . .
> Denn Dein ist Kraft und Ruhm,
> Das Reich und Heiligtum,
> Da mich Entsetzen mir entreisset.
> Bei Dir ist Majestät
> Die über alles geht,
> Und heilig, heilig, heilig, heisset.

That goes farther than Gellert. And yet even here there is still something lacking, something that we find in the Song of the Seraphim in Isaiah vi. Even Lange, despite his 'numb amazement', sings ten long stanzas; the angels sing a bare two lines. And he incessantly speaks to God in the second person singular; whereas the angels speak before Yahweh in the *third* person.[1]

---

[1] In point of fact one cannot always speak of God as 'Thou', and sometimes not at all. St. Theresa addresses God as 'Eternal Majesty', and the French readily use '*Vous*' for '*Tu*'. And Goethe came very near to the *tremendum mysterium* when he said to Eckermann (31 Dec., 1823): 'People treat the name of God as though the inconceivable and wholly incomprehensible supreme Being were not far more than such as they. Else they would not say: "The Lord

A liturgy unusually rich in numinous hymns and prayers is that of *Yom Kippur*, the great 'Day of Atonement' of the Jews. It is overshadowed by the 'Holy, Holy, Holy' of the Seraphim (Isa. vi), which recurs more than once, and it has prayers in it as wonderful as the *ubekēn tēn pachdekā*:

'So then, let Thy fear, O Yahweh our God, come over all Thy creatures, and reverent dread (*ēmātekā*) of Thee upon all that Thou hast made, that all Thy creatures may fear Thee and every being bow before Thee and that they may all become bonded together to do Thy will with all their heart, even as we know, O Yahweh our God, that Thine is the lordship, that might is in Thy hand and power in Thy right hand and Thy name exalted above all that Thou hast created.'

APPENDIX III

ORIGINAL NUMINOUS SOUNDS

FEELINGS and emotions, as states of mental tension, find their natural relaxation in uttered sounds. It is evident that the numinous feeling also, in its first outbreak in consciousness, must have found sounds for its expression, and at first inarticulate sounds rather than words; but it is improbable that it devised special and peculiar sounds for itself. Analogous as it is to other feelings, it no doubt adopted the already familiar sounds expressive of the emotions of terror, amazement, joy, and the like. But it could, and sometimes did, put, as it were, a special stamp upon sounds coined for a different use. The German interjection '*Hu!*', for instance, expresses to-day invariably and exclusively, not terror in general, but terror accompanied by shuddering, i.e. numinous 'terror'. So, too, whereas *hus* in vulgar Arabic is, I am told, a sound expressive of soothing in general, the corresponding Hebrew sound *hās* is only found in a numinous context. (Cf. Amos vi. 10: 'Hold thy tongue (*hās*), for we may not make mention of the name of the Lord.' Zeph. i. 7: 'Hold thy peace at the presence of the Lord God.' Hab. ii. 20; Judges iii. 19; also Amos viii. 3.) Such a specialization of a common interjection has very possibly often come about. When the ecstatic Dervishes of Islam

God," "the dear God," "the good God." Were they penetrated through and through by a sense of His greatness, they would be dumb and unable to name Him for very veneration.'

bring their '*Zikr*' to an end, they break into ejaculations, such as '*Allāh Akbar*', which end finally in a protracted groaning *Hū*. This *Hū* has indeed been explained on rational grounds as the Arabic personal pronoun of the third person, '*He*', i.e. Allah. But any one who has actually heard these ejaculations finds it hard to think of them simply as pronouns. Rather we have the impression that in this sound the numinous feeling is seeking to discharge itself.

This specialization is perhaps the clue to the understanding of the Sanskrit word *āścarya*, to which reference has been made more than once. Its derivation has been hitherto an enigma; but one may conjecture that the explanation is in fact very simple, and that the word is just a compound of the two words *as* and *carya*. *Carya* = '*agendum*', that which is done or is to be done; while *as* is a primitive sound to express the '*stupendum*', the long-protracted open vowel of wonder (ā, oh, hā), combining with the sibilant, which in all languages is used to express or produce a terrified silence (cf. Hist! Sh! Sst!). An '*āś-carya*'[1] would not then be properly and primarily anything conceptual at all, nor even a 'marvel', but simply 'that in the presence of which we must exclaim "ās! ās!"'. If this interpretation is correct, we can detect in this word just the original 'shudder' of numinous awe in the first and earliest form in which it expressed itself, before any figure of speech, objective representation, or concept had been devised to explicate it; it bursts forth crudely and vehemently in this primal cry and is unable to name its object otherwise than as a something before which such sounds must involuntarily be uttered. Professor Geldner has kindly sent me a reference to a passage in the *Kena-Upanishad* (iv. 29) which seems to me to be an excellent confirmation of this and at the same time to illustrate how the primal numinous feeling did originally emerge as pure feeling, before any concept or concrete representation of it had come into being. The fine, naïve old *Kena-Upanishad* aims at making perceptible to the disciple that before which 'all words turn back', and proceeds just as we do, by trying to produce in him an appropriate feeling-reflex by means of a simile. The lines run:

> This is the way It (*sc.* Brahman) is to be illustrated:
> When lightnings have been loosened:
> aaah!

---

[1] Compare the exactly parallel forms *ā-kāra*, *ahan-kāra*: and *vide* Söderblom, *Das Werden des Gottesglaubens*, 1916, p. 96, on the *Manitu* of the Indians.

When that has made the eyes to be closed—
aaah!—
So far concerning Deity (*devatā*).

What, then, is the *devatā*, the *Brahman*? It is an *ā-caryam*, i.e.
'that in whose presence we must exclaim "aaah!"' And one
cannot 'illustrate' the numinous character of this 'aaah' by any
better analogy than that of the lightning here given. The un-
expectedness and suddenness of the lightning-flash, its dreadful
weirdness, its overpoweringness and dazzling splendour, the
fright and the delight of it, give it an almost numinous impressiveness, and indeed often do produce an actual numinous impression
on the mind.

This reference of Professor Geldner's seems to me all the more
significant from the fact that it appears to me to adumbrate quite
a new method of solving the old puzzle of the *Brahman*, and what
it means. For this task philosophical speculation is too elevated,
mere etymology too insufficient, a method. What is necessary in
order really to get at the heart of the matter is to have rediscovered
and recaptured the *feelings* which this word originally connoted
and which thrill through it. And for this we have again a very
instructive passage in that which, immediately preceding the one
just quoted (Kena, iii. 15), at the same time serves to elucidate it.
It is where the *Devas* catch for the first time an intimation of the
Brahman. They ask, in amazement, and yet obviously also in
extreme eagerness: '*Kim idam yakṣam?*' of which Deussen's translation 'What marvellous thing (*Wunderding*) is this?' is too tame
a rendering. It is more exactly: 'What un-thing (*Unding*) is
this?' in the sense in which this expression is popularly used for
a thing of which no one can say what it is or whence it comes,
and in whose presence we have the feeling of the uncanny.
'*Yakṣa*', like '*Unding*', is sometimes a word for a ghost, and is
originally the '*ungeheuer*', 'monstrous', in the sense of the uncanny,
eerie, 'apparition', or spectre. And it is just as such that the
Brahman in this passage behaves. It does the things goblins and
magical creatures usually do, vanishing suddenly like a true
phantom at the climax of the transaction. Such feelings, which
we meet at the commencement of the great Mysticism of Brahman, attend its course continually, and he who cannot recognize
and detect their presence there cannot do more than reconstruct
the meagre skeleton of concepts they have left behind. And the
same thing, *mutatis mutandis*, holds good also for western Mysticism.

Another original sound in which the numinous feeling is arti-

culated is certainly the holy syllable 'om'. It likewise has no sort
of conceptual connotation. Like the particle ās, it is simply an
articulated sound—no word, nor even a complete syllable, for the
m in which it ends is not an ordinary 'm', but simply the long-
protracted nasal continuation of the deep 'o' sound. It is really
simply a sort of growl or groan, sounding up from within as the
quasi-reflex expression of profound emotion in circumstances of a
numinous-magical nature, and serving to relieve consciousness
of a felt burden, almost physical in its constraining force. And
this constraint and compulsion to expression are still recoverable
to our feeling when we recapture this mood of submergence and
absorption in the 'wholly other'.

This Om is exactly parallel to the similar sound in Sanskrit,
Hum—like it, nothing but a numinous ejaculation, with probably
no further significance.

It would be a task for the history and psychology of religion
alike to examine the innumerable names of gods and demons, and
perhaps also the various designations for ghost, soul, and spirit,
with a view to seeing whether many of them may not simply have
arisen from original numinous sounds and thus be parallels to the
name āścarya, already considered.[1]

Appendix IV

'SPIRIT' AND 'SOUL' AS NUMINOUS ENTITIES

THE non-rational which we were looking for in the idea of the
divine was found in the numinous, and in our recognition of this
we came to see that rationalistic speculation tends to conceal the
divine in God, and that before God becomes for us rationality,
absolute reason, a personality, a moral will, He is the wholly non-
rational and 'other', the being of sheer mystery and marvel. We
had to turn to the feelings of horror and shudder and spectral

---

[1] K. Müller suggests that the divine name Yah, Yahū, may have had this
origin. 'Euoios', the secondary name of Bacchus, may also denote simply him
in whose presence one ejaculates 'Euoi'. He could cite in his support Jelaleddin,
who says in Divan 31. 8: 'I know no other than Yahū.' This is here certainly
nothing but 'one of the most familiar dervish cries' (as the translator adds in a
note, p. 282), and will then mean, in accordance with the usual rendering,
'O he', or, as we rather suspect, simply 'O hu'. Nicholson puts 'Yahweh' in
brackets, without further justification. Cf. R. A. Nicholson, Selected Poems from
the Divani Shamsi Tabriz, Cambridge, 1898.

haunting in order, by means of these caricatures of the authentic numinous emotions, to break through the hard crust of rationalism and bring into play the feelings buried deep down in our religious consciousness.

Now what is true of our apprehension of the divine is true also of its counterpart in the creature—soul and spirit. Gregory of Nyssa well says: 'Since one of the signs of the Divine Nature is its essential incomprehensibility, in this also must the copy be like the original. For were the nature of the copy comprehended, when the original was above comprehension, the copy would be a mistaken one. But, inasmuch as the nature of our spirit is above our understanding, it has here an exact resemblance to the all-sublime, representing by its own unfathomableness the incomprehensible Being of God.' Here, too, we need to break up anew our hardened and crusted feelings and to withstand the intellectualizing tendency to which we are so prone in our doctrine of the soul and its creation in God's image. For this divine image in man also does not merely consist in the fact that he is reasonable, moral, intelligent, and a person, but primarily in the fact that in its profoundest depths his being is indeed for religious self-consciousness something numinous—that the soul is mystery and marvel. This is how mysticism apprehends it, and we can understand at once why this is so from our definition of mysticism as the tendency to stress up to an extreme and exaggerated point the non-rational aspect of religion. And what was already stirring in crude fashion at the earliest and lowest stage of numinous feeling recurs at the most exalted level of mysticism with after-effects that colour the whole experience. In the mystic's praise of the soul, and in that '*fundus animae*' of which he tells the mysteries, there echoes the '*stupor*' before the 'wholly other' that characterized the primitive belief in souls and even primitive feeling of the presence of ghosts.

We said above (p. 120) that the most interesting point in the primitive idea of soul is not the form given to it in fantasy, multifarious in its variations, but the element of feeling—*stupor*—which it liberates, and the character of 'mystery' and 'wholly otherness' which surrounds it. This fact is obscured in the measure in which the 'soul' becomes later the subject of myth, fairy story, and narrative, speculation and doctrine, and finally of psychological investigation. It then becomes more and more something entirely rational; its origin in magic and mystery becomes overlaid with concepts, scholastic terms, and classifications. The Doctrine of souls or *Ātman* of the Indian *Sānkhya* system is the best example of this. But even this cannot entirely conceal the fact that 'Soul' or *Ātman* is *properly* the thing of marvel and stupefaction, quite undefinable, outsoaring all conceptions, 'wholly alien' to our understanding. And this finds wonderful expression in the verses of the Gītā, 2. 29, which we transcribe here of intention in the original:

> Āścaryavat pašyati kašcid enam.
> Āścaryavad vadati tathaiva cānya<u>h</u>.
> Āścaryavac cainam anya<u>h</u> šrinoti.
> Šrutvā 'pyenam veda na caiva kašcit.

The sound of these verses suggests a magic formula, almost a conjuration, especially when they are heard intoned in the peculiar sacred sing-song in which such lines are commonly recited. The note of magic and mystery is very palpable in them. As for the translation, it is usual to render *Āścaryam* by 'strange', 'wondrous', 'a thing of wonder' or 'marvel'; but we should perhaps catch the emotional accent in the lines more exactly as follows:

As 'wholly other' doth one gaze upon it (*sc.* Ātman).
He speaketh of the 'wholly other', who speaketh of the Ātman.
Something 'wholly other' hath he learned, who hath learned the Ātman.
Yet none, albeit he hath learned it, may come to know it.

But, however they be rendered into another language, there is living in these old phrases a profoundly numinous self-feeling, which still retains a trace of the *'stupor'* before an apparition of spirits. And it is continued where the Gītā (2. 25) designates the *Ātman* the *'acintya'*, i.e. that which is incomprehensible by thought. In this it is exactly like the *'fundus animae'*, the 'spark', 'Synderesis', or 'Inner Abyss' of our own Western mystics. In both cases we have, surviving in an ennobled form, the primal awe and shrinking before the presence of *'āścaryam'* and *'adbhutam'*, the haunting presence that prompts the earliest numinous feelings. For, as an old mystic tells us, the soul and its bottommost depth lie hidden away, ineffable as God himself—'so that no human skill ever attains to be able to know what the Soul is in its bottommost depth. For that a supernatural skill is needed. It is what is without a name.' And 'the heights and depths which are disclosed in these Men can be grasped by no human sense or reason, for they surpass in their profundities all understanding'.[1]

---

[1] Greith, pp. 70 and 80.

Finally, it may be said that we catch a last reflection of the numinous wonder in the wonder, one might almost say in the eager curiosity, with which Augustine roves through the chambers of the soul, even when he is pursuing 'psychological' discussion. He feels that he has a story of marvel to tell when he describes the soul. His psychology is half 'numinology'. Cf. *Confessions*, x. 6–27.

The clearer insight into the inmost marvel of the soul is not set free as a sort of reflex: it comes in the experience as an uprush, an irruption, a burst of illumination, 'like a flash', in the English phrase, as a 'sudden *aperçu*', in Goethe's. And so it easily shows the two elements; on the one hand there is an entry or penetration into consciousness of inspiration, sudden, unmeditated, once and for all achieved; and on the other hand there is a reminiscence (*anamnesis*), a recollection of something that was a familiar possession in the obscurity of feeling even before the moment of insight. Both of these elements are indicated in the old *Kena-Upanishad*, when (iv. 30), after speaking of the *Brahman* in the significant verses we have already considered (p. 191), the text goes on at once to speak of the *Ātman*, in words which may be rendered thus:

Now in respect to the Ātman:
It is as though something forces its way into consciousness
And consciousness suddenly remembers—
Such a state of mind illustrates the awakening of knowledge of the Ātman.

We may compare the saying of Plato, already quoted (p. 95 n.); and, finally, the words of Meister Eckhart:

'Upon this matter a heathen sage hath a fine saying in speech with another sage: "I become aware of something in me which flashes upon my reason. I perceive of it that it is something, but what it is I cannot conceive. Only meseems that, could I conceive it, I should comprehend all truth." ' (W. Lehmann, *Meister Eckhart*, Göttingen, 1917, p. 243.)

And the 'obscure' Heracleitus says: 'Thou canst not discover the bounds of the soul albeit thou pacest its every road: so deep is its foundation.'

Appendix V

THE SUPRA-PERSONAL IN THE NUMINOUS

We said above that the feeling of the 'wholly other' gives rise in mysticism to the tendency to follow the *'via negationis'*, by which every predicate that can be stated in words becomes excluded from the absolute Numen—i.e. from Deity—till finally the God-head is designated as 'nothingness' and 'nullity', bearing in mind always that these terms denote in truth immeasurable plenitude of being. Now this is also the origin of that tendency to let the conception of *personality* and the personal also be submerged in the same 'nothingness', a tendency which is in appearance so irreligious. We need not dispute that the denial of personality to God does often in fact denote a wholly irreligious attitude; mostly it is simply a disguised form of atheism, or betokens a desperate attempt to equate faith in God with belief in natural law and with naturalism. But it would be a huge error to suppose that anything of this kind is in the minds of the mystics when they set themselves to oppose the idea of personality in God. We shall be in a better position to understand what they are contending for if we take mysticism—following our previous definition—as meaning the preponderance in religious consciousness, even to the point of one-sided exaggeration, of its non-rational features. What we have, then, is a sort of antimony, arising from the inner duality in the idea of the divine and the tension of its more rational and its more non-rational elements. (The non-rational assumes thus an apparently *irr*ational character.) It is the 'wholly other' aspect of the numen, resisting every analogy, every attempted comparison, and every determination; so that it is here really true that *'omnis determinatio est negatio'*.

Now this holds good not only in the case of the most lofty and reverent feelings, in which devotion and worship reach their consummation, but also in the case of that primary and elemental 'awe' of which we spoke on pages 125–8. Let us glance once more at the experience given in the story of Jacob at Bethel, there cited (Gen. xxviii. 16–17). If we use as a clue to it our own power of imaginative sympathy, introspection will show that even this experience contains a clear antimony, a conflict of opposites. We said that the pure elemental 'awe' mirrored in Jacob's first words, 'How dreadful is this place!', is rendered explicit in the words that follow. The simple experience of *'awefulness'* is *interpreted*—all but instinctively, and apart from reflection—and the interpretation is, in the English phrase, 'a presence', a real, present, and personal being. Now though we certainly feel that such an interpretation is needed and in some sense right, and that we should in Jacob's place have found no other to 'explicate' our feeling, yet we are no less certainly conscious of a counter-impulse in us which resists it, suggesting that, when all is said, such expressions as 'Being', 'Person', 'Thou', 'He', are strangely alien and repugnant to the very import of the experience. Does this Power that impresses us with such awe admit of being comprised in such a firm outline, admit of question and answer in the second person? Is not this interpretation at first glance distinctly anthropomorphic? The abstract English expression, 'a presence', is itself a good indication of this—for 'a presence' is simply felt, and the English usage of words is chary of saying anything more specific. The 'Personalism' of the later-developed mythology and the later developments of ordered worship (mostly practised on a wholly 'personalist' basis) have tended more and more to extrude this authentic and sensitive element of feeling from the religious experience; and the 'daemon' or 'god', which they both contributed to shape, is not richer but poorer in content than the object of that primal 'awe', corresponding only to certain sides and aspects of it. Before the 'gods' were the hard-outlined, clear-featured gods of the myths, they were *numina*, and, though the numen certainly gains something from subsequent mythology in definiteness and fixity of representation, it also certainly loses something of its original wealth of meaning in the process. In drawing more near to earth and to humanity, it comes itself to acquire human traits, and, that this tendency may not be carried too far, it is necessary now and then to melt down, as it were, the human lineaments of God in the more elemental entirety of the original experience. The numen has, no doubt, in itself personal features, which somehow enable the worshipper to refer to it by a pronoun, as 'he' or 'she'. But, while the limits of the personal are at this stage still fluid, they cannot (any more than in the case of the more definite figure of the 'God') quite comprise the full import of the inapprehensible and unnameable, which presses out beyond them.

Thus already, at the outset, we find in the numen of primitive religious feeling that tension between the personal and the supra-personal which recurs again in the maturer stages of the developing experience of God. It is to be found next in the comparatively

low level of 'the daemonic', where it is disclosed in an actual
difference in the verbal forms employed. The Greek δαίμων is
indisputably a single, concrete, personal Being; the δαιμόνιον,
that, for example, of Socrates, is certainly none of these—neither
concrete, nor personal, and hardly even to be called a being or
individual entity. Yet in the impressiveness and devout awe
which it suggests δαιμόνιον is, if anything, the richer of the two
terms. In Indian terminology *rakṣás* is the concrete, personal,
and masculine 'Daemon', but a transposition of the accent to the
first syllable gives *rákṣas* (the neuter), 'the daemonic', or rather
'demonic'; a word, perhaps, more charged with terror than is
rakṣás; and the fact that the difference is merely one of accent
shows very clearly how easily the one meaning passes into the
other. But exactly the same thing is seen again at that highest
stage, at which the unfolding of the numinous consciousness
reaches its climax in India: *brahmán* is the everlasting Lord and
God, the personal *Brahmá*; while *bráhman* is the divine Absolute,
the supra-personal *Bráhma*, an 'It' rather than a 'He'. And the
two are bound together in indissoluble union as the two essential
poles of the eternal unity of the Numen. And here, again, the
closeness of their interconnexion is emphatically shown by the
fact that they are denoted by one and the same word and distinguished by a mere change of accent and gender.

Now it is generally supposed that there is something peculiarly
and specifically 'oriental' in this characteristic of Indian religion.
But this is by no means the case. On the contrary, one may
venture to assert that *all* gods are more than mere (personal) gods,
and that all the greater representations of deity show from time to
time features which reveal their ancient character as '*numina*' and
burst the bounds of the personal and theistic. This is obviously
the case where the experienced relation of the worshipper to his
god does not exclusively take the form of contact with a 'beyond'
and transcendent being, but comes somehow as the experience of
seizure and possession by the god, as being filled by him, an
experience in which the god wholly or partially enters the
believer and dwells in him, or assimilates him to his own divine
nature, commingling with his spirit and becoming very part of
him; or, again, where the god becomes the sphere in which 'we
live and move and have our being'. And what god has not in
some sense had this character? It is certainly true of the personal
'*Īśvara*' of India, who, besides his personal character, pervades
his '*Bhakta*' as '*antaryāmin*', the immanent Indweller; it is true of

Ahura-mazda, who by his spirits does the same; and it is true of Dionysus, Apollo, and Zeus. No less than the mere crude 'daemon' can the 'god' become πνεῦμα and permeate the soul of man. And in so far the notion of a 'god' passes beyond the sphere of social and personal ideas and breaks through the confines of the merely personal. *Persons* cannot strictly interpenetrate, cannot become one inclusive of another. Such relations experienced between man and deity become altogether irrational, if we judge them by the standard of personality.

The Yahweh of the Old Testament is also more than a 'god' in the merely personal sense, for though it is a sign of his superior value to all tribal gods, that the personal traits are so incomparably more strongly marked in him, yet other and non-personal features are not lacking. We come up against these in groping fashion in the comparison made between God's dealings with men and the working of an inexplicable 'force' spontaneously released. But the second name of Yahweh, 'Elohim', is also a proof of their existence. Elohim is 'gods', in the plural; and 'in the beginning created (sing.) "gods" heaven and earth'. Our way to-day, when we try to escape from the too narrow confines of the notion of unitary personality applied to God, is to use either an abstract noun, 'deity' (*die Gottheit*), or an adjectival neuter expression, 'the divine' (*das göttliche*). In Israel the same groping instinct had recourse to the adoption or adaptation of a plural substantive form, which was yet made to govern a verb in the singular! There cannot be a more uncompromising expression of what we called the antinomy or conflict of opposites in the experience of the numinous. It is very similar when later *Shāmayim*, 'Heaven', becomes a name for God—to be used once as such also in the Gospel. It does not in the least signify an 'abstract' way of conceiving God; but rather the feeling that endeavours to escape from any too anthropomorphic conception. Above all does the God of Job burst the bounds of interpretation by mere personality, as we have already seen. Moreover, Yahweh also is the numen which, blowing in the form of spirit, enters as '*ruach*' and πνεῦμα into his chosen, mingling with their spirit, an *antaryāmin* in full completion.

And so, when we turn to the New Testament, we see that the 'Pneumatology' and doctrine of Immanence in Paul and John, which give such unmistakable expression to the supra-personal aspect of the divine as the 'Light' and the 'Life', do not mean a sudden irruption into religion of a wholly novel and alien element, but merely the complete realization of what was all the while potential in the character of Yahweh in his essence as a numen. And what of the loftiest of all Christian claims, 'God is Love'? Usually we hear this saying without remarking how extraordinary it is. If we think of God in strictly and narrowly personal terms, He can indeed be 'He that loves', 'the loving One'. But the God who is *Love*, who pours Himself out as love and becomes the love whereby Christians love, is something more even than this.[1] In fine, even our GOD is more than merely 'god'. And, when Meister Eckhart says that one must stand apart from God in order to find deity, his error is certainly grave, but it is one which we can easily conceive as springing from the very heart of religion.[2]

But it is very evident that the religious attitude in face of this supra-personal aspect of the numen must be different from the ordinary attitude in personal intercourse by petition, prayer, colloquy. These have all assuredly pertained to the essence of religion from the earliest times, yet from the beginning they were not the only forms of intercourse. The numen on its side 'has intercourse' with man in attracting him to it, seizing upon him, possessing him, breathing upon him, filling and permeating him. Its function is $\dot{\epsilon}\nu\epsilon\rho\gamma\epsilon\hat{\iota}\sigma\theta\alpha\iota$, and on his side the man, the $\dot{\epsilon}\nu\epsilon\rho\gamma o\acute{\nu}\mu\epsilon\nu o\varsigma$, is filled, possessed, made one with the numen. And what is true at the lower levels is true also at the highest. The Divine, experienced as 'light', 'fire', and $\pi\nu\epsilon\hat{\upsilon}\mu\alpha$, cannot properly accost or be accosted. It is a penetrating glow and illumination, fulfilment, transfiguration—most of all where it is experienced as 'Life', or

---

[1] There is an echo of this antinomy in the dispute of the Scholastics whether the love whereby we love is the 'Spiritus Sanctus', i.e. God Himself, or merely His 'donum'.

[2] We have seen that it is an indication of its superiority that in the Biblical conception of God the pole of the personal rather than of the impersonal is altogether preponderant. Taoism stands at the opposite extreme; but it too is genuine and deeply felt religion, moving as it does wholly in the numinous. H. Hackmann says of it: 'Taoism originates in the contemplative speculation upon the secret of the world, the mystery of existence. Its basic instinct is to pay reverent and surmiseful heed to the marvellous forces operative in our phenomenal life, which give to its particular details system and connexion with the great unknown background of the universe. The word "mystery"—the *mysterium tremendum*—occupies a more central position in Taoism than in almost any other religion. . . . Here sounds a genuine note in the prodigious symphony of that life of the soul—the religious life—which searches and surmises a deeper unity and a firm foundation in the beyond behind the happenings upon earth.' (H. Hackmann, 'Die Mönchsregeln des Klostertaoismus', *Ostasiatische Zeitschrift*, vii. 170.) For this whole question cf. the same author's essay: 'Über Objekt und Gebietsumfang der Religion', in *Nieuw Theologisch Tijdschrift*, 1918.

(what is but the intensification of this) as very 'Being'. One can make a petition *for* life, but not *to* Life. One is simply quickened through and through by it; one cannot address it as 'Thou'. And so intercourse with the numen comprises a way other than that of personal intercourse, that of the 'mystic'. Each of the two, the personal and the mystical, belongs to the other, and the language of devotion uses very naturally the phrases and expressions of both commingled. They are not different forms of religion, still less different stages in religion, the one higher and better than the other, but the two essentially united poles of a single fundamental mental attitude, the religious attitude. In Luther's conception of 'faith' they are found in this relation openly manifested, where *'fides'* denotes both *'fiducia'* or trust—a term implying personal intercourse—and *'adhaesio'*, or intimate contact, a term essentially mystical.

It is in the light of this primal fact of religion that we must seek an answer to the question as to the general place of 'Personalism' and 'Supra-personalism' in religious history, and only so are we likely to avoid confounding this question with the question of Theism and Pantheism, with which it has nothing in common. In my books *Vishnu-Nārāyana* (pp. 59, 63) and *Siddhāntā des Rāmānuja* (pp. 2, 80) I have referred further to the subject. And I have shown in a paper, 'Neues Singen' (*Christliche Welt*, 1919, No. 48), its important practical bearings for religious conduct and its expression in prayer and hymn. I reproduce the relevant passage:

'Our usual prayers and hymns confine themselves to the region which I call the "rational". They lack that element which I call the non-rational or the "numinous". But this is the other half of religion, its profounder and more mysterious background and basis. Yet only seldom has hymnody hitherto done justice to it. Consequently we are very deficient in the great and impressive "hymns of reverence", the hymns of the (grammatical) third person, and our hymns are almost entirely in the second person, "Thou", not "He". Now there is something lacking in this constant, direct, obvious mode of accosting God in the second person singular. The Seraphim in Isaiah vi do not venture on such an address, and many a glorious Ekteny and Litany of the older Liturgies follows their example. The creature is simply unable to stand face to face with the Eternal without interruption; his vision cannot bear the perpetual sight of Holiness without an occasional screen. He needs sometimes the oblique as well as the straight, frontal approach, the indirect relationship with face half averted and covered, as well as the direct; and consequently his utterance should not be so continually in the form of an address *to* God as to exclude prayerful and thoughtful discourse *about* Him. The same holds good of prayer in general, not merely of hymns. "Third person" hymns in this sense are not necessarily less, but under certain conditions may even be more genuine and first-hand utterances than those which address God as "Thou". There is a further consequence. It is often thought that the designations of deity in impersonal, neuter terms ("It"), rather than in terms of person and masculine pronoun ("He", "Thou"), are too poor and too pale to gain a place in our Christian thought of God. But this is not always correct. Frequently such terms indicate the mysterious overplus of the non-rational and numinous, that cannot enter our "concepts" because it is too great and too alien to them; and in this sense they are quite indispensable, even in hymns and prayers. It is a defect in our devotional poetry that it hardly knows any other image for the eternal mystery of the Godhead than those drawn from social intercourse and personal relationship, and so it tends to lose sight of just the mysterious transcendent aspect of deity. Assuredly God *is* for us "Thou" and a Person. But this personal character is that side of His nature which is turned manward—it is like a "Cape of Good Hope", jutting out from a mountain range which, as it recedes, is lost to view in the *"tenebrae aeternae"*—only to be expressed by the suspension of speech and the inspiration of sacred song.'

So far we have spoken of the personal and supra-personal as applied to the supreme, spiritual Being. But what is true here is no less true of that which was created in its image, our own human soul or spirit. In us, too, all that we call person and personal, indeed all that we can know or name in ourselves at all, is but one element in the whole. Beneath it lies, even in us, that 'wholly other', whose profundities, impenetrable to any concept, can yet be grasped in the numinous self-feeling[1] by one who has experience of the deeper life.

---

[1] We say 'numinous self-*feeling*', not 'numinous self-*consciousness*', as Schleiermacher called it, who may be said to have re-discovered it. The ambiguity of his nomenclature, however, does not detract from the importance of his discovery.

Appendix VI

THE MYSTICAL ELEMENT IN LUTHER'S CONCEPTION OF 'FAITH'

In connexion with the discussion of Luther's conception of faith on pp. 103–4, I would refer to my book, *Die Anschauung vom Heiligen Geiste bei Luther*, the chapter 'Geist und Glaube' (pp. 25–46), which includes the inquiry into Luther's conception of Faith and how far Faith for him is not merely confidence and trust (*confidere, fiducia*), but also a 'cleaving to God' in feeling and will (*adhaerere Deo*). And then let the reader study the noble little work of Johann von Kastl, *De Adhaerendo Deo*, to recognize the inner connexion of Luther with mysticism in regard to his conception of faith, especially the 12th chapter, 'De Amore Dei quod efficax sit.' Luther says *nothing* of the impelling power of Faith to bring to new birth, to justify and to sanctify, that is not also said in this chapter of the 'Amor Mysticus'.

'Solus amor est, quo convertimur ad Deum, transformamur in Deum, adhaeremus Deo, unimur Deo, ut simus unus spiritus cum eo, et beatificemur cum eo.'[1]

Here '*amor*' is the 'potent, active, creative thing that changes us and brings us to new birth'. 'Love', too, like faith, is the 'affect' that knows no quiescence.

'Proinde nihil amore acutius, nihil subtilius, aut penetrabilius. Nec quiescit, donec universaliter totam amabilis penetravit virtutem et profunditatem ac totalitatem, et unum se vult facere cum amato. *Vehementer tendit* in eum et ideo *nunquam quiescit*, donec omnia transeat et ad ipsum in ipsum veniat.'[2]

The effect of this '*adhaesio*' is thus exactly that which Luther also frequently describes:

'Quippe qui Deo adhaeret, versatur in lumine . . . qua ex re est hominis in hac vita sublimior perfectio, ita Deo uniri, ut tota anima cum omnibus potentiis suis et viribus in Dominum Deum suum sit collecta, et unus fiat spiritus cum eo.'[3]

[1] 'It is Love alone whereby we are turned to God, and changed into the form of God, whereby we cleave to God and are made one with God, so that we are one spirit with Him and are beatified with Him.'

[2] 'For nothing is keener, nothing more subtle or more penetrating, than Love. Nor does it rest until it has penetrated the whole power and depth and entirety of its object, and its will is to make itself one with the loved one. It strives towards him with vehemence and so never has rest until it has passed through all things and reached him and entered into him.'

[3] 'He indeed who cleaves to God abides in light. . . . Wherefore is it man's

Luther calls this, in a still more violent expression, '*mit Gott ein Kuche werden*' (to become kneaded into one cake with God).

It should at the same time be noted that in Johann von Kastl this *amor* is already permeated through and through by faith, trust, comfort, and the longing for certitude, and that for him no less than for Luther the 'Remission of Sins' stands as the first step in the *ordo salutis*, the order of salvation. Thus:

'Sic scilicet in Domino Deo de omni sua necessitate *audeat plene totaliter confidere*. Hoc ipso facto in tantum Deo complacet, ut suam ei gratiam largiatur et per ipsam gratiam veram sentiat caritatem et dilectionem, omnemque *ambiguitatem et timorem expellentem* in Deoque *confidenter sperantem*'[1] (op. cit., ch. 5).

And so *adhaesio* may come about just as well by means of 'faith': '*sed tantum fide et bona voluntate adhaerere Deo*'[2] (ch. 6).

Here, too, are freedom from care and the assurance of consolation the things to be prized: '*et eius consolatione suaviter reficitur*'[3] (ch. 7).

And the whole series of religious experiences, so often recurring in Luther, are already displayed in Johann von Kastl in their characteristic order:

'. . . peccatorum remissio, amaritudinis expressio, collatio dulcedinis et securitatis, infusio gratiae et misericordiae, attractio et corroboratio familiaritatis atque abundans de ipso consolatio, firmaque adhaesio et unio.'[4]

But a complete judgement upon Luther's connexion with mysticism will only be possible when all the manuscript remains of the popular mystical preaching of his time become known, which as yet lie undisturbed in our libraries. They will show the background and setting of Luther's thought and phraseology, the soil out of which they grew, and how many similarities and analogues there are to the feelings to which Luther gives expression. Were

---

loftier perfection in this life to be so united to God that the whole soul with all its strength and all its powers is gathered into its Lord and God and becomes one spirit with Him.'

[1] 'So then let (the soul) of its very necessity make the venture to trust wholly and completely in the Lord God. In this very wise is the soul so pleasing to God, that He bestows His own grace upon it, and by that very grace it comes to feel the true love and affection which drives away all doubt and all fear and hopes confidently in God.'

[2] 'but only to cleave to God in faith and good will.'

[3] ' and by his consolation is (the soul) sweetly restored.'

[4] 'The forgiveness of sins, the expelling of bitterness, the bestowal of sweetness and security, the inpouring of grace and of mercy, the attraction and the strengthening of friendship with Him and abundant comfort in Him, and a firm cleaving to Him and union with Him.'

we unaware that the pamphlet *Of the Liberty of a Christian* was by Luther, we should probably count it among these writings. And in any case there are to be found within the limits of the so-called 'mystical' literature contrasts in mental attitude that go farther than that between this work of Luther's and that of Johann von Kastl from which we have been quoting. And Luther is really far more akin to such a mystic as Meister Eckhart in his attitude than are either Plotinus on the one hand or, on the other, the crowd of God-enamoured monks and nuns, the '*doctores ecstatici*' and '*seraphici*', such as Ignatius and John of the Cross, Theresa and Madame Guyon.

But such comparisons as this are illuminating not only upon the question of the historical relation between Lutheranism and mystical religion, which is, after all, not a very important issue, but also upon the question as to the connexion between the two in their essential nature. It has been said that for a Protestant to love mysticism is mere dilettantism: if he is in earnest, he must become a Catholic. But then 'mysticism' is an ambiguous term. If we mean by it the melting transport of a transcendent quasi-nuptial rapture, then the assertion may be justified. But the really typical 'moments' of mysticism—'creature-feeling' and 'union'—are not *less* but *more* possible upon the basis of Luther's '*fides*' ('faith' as '*fiducia*' and '*adhaesio*') than upon the basis of the '*amor mysticus*'.

Johann Arndt says at the commencement of his *Four Books of True Christianity* (ch. 5): 'By this heart-felt confidence and heart-felt trust man gives his heart to God utterly, reposes only in God, surrenders himself and attaches himself to Him, unites himself with God, becomes a sharer in all that is of God and of Christ, becomes one God with God.' This is simply Luther's doctrine (his '*fides*' as '*fiducia*' and '*adhaesio*'), clarified and raised to a higher power. These expressions might well be found in Luther's *Of the Liberty of a Christian*—indeed their meaning is to be found there. St. Paul says the same, only more forcibly still, in Gal. ii. 20 and 1 Cor. vi. 17.

But this question of the possibility of the transition from '*fides*' to the experience of union is not to be definitely decided by a citation of texts from Luther or from the Bible, but by a consideration of what 'faith' is in essence. Faith is more than a conviction of the truth of the eternal verities. It is a deeply felt state of tension with regard to them and of absorption in them; and, as 'trust', it is the most intimate feeling of nearness. But in all this it contains in itself the core of that which is meant by mysterious terms like 'union', something that is more than the 'knowledge' or the 'love' of the earlier mystic schools. And this becomes still plainer to anyone who has clearly recognized by deeper contemplation the profoundly non-rational elements to be found in the very act of faith.

APPENDIX VII

'SIGNS FOLLOWING'

(I GIVE here a passage from my *Leben und Wirken Jesu* relevant to this subject, touched upon on p. 172.)

Jesus begins his work on the shore of the Sea of Galilee, and the Gospels present us with its main features unmistakably. He preaches in the synagogues, in the houses of his friends, on every sort of occasion at table and under the open sky, now sojourning in one spot, now journeying from place to place. His fame is spread abroad especially by means of the mysterious gift of healing which is active in him.

What are we to say of this? The Jesus who works the miracles in the Synoptic narrative is, as we saw above, not the wonder-worker *par excellence*, of whom we read in St. John's Gospel or whom the traditional view presents to us. But even in those passages which can be least impugned by criticism there is something incommensurable with our rational standards in the setting in which we see his figure, and this gift of healing is an example of it. The narratives of these acts of healing stand out with such an assured and plain simplicity, with a clarity so well-nigh disconcerting, that they cannot be the fabrications of legend. We have only to read the sober account—it is almost like an official report—of the healing of Peter's wife's mother (Mark i. 29–31), or that of the healing of the man with the palsy (Mark ii. 1–12), with its concreteness of detail. And it is the same with many other cases. The story of the centurion of Capernaum, and Jesus's astonished wonder at the faith of this Gentile; the story of the woman of Canaan, and of how Jesus, at first reluctant, comes to be inwardly won over; this is not the way of imagination and legend. Moreover, there is the fact that we encounter exactly similar occurrences among the early Christian communities. Even if we are ready to impugn the accounts of Jesus's miracles of healing in the Gospels, we cannot impugn the accounts in the Pauline epistles of the same thing as happening among the Corinthians,

Galatians, and Romans, and to Paul himself. Here they stand in
the full light of history and with the fullest testimony of history.
It is quite evident that both Paul and the first Christian communities were firmly convinced that they had the '*charismata*',
the 'gifts', among them. St. Paul gives, in 1 Cor. xii. 4–11, a
formal catalogue of these, in which the gifts of healing the sick
and of the exercise of super-normal physical power and other
abnormal psychical gifts take their place alongside the gifts of
tongues and prophecy. No doubt he says (1 Cor. xiii) that something is higher and more precious than all 'gifts', namely, the
simple Christian virtues of faith, hope, and love, and love 'the
greatest among these'. But it is implied thereby that those other
gifts, too, are a reality and a present possession. He has them in
himself and frequently exercises them, and in every Christian congregation they make their appearance. In fact we have sure
historical warrant for holding that 'gifts' of this kind were in
evidence for a long time beyond the borders of the early Church
—just as, for that matter, we have similar warrant for recognizing
that analogous phenomena have been since observed in other than
Christian surroundings. Will this mysterious region one day be
clearly revealed to us? We can at any rate say this: that our
procedure is very uncritical if we propose to rule it out as
non-existent simply because it does not square with our current
conceptions of 'agreement with the natural order'.

Now the fewer the preconceptions which we bring to our reading of the narrative-material of the Gospels, as reviewed and
guaranteed by a thorough criticism, the stronger becomes the
impression that in Jesus these powers were present with a rare
potency. We have in a sense a key to the matter in the peculiar
predisposition and endowment for their calling which marked the
great prophets of the Old Testament. What characterized them
really was not omniscience and not the capacity of predicting a
future many hundred years distant: it was beyond question in
many cases a unique power of forefeeling and foreboding impend-
ing supernormal occurrences that threatened to break in upon
the natural course of events. This gift we have held to be not
something 'supernatural' and miraculous in the old sense of the
word, i.e. something that falls altogether outside all analogies of
what happens elsewhere; on the contrary, analogies in plenty for
this extraordinary prophetic gift are to be found in the phenomena
of clairvoyance, presentiment, second-sight, &c. Now it is possible
that the gift of healing of Jesus which appears so puzzling was

'merely' a heightened and intense form of capacities which lie dormant in human nature in general. But for a manifestation of the influence exerted by the psychical upon the physical we need in fact go no farther than the power of our will to move our body —the power, that is, of a spiritual cause to bring about a mechanical effect. There assuredly is an absolutely insoluble riddle, and it is only the fact that we have grown so used to it that prevents it from seeming a 'miracle' to us. But, this granted, who can pronounce beforehand what intenser and heightened manifestations of this power may not be possible? Who can presume to determine what direct results a will may not achieve which, wholly concentrated and at one with itself, rests altogether upon God? We have had in recent years many indications of parallels and analogies to the miraculous power of Jesus in the newly discovered methods of suggestion and hypnotism, in telepathy, 'action at a distance', and (in my opinion) animal magnetism. All these suppositions may be accepted without misgiving, only with this addition, that what Jesus did passed gradually far beyond anything known to us in these fields; and moreover, that Jesus's whole power grew out of his consciousness of his mission, and his will, unusually strong as it was, drew its strength only from his religious and moral consciousness, from the fact that he was rooted and grounded in God.

If it be granted that Jesus really had an abnormal power in action, it is evident that this very fact would stimulate rumour and imagination to exaggeration and embellishment and invention of miraculous incident. It is evident that we may quite properly approach the miracle narratives with a certain expectation of finding such features in them; and that it will not do, in face of some sheer prodigy, to rest content with 'the mysterious gift' as a solution to every difficulty. Thus a raising from the dead, as that of Lazarus, or a changing of water into wine (both stories only in St. John), is excluded from the region of the historically conceivable and admissible. And there is in the Synoptists also matter enough that passes these limits, e.g. the walking on the sea, the feeding of the five thousand, the tale of the Gadarene swine. When such stories have been deducted, then practically all that is left in the Synoptic narrative are cases of healing, though of course some of these are of an astonishing character. There are also two cases of raising from the dead—that of Jairus's daughter and that of the young man of Nain. Criticism will be inclined to reject these. It must, however, be granted that there is a real

P

difference between these stories and that in St. John of the raising of Lazarus. Jairus's daughter had not lain three days in the grave, like Lazarus; she had only lost consciousness a short time before the miracle. Where is the margin that divides complete death from the last faint glow of the spark of life, very likely already passed into unconsciousness? May not he who by his will had power to restore a consciousness confused by madness have had also the power to arrest a consciousness just vanishing over the borders of life, and even awaken again in the body one that has but just vanished? Here the account is strikingly concrete. Even the very words Jesus uses to awaken the girl as uttered in Aramaic—'talitha cumi'—are still given in the Aramaic form by the Greek narrator. There is nothing grandiose or theatrical, as is customarily the case with a miracle designed for display. Jesus only admits the most intimate even of his disciples, and the whole incident closes with the soberly practical injunction to give the newly restored child food, and with the direct prohibition to talk further about the event. We have only to compare with this the raising of Lazarus; here is the exact opposite, a genuine miracle of display. The wonder-worker designedly delays his arrival, so that a miracle becomes necessary; the whole proceeding, with its solemn *mise-en-scène*, takes place in public, and is accompanied by a prayer, which is at the same time a sort of address to the surrounding spectators. The act is to be performed expressly 'because of the people which stand by'. This is how a miracle-narrative looks when it is the offspring of literary art. The raisings from the dead given in St. Mark are quite other than this, and consequently a circumspect criticism may perhaps in their case suspend judgement.

APPENDIX VIII

SILENT WORSHIP

Still-born Silence, thou that art
Flood-gate of the deeper heart.

I TAKE these lines[1] from a little Quaker book on *Silent Worship*[2] which, recently translated into German, should give the German public a good impression of the worship of silent waiting upon

---

[1] They are quoted from Charles Lamb's essay, 'A Quakers' Meeting'. (*Trans.*)   [2] *Silent Worship: The Way of Wonder*, by Violet Hodgkin.

God which has been a feature of the Quaker community from the days of George Fox up to the present day. It is the most spiritual form of divine service which has ever been practised, and contains an element which no form of worship ought to be without, but which, as has been hinted on a former page, is unduly neglected in our Protestant devotional life. We must learn it once again from the Quakers, and thereby restore to our divine service a spirit of consecration the loss of which has cost it dearly.

I

Devotional Silence may have a threefold character. There is the numinous silence of Sacrament, the silence of Waiting, and the silence of Union or Fellowship.

1. The first of these is that silence meant in the verse of the Prophet (Hab. ii. 20), 'Let all the earth keep silence before him.' Such impressive moments of silence were known not only in the worship of Israel but in that of other peoples. They are the culminating sacramental point in the worship, denoting as they do the instant when 'God is in the midst', experienced as '*numen praesens*'. All the preceding part of the service is but a preparation for this, a preparation for the moment of which the words hold good, '*Das Unzulängliche, hier wird's Ereignis*,' 'the Insufficient here becomes Event'. For what was previously only possessed in insufficiency, only longed for, now comes upon the scene in living actuality, the experience of the transcendent in gracious intimate presence, the 'Lord's Visitation of His people'. Such a realization is Sacrament, and what occasions it, attends, or prepares for it, must be termed sacramental. Such a silence is therefore a sacramental silence. It was found in the forms of worship of ancient Israel, and it is found to-day in the Roman Mass, in the moment of 'transubstantiation'.

2. Next there is the silence of *Waiting*. The meaning of this is primarily other than sacramental. When the Quakers assemble for a quiet time together, this is first and foremost a time of waiting, and it has in this sense a double value. It means our submergence, i.e. inward concentration and detachment from the manifold outward distractions; but this again has value as a preparation of the soul to become the pencil of the unearthly writer, the bent bow of the heavenly archer, the tuned lyre of the divine musician. This silence is, then, primarily not so much a dumbness in the presence of Deity, as an awaiting His coming, in expectation of the Spirit and its message. But it passes over

naturally into the Sacramental Silence of which we have spoken. And in fact 'Silent Worship' may remain without words from first to last—it may exclude all *utterance* of the Spirit's message in vocal form, and in that case the worshippers part, as they met, without any audible exhortation or thanksgiving. Yet the worship need not have been in any way defective, for the silence may have been a direct 'numinous' experience, as well as a waiting upon God. The Eternal was present in the stillness and His presence was palpable without a word spoken. The solemn observance of silence became a Sacrament.

3. The consummation of the Sacrament is the achievement of unity, i.e. fellowship and *Communion*. This third silence is the completion of the waiting and the sacramental silences. The Silent Worship of the Quakers is in fact a realization of Communion in both senses of the word—inward oneness and fellowship of the individual with invisible present Reality and the mystical union of many individuals with one another. In this regard there is the plainest inward kinship between the two forms of worship which, viewed externally, seem to stand at the opposite poles of religious development, viz. the Quaker Meeting and the Roman Catholic Mass. *Both* are solemn religious observances of a numinous and sacramental character, *both* are communion, *both* exhibit alike an inner straining not only 'to realize the presence' of God, but to attain to a degree of oneness with Him.

II

'Silent Worship', in the fully formed character in which the Quakers practise it, is not possible in a 'Church', as we understand the word to-day, but only within the narrower limits of a more intimate 'Brotherhood of the Spirit'. May God grant that such a brotherhood may one day arise among us, not as a sect or a Church alongside our other Churches, but as a circle of self-dedicated enthusiasts, who have rediscovered the ancient heritage of the early Church—the Spirit and its sevenfold gifts!

But if the Quaker Silence is excluded, still less is any imitation of the Sacramental Silence in the form of the Catholic Mass possible in our Protestant services. All that tends in this direction is bound to go astray. The Communion Service does, it is true, celebrate Christ's Passion, that event which in all world history is the numinous event *par excellence*, the entry of the divine in fullest and loftiest presence upon the human scene. But the Communion Service is emphatically not a Mass, and the Mass has grown to be a distortion of its true form. The Communion Service is, in the original intention of its first celebration or institution, not a piece of public ceremonial at all, far less a drama to be performed by one or at most a few participants in the presence of spectators, but a tender mystery, restricted to a fellowship of brothers, pertaining to a special time and hour, and needing particular preparation—in short, something that should be precious and rare. For Protestants it is to be kept entirely apart from the regular and congregational Divine Service, and should be reserved for particular feasts, for celebration at evening or in the night stillness. It ought to be withdrawn altogether from the use and wont of every day and become the most intimate privilege which Christian worship has to offer.

But though these two means are excluded, it is yet possible to find another way to introduce Silent Worship into our ordinary Sunday services, and so to give these a consecration which is as yet lacking to them. We can make the service culminate and find its climax in a short period of silence, which shall be at once the silence of sacrament and the silence of waiting, and which may become, at least for the more practical, also a realization of union. We may devise an opportunity of silent dedication which will avoid the ceremonial apparatus and mythology of the doctrine of 'Transubstantiation', and yet in its simplicity and pure spirituality may be more deeply sacramental than the Mass, for which many are again beginning to crave. We have only to follow the indications afforded by the example of the 'Silent Worship' of the Quakers.

Where lies the essence of the sacramental? It is in fact—in the expression of the English High Churchmen—the 'real presence', the real presence of the transcendent and holy in its very nature in adoration and fellowship, so as to be laid hold of and enjoyed in present possession. No form of devotion which does not offer or achieve this mystery for the worshipper can be perfect or can give lasting contentment to a religious mind. And it is just because our usual Divine Services fall short in this that we see to-day again—quite comprehensibly—such a ferment and stirring of all sorts of uneasy 'High Church', 'Ritualistic', and 'Sacramental' movements.

But—we may well be asked—has it any meaning to ask for 'the presence of the divine'? Does not that Sacramental idea at once cancel itself, when thought out? Is not God 'omnipresent' and 'really present' always and everywhere?

Such a view is often put forward, and with a confident air of assurance which is in sharp conflict with the testimony of genuine religious experience; so much so, indeed, that one is tempted to venture a very blunt reply to it. We say, then, that this doctrine of the omnipresence of God—as though by a necessity of His being He must be bound to every time and to every place, like a natural force pervading space—is a frigid invention of metaphysical speculation, entirely without religious import. Scripture knows nothing of it. Scripture knows no 'Omnipresence', neither the expression nor the meaning it expresses; it knows only the God who is where He wills to be, and is not where He wills not to be, the *deus mobilis*, who is no mere universally extended being, but an august mystery, that comes and goes, approaches and with-draws, has its time and hour, and may be far or near in infinite degrees, 'closer than breathing' to us or miles remote from us. The hours of His 'visitation' and His 'return' are rare and solemn occasions, different essentially not only from the 'profane' life of every day, but also from the calm confiding mood of the believer, whose trust is to live ever before the face of God. They are the topmost summits in the life of the spirit. They are not only rare occasions, they must needs be so for our sakes, for no creature can bear often or for long the full nearness of God's majesty in its beatitude and in its *awefulness*. Yet there must still be such times, for they show the bright vision and completion of our sonship, they are a bliss in themselves and potent for redemption. They are the real sacrament, in comparison with which all high official ceremonials, Masses, and rituals the world over become the figurings of a child. And a Divine Service would be the truest which led up to such a mystery and the riches of grace that ensue upon the realization of it. And if it be asked whether a Divine Service is able to achieve this, let us answer that, though God indeed comes where and when He chooses, yet He will choose to come when we sincerely call upon Him and prepare ourselves truly for His visitation.

Appendix IX

A NUMINOUS EXPERIENCE OF JOHN RUSKIN

My attention has been called by Professor Deutschbein to the following passage in Ruskin, in which he recounts experiences of his youth that repeatedly recurred. They are purely numinous in character and well-nigh all the 'moments' which we discovered reappear here quite spontaneously. I give the passage without detailed comment:

'Lastly, although there was no definite religious sentiment mingled with it, there was a continual perception of Sanctity in the whole of nature, from the slightest thing to the vastest; an instinctive awe, mixed with delight; an indefinable thrill, such as we sometimes imagine to indicate the presence of a disembodied spirit. I could only feel this perfectly when I was alone; and then it would often make me shiver from head to foot with the joy and fear of it, when after being some time away from hills I first got to the shore of a mountain river, where the brown water circled among the pebbles, or when I first saw the swell of distant land against the sunset, or the first low broken wall, covered with mountain moss. I cannot in the least describe the feeling; but I do not think this is my fault, nor that of the English language, for I am afraid no feeling is describable. If we had to explain even the sense of bodily hunger to a person who had never felt it, we should be hard put to it for words; and the joy in nature seemed to me to come of a sort of heart-hunger, satisfied with the presence of a Great and Holy Spirit. . . . These feelings remained in their full intensity till I was eighteen or twenty, and then, as the reflective and practical power increased, and the "cares of this world" gained upon me, faded gradually away, in the manner described by Wordsworth in his "Intimations of Immortality".' (*Modern Painters*, Popular Edition (George Allen), vol. iii, p. 309.)

Schleiermacher calls such an experience 'intuition and feeling of the infinite'; we give it the name 'divination'. Schleiermacher was right in saying that even greater than all this divination in the sphere of nature is divination in the sphere of history.[1] Will not a Ruskin arise to divine and reveal the non-rational and numinous character of our own epoch?

[1] See Appendix X, p. 219.

Appendix X

THE EXPRESSION OF THE NUMINOUS IN ENGLISH[1]

ALTHOUGH it could hardly be disputed that the German philosophical vocabulary is superior to the English both in fullness and in precision, in regard to the subjects discussed in this book our language does not seem to be altogether at a disadvantage. Indeed, the English wealth of synonyms has presented the translator with an embarrassment at the very outset. In place of the single German adjective *heilig*, with its derivative noun and verb, we have the words *sacred* and *holy*, *sacredness*, *holiness*, and *sanctity*, *hallow* and *sanctify*. *Gottheit* again gives us a triad of synonyms, *deity*, *divinity*, *Godhead*. Each of these alternatives is probably the most appropriate rendering in some special context, and in choosing any one of them we are bound to sacrifice subtle differences in meaning which would be suggested by the others, and which are perhaps implicit in the single German equivalent. The deciding factor in the choice of *holy* rather than *sacred* as the regular rendering of *heilig* was the fact that it is the Biblical word, found especially in those great passages (e.g. Isa. vi) of which this book makes repeated use, and which seem central to its argument. *Holy* will be felt, I believe, to be a distinctly more numinous word than *sacred*: it retains about it more markedly the numinous atmosphere. And although, as is urged in the text with perhaps still more reason of its German equivalent, it refers mainly to the higher levels of religious experience at which the numinous has been interpreted in rational and moral terms, and therefore means to us mainly *goodness*, the word 'holy' is found also in contexts where this more exalted meaning is excluded, and where it is simply the numinous at an early and savage stage of development. The well-known lines from Coleridge's *Kubla Khan* give an example of such a use:

> A savage place! as holy and enchanted
> As e'er beneath a waning moon was haunted
> By woman wailing for her demon-lover!

This is a finely numinous passage, but it is the numinous at the primitive, pre-religious, 'daemonic' level: it conveys nothing of *sanctity*. For, while the daring use of 'holy' in this context may

---

[1] Added by the translator.

be just permissible, we reserve 'sanctity', if I mistake not, for the more restricted and elevated meaning.

Apart from these words it would appear that the English language is in general rich in numinous terms. Dr. Otto has himself noted (p. 14) that the English 'awe' has a numinous suggestion lacking in the German *scheu*, and (p. 127 n.) that 'haunt' has no precise German equivalent in all its range of significance. And besides 'uncanny' (a more or less exact rendering of *unheimlich*) I have made use of words like *weird* and *eerie*, which convey the indefinable numinous atmosphere unmistakably. The old word *freit* (a supernatural intimation or sign) may be another such; and possibly the obsolete verb-form *oug*, which gives us *ugly*, may have conveyed originally a suggestion of unnatural, uncanny daunting or repulsion. It should be noticed that these numinous words are all (except 'awe') concerned *primarily* with the cruder and more primitive forms of the experience: they are not in the first instance *religious* words in the higher sense, though, unlike such words as *grue*, *grisly*, and *ghastly*, they can be used with a loftier and more ennobled, as well as with a lower and more primitive meaning. And it can, finally, be hardly an accident that they all, or nearly all, are northern in origin. A peculiar susceptibility to numinous impressions—what Dr. Otto would call a peculiarly sensitive faculty of 'divination'—would seem, indeed, to be a characteristic of the North British. Such phenomena as those of clairvoyance and second-sight would seem to make for the same conclusion.

Apart from the expressiveness of single English words, it would be easy to amass from English poetry and prose alike passages (like that from Coleridge already quoted) illustrative of the different elements in numinous apprehension which have been discussed in this book. I venture to give three further citations.

On page 189 the contrast between the piety in which the 'rational moments' predominate and that in which a more numinous feeling is to be noted is illustrated from two German hymns of praise.

The same antithesis could hardly be shown more clearly than by the contrast between two poems familiar to every English reader, Addison's hymn based on Ps. xix, and Blake's poem 'The Tyger'. Both poets are hymning the Creator as revealed in his creation, but the difference of temper is unmistakable. On the one hand there is the mood of tranquil confidence, serene dignity, thankful and understanding praise; on the other, a mood of trepidation, awed surmise, the hush of mystery, in which rings none the less a strange exultation.

> The spacious firmament on high
> With all the blue ethereal sky,
> And spangled heavens, a shining frame,
> Their great Original proclaim.
> The unwearied sun, from day to day,
> Does his Creator's power display
> And publishes to every land
> The work of an Almighty hand.
>
> Soon as the evening shades prevail
> The moon takes up the wondrous tale
> And nightly to the listening earth
> Repeats the story of her birth;
> While all the stars that round her burn,
> And all the planets in their turn,
> Confirm the tidings as they roll
> And spread the truth from pole to pole.
>
> What though in solemn silence all
> Move round the dark terrestrial ball;
> What though no real voice or sound
> Amid their radiant orbs be found?
> In reason's ear they all rejoice,
> And utter forth a glorious voice;
> For ever singing as they shine:
> 'The hand that made us is Divine.'

This is, confessedly, *rational* piety; it is 'reason' that listens to nature's hymn of praise. As such it is characteristic not only of a certain type of mind, but of the particular age in which it was written. And the contrasted numinous note can hardly be missed in Blake's wonderful verses:

> Tyger, Tyger, burning bright
> In the forests of the night,
> What immortal hand or eye
> Could frame thy fearful symmetry?
>
> In what distant deeps or skies
> Burnt the fire of thine eyes?
> On what wings dare he aspire?
> What the hand dare seize the fire?

And what shoulder and what art
Could twist the sinews of thy heart?
And, when thy heart began to beat,
What dread hand and what dread feet?

What the hammer? What the chain?
In what furnáce was thy brain?
What the anvil? What dread grasp
Dare its deadly terrors clasp?

When the stars threw down their spears,
And watered heaven with their tears,
Did He smile his work to see?
Did He who made the lamb make thee?

Tyger, Tyger, burning bright
In the forests of the night,
What immortal hand or eye
Dare frame thy fearful symmetry?

The remark of the author on page 215 suggests my last quotation. Wordsworth, in the tenth book of *The Prelude*, recounts the
profound impression made upon him by the terrific events in
which the French Revolution culminated. Then, as now, outward convulsion and catastrophe had their inward counterpart in
spiritual tumult and overthrow, in widespread disillusionment
and despair. And Wordsworth tells us in effect how the very
tremendousness of the time, its 'portentousness', became to him
a revelation of the sustaining presence of the holy and the divine
(see *The Prelude*, x. 437–69):

> . . . 'So, with devout humility be it said,
> So, did a portion of that spirit fall
> On me uplifted from the vantage-ground
> Of pity and sorrow to a state of being
> That through the time's exceeding fierceness saw
> Glimpses of retribution, terrible,
> And in the order of sublime behests:
> But, even if that were not, amid the awe
> Of unintelligible chastisement,
> Not only acquiescences of faith
> Survived, but daring sympathies with power,
> Motions not treacherous or profane, else why
> Within the folds of no ungentle breast
> Their dread vibration to this hour prolonged? . . .

Then was the truth received into my heart,
That, under heaviest sorrow earth can bring,
If from the affliction somewhere do not grow
Honour which could not else have been, a faith,
An elevation, and a sanctity,
If new strength be not given nor old restored,
The blame is ours, not Nature's.'

APPENDIX XI

THE *MYSTERIUM TREMENDUM* IN ROBERTSON
AND WATTS

A PROFOUND expression of the *Mysterium Tremendum* may be found
in the sermon of F. W. Robertson on 'Jacob's Wrestling' (*Ten
Sermons*), point 2, The revelation of mystery.

'It was revealed by *awe*. Very significantly are we told that the
divine antagonist seemed, as it were, anxious to depart as the day
was about to dawn; and that Jacob held Him more convulsively
fast, as if aware that the daylight was likely to rob him of his
anticipated blessing: in which there seems concealed a very deep
truth. God is approached more nearly in that which is *indefinite*
than in that which is definite and distinct. He is felt in *awe* and
wonder and *worship* rather than in clear *conception*. There is a sense
in which *darkness* has more of God than light has. He dwells in
the thick darkness. Moments of tender, vague mystery often
bring distinctly the feeling of His presence. When day breaks and
distinctness comes the Divine has evaporated from the soul like
morning dew. In sorrow, haunted by uncertain presentiments,
we feel the infinite around us. The gloom disperses, the world's
joy comes again, and it seems as if God were gone—the Being
who had touched us with a withering hand and wrestled with us,
yet whose presence, even when most terrible, was more blessed
than His absence. It is true, even literally, that the darkness
reveals God: every morning God draws the curtain of the garish
light across His eternity, and we lose the Infinite. We look down
on earth instead of up to heaven, on a narrower and more contracted spectacle—that which is examined by the microscope
when the telescope is laid aside—smallness, instead of vastness.
"Man goeth forth unto his work and to his labour till the even-

ing"; and in the dust and pettiness of life we seem to cease to behold Him: then at night He undraws the curtain again, and we see how much of God and Eternity the bright distinct day has hidden from us. Yes, in solitary, silent, vague darkness, the Awful One is near—

'Names have a power, a strange power of *hiding* God.

'Who does not know how we satisfy ourselves with the name of some strange bird or plant, or the name of some new law in nature? It is a mystery perplexing us before. We get the name and fancy we understand something more than we did before; but in truth we are more hopelessly ignorant: for before we felt there was a something we had not attained, and so we inquired and searched—now, we fancy we possess it, because we have got the name by which it is known: and the word covers over the abyss of our ignorance. If Jacob had got a word, that word might have satisfied him. . . . God's plan was not to give names and words, but *truths of feeling*. That night, in that strange scene, He impressed on Jacob's soul a religious awe, which was hereafter to develop—not a set of formal expressions, which would have satisfied with husks the craving of the intellect and shut up the soul: Jacob felt the Infinite, who is more truly *felt* when least *named*.'

The following hymn of Watts expresses the numinous feeling more adequately than many that are more familiar.

> Eternal Power, whose high abode
> Becomes the grandeur of a God,
> Infinite length beyond the bounds
> Where stars revolve their little rounds:
>
> Thee while the first Archangel sings,
> He hides his face beneath his wings;
> And ranks of shining ones around
> Fall worshipping and spread the ground.
>
> Lord, what shall earth and ashes do?
> We would adore our Maker too:
> From Sin and dust to Thee we cry,
> The Great, the Holy, and the High!
>
> Earth from afar has heard thy fame
> And we have learned to lisp Thy name;
> But oh the glories of Thy mind
> Leave all our soaring thoughts behind.

God is in Heaven, and men below;
Be short our tunes, our words be few;
A sacred reverence checks our songs,
And praise sits silent on our tongues.

APPENDIX XII

THE RESURRECTION AS A SPIRITUAL EXPERIENCE

I

'I *know* that my Redeemer liveth': 'I *believe* in Jesus Christ, risen from the dead': such is the Christian's confession.

'I know' and 'I believe' or 'have faith'—these are not here mutually exclusive expressions. This 'knowing' is not that with which scientific theory is concerned, based upon empirical sense-knowledge; it is rather *faith-knowledge*, and faith-knowledge does not rely on the evidence of the senses, but is, in the scriptural phrase, 'the evidence of things not seen', that is, not presented to sense-perception; and it would lose its essential nature and be transformed into a mere sorry empirical knowledge, if it relied on any other evidence than 'the witness of the Holy Spirit', which is not that of sense-experience. And so we cannot afford to account Christ's Resurrection, and our own, known facts, in this lower 'scientific' sense of knowledge. The simplest understanding feels this. To speak of 'resurrection' is to utter a mystery, and mystery is a subject for faith, not science. And, for Christianity, how this faith itself comes to be is no less a mystery, indeed the greatest of all mysteries. But if 'faith' were knowledge, directly attested by the senses or based upon the tradition of a former occurrence attested by the senses, this mystery would wholly disappear.

And so we hold that in endeavouring to account for our assurance of the Risen Christ two sorts of interpretation must be excluded, the naïvely supernaturalistic and the rationalistic. The former is that which has recourse to the 'Empty Tomb'. It holds that Christ's tomb was proved to be empty by the evidence of the senses, that the Risen Christ was perceived by the senses, and that the truth of the facts so certified in sense-experience was then handed down by human testimony. On this view the conviction of the resurrection was from the first not *faith*, but a piece of empirical knowledge. This is the most serious objection that can be brought against the naïve 'supernaturalist' interpretation, a more serious objection than the uncertain and legendary character of the 'Empty Tomb' narrative or the fact that the earliest and most authentic witness to the resurrection of Christ—that of St. Paul in 1 Cor. xv—makes no mention of the empty tomb, although there the Apostle is at pains to assemble all possible reasons for assurance in the reality of the Resurrection.

But the ordinary rationalistic interpretation is equally inadmissible. A deep 'impression' of the person of Jesus had remained, so it is said, with the disciples and especially with Peter, and from this impression grew their conviction after His death, 'Such a one cannot have remained dead.' And this conviction, thus born in their minds, took imaginative and figurative form in visions, which must therefore be regarded as purely subjective. But this explanation is patently forced and unsatisfactory, and seems to us to miss altogether the uniqueness and coherence of the experience centring in the Resurrection. The two lines of interpretation have this in common, however: they both entirely ignore the fundamental fact about the experience, that it was a *mystery*; both agree in disregarding altogether its mysterious character.

We can only get beyond the opposition between supernaturalism and rationalism by frankly recognizing that the experiences concerned with the Resurrection were *mystical experiences* and their source 'the Spirit'. It is only 'of the Spirit' that the higher knowledge is born. It is the eye of Spirit, not the eye of sense that beholds the eternal things; but what it sees is not a mere insecure, half-woven fabric of 'convictions', but the adamantine certainty of the eternal truth itself.

II

To understand the matter truly we need to make clear to ourselves by examples drawn from occurrences in the Bible record to what more general class of experience those that are concerned with the Resurrection belong, and then to grasp what the essential character of this wider class is. Isaiah tells (ch. vi) how in that mysterious experience in the Temple his inward eye was opened to behold Yahweh in His holiness and majesty, how he received His command and became thereby the messenger of Yahweh to His people. This supreme, mysterious vision becomes thus for Isaiah his summons and his ordination, and his whole subsequent activity as prophet in its wider significance is founded upon this experience. And the occurrence is not one without a parallel, but rather is typical of all the great men who received God's summons (compare Jer. i, Ezek. i and ii, Amos i, Hos. i).

But what really took place in these mystical experiences? Has God a body? Is He really seated upon a throne, or has He any place in a physical sense? Do beings such as the Cherubim and Seraphim are described surround Him in visible form? Has He a voice audible to our actual sense of hearing? Even those who, so far as concerns the Resurrection of Christ, think to base their faith upon an actually perceived Empty Tomb and a Body which, however 'transfigured', yet remained an object to see and touch— even they will answer these questions with a decided negative as regards the vision of Isaiah. Even they will admit that these forms of imagery, in which the experience of Isaiah clothes itself, are nothing more than forms of imagery, born of the ideas of the time and merely a vesture for something seen and apprehended by other means than by stimulation of the senses, with which it indeed has nothing to do.

On the other side, the naturalistic rationalist will set up some sort of plausible psychological 'explanation', differing according to the empirical psychology that is at his disposal; or, resorting to a still simpler mode of explanation, he will be inclined to say that such occurrences never occurred at all. But whoever knows anything of the Spirit and its miraculous nature, whoever feels in himself the Spirit active in those mysterious experiences that build up the Christian's life, will reject such explanations. He alone has the key to the truth of the matter. Just as the Scriptures as a whole, as the Christian believes, require the Spirit if they are to be taught or understood, so too is it with these occurrences. Only a first-hand spiritual experience teaches a man to see and enables him to estimate a spiritual experience of a former day. Possession of the Spirit at first hand becomes here a faculty of 'retrospective prophecy', which is recognition in the sense of re-cognition or knowing again for oneself. And so only on the basis of a first-hand religious experience, of and from the Spirit, is there any possibility of obtaining a real and genuine historical knowledge of these things, for only such an experience is acquainted with and can estimate the effect of *all* the factors of the explanation. What the Spirit gives is not a view that transcends the historical, but the genuine historical view. And the naturalistic view gives on the other hand a falsification of history, for it has ignored an essential part of the facts it seeks to explain.

III

Let us now turn to the New Testament. Once we have come to understand aright, that is, in the Spirit, the experiences of the great prophets, we can recognize plainly how similar they are to the narratives of the great visions of Jesus at the outset and at the full height of His ministry—the vision at His Baptism and the vision at His 'Transfiguration'. As with the prophets, so with Jesus: these, too, are manifestly spiritual and mystical experiences; but these, too, were objectively real occurrences. And they are also to be counted as belonging to the same class of experiences for the reason that they too are manifestly visions of Call and Ordination. As before, we do not doubt that all that is recounted in perceptual terms stands upon just the same footing as the perceptual imagery that invests the mystical experience of Isaiah, the essential and unshakeable truth of which lies not in that vesture, but in the knowledge and assurance born 'of the Spirit'.

And if we pass on to the Resurrection-experience of Paul on the road to Damascus, do we not at once recognize the same characteristic features? Have we here sense-perception or spiritual experience? Paul nowhere describes how and in what form he beheld the Risen Christ. That does not in itself make it the less likely that he did see Him in some form, probably as a royal figure of radiant glory rather than merely as a dazzling light. The material of his vision was no doubt supplied him by the current ideas of his time concerning royal splendour and messianic kinghood, and then his faculty of vision gave this material an individual and special form. That is but to say that the vision would have a vesture of outward form just as that of Isaiah did; but this does not, for Paul any more than for Isaiah, touch the inmost import of the experience, which is here: '*He lives*; He lives as the accepted of God, the preserved of God, the exalted of God, the transfigured of God, as the conqueror of Judgement, of the Cross, and of Death.' And at the same time that further point of resemblance with the occurrences already mentioned is manifest, which, strangely enough, is here not generally noticed. For this vision of Paul, like those others, is not merely a vision of the Risen Christ, but again precisely inaugural, a vision of Calling and Ordination.

At the same time this experience of Paul has its place among a second class of experiences, which in turn stand fully illumined

Q

in the Pauline writings. For it is but the first link in a whole chain of spiritual happenings which develop in him and in his congregations. These are the *charismata* or 'gifts of the Spirit', and among them is included the gift of *horasis* or mystic vision which Paul himself possessed. And what took place on the road to Damascus is not only the first link in the chain, but more fundamental and potent than all that followed. There it was that the *pneuma* first broke through, the Spirit which man makes not nor can bestow upon himself, which blows whither it lists, and kindles what it wills, and whose 'prick' was already felt in Paul's heart.

Paul puts his experience on a parity with those of Peter and others, an indication that these also were of the same class as his own. And we could ourselves recognize as much even without Paul's express testimony. According to Paul's statement Peter was the first to receive the new revelation of the Risen Christ, and what we know otherwise of Peter is in accord with this. He has the gift of 'vision', as the story in Acts x shows, and it had been manifested more than once while his Master was still on earth, as at the time of the Transfiguration on Mount Tabor. And the Synoptic record gives other more general indications of his rare spiritual endowment. Further, for Peter and the others to whom the experience came, the vision of the Risen Christ is once again an inaugural experience of Call and Ordination, as is indicated in the words, 'Go ye therefore and teach all nations', which we are to take as a spiritual realization of mission just in the same way as the command of Yahweh to Isaiah: 'Go and tell this people', and which, no less than the experience of the prophets, attest themselves as having been really 'heard' in spiritual perception at a definite place and time. And again in the case of these original witnesses to the Resurrection, the vision of the Risen Christ is no more an isolated experience than in the case of Paul. For Paul and his converts are not the first to receive 'the Spirit' and its sevenfold gifts. These gifts are the possession of the earliest Christian community from the first, and characterize it, as Paul himself avows, when he justifies his position as an apostle in showing that he and his converts *also* possess the same spiritual gifts which the Christians of Jerusalem had from the first.

And so the consciousness of the Risen Christ loses its isolated character and is already manifested as one of a class of spiritual experiences, a mystical and spiritual apprehension of truth, beyond the opposition of supernaturalism and rationalism.

IV

The apostles proclaim their Lord not only as 'raised from the dead', but as 'exalted' and 'ascended' into heaven. That is in harmony with the picture of the universe which they shared with antiquity as a whole. But whoever thinks it necessary to retain the bodily, physical idea in 'raised from the dead' ought to realize that he is bound to do the same with the expression 'exalted'. For that also conveys in its literal sense a *spatial* idea; it presupposes the old notion that 'Heaven', God's eternal realm, is somewhere high above us in space. This notion was natural enough in antiquity; but for us heaven and the eternal world of God is no more in space or time than God Himself is: it is in God's eternity, which is apart from space and time. This does not at all mean that the expressions 'resurrection', 'raising from the dead', lose their meaning. In contrast to the idea of 'immortality', which properly is the denial of any state of real death, they affirm the *restoration* from real death to real life, or rather the admittance for the first time into plenary and genuine life. Nor have they in the Biblical view reference solely to the body. It is not the body merely, but the *man* that dies; and it is as soul as well as body that he sinks into the state of death,[1] the 'dread night of death', from which he can only be delivered and raised up by the power of God. If he is to live, man needs to be thus *awakened*, brought up out of Hades and from the shadow of death, and raised again 'from the dead'. To be sure, according to Paul's idea, there is *combined* with this at the same time a bodily restoration. But, as is often noticed, this is for him *not* a raising up of the *old* body, a 'resurrection of the flesh'. Rather he would on his own presuppositions have emphatically rejected such a notion; for 'the flesh'—which is for him the essence of antagonism to God—is to pass away like the seed of corn sown in the earth, and the 'resurrection of the body' is for him rather the bestowal of a *new* and quite other 'spiritual' body, provided and prepared of God. This

---

[1] To die is to lose not *being* but *life*. The fleshly body does not cease at first to *be* but to exercise the function we call 'living'. . . . And so the soul sinks not into not-being, nonentity, but into death, i.e. the cessation of its living function. This state is spoken of in Scripture as passing into 'Hades' (wrongly rendered 'Hell') and is compared to sleep, which is essentially life whose potentiality has been suspended. A closer analogy still to the state of 'soul-death' is that of cataleptic lethargy or impotence. We have to think of the condition of the soul sundered from the organ necessary to its essential nature as that of utter impotence, deprivation of life but not of being.

is also the direction in which our thought must turn if we are to attempt to represent to ourselves the new life of the resurrection. We too are unable to think of the completed perfected life of the Spirit without ascribing to the Spirit some *instrument* or 'organ' whereby it realizes itself in practice. Now 'body' is the instrument of spirit, and the phrase 'spiritual body' affirms in an unambiguous manner that this instrument is not a fleshly body, not even 'transfigured flesh'—a contradiction in itself—but is itself spiritual in kind. And that implies that it is not bound up with any one point in space or time, and so is in no sense a *physical* body, which cannot be severed from material and spatial determination.

But whatever our thought may be upon this matter, one thing at any rate holds good: the meaning of the Christian knowledge that is by faith lies in this, that Christ Himself who really died was brought again by God to real life and perfected unto the glory of the eternal life of God; and that we live in expectation of the same with Him. This is a 'knowing' which, for us to-day no less than for the apostles, can be born of the Spirit, but only of the Spirit. Whether the body belongs to the being of this Christ and to our own completed being is a physiological not a religious question, and one which pertains not at all to our confession of faith. But to any one who has to meet this issue we would say, the 'Risen Christ' is to be 'our comfort', not a source of trouble in our conscientious fidelity to truth; and for a true understanding of the experiences bearing on the Resurrection we would refer him to the nature of spiritual revelation as recounted in Isaiah vi.

As regards the narratives of the 'Empty Tomb', we shall judge of these as of the narratives of a later date which gathered about the birth of Jesus, appraising them as a holy legend, in which the supra-rational relation of the eternal to the temporal is mirrored in the medium of contemporary thought. They have an enduring value to us from the incomparable beauty and power with which they symbolize the essence of the 'mystery'. We would not be without them in our Bible, nor yet in the pictorial art of the churches, nor in the hymns that express our devotion. And we can retain them thus without being false to the obligation of the most rigid honesty if we remain fully conscious of that other obligation, without fulfilling which we neither can nor indeed should have either Biblical instruction or Christian doctrine. And that is the obligation we are under to train ourselves and the mind of our time to a sincere and devout understanding of three things. In the first place we need to realize the fringe of legend that surrounds the entire narrative of Holy Scripture and recurs as a constant problem from the first page of the Bible to the last. Secondly, we need to appreciate the signal value and beauty and the profound import which distinguish the Biblical narrative, even where it is of the nature of legend; and, finally, the fact that even in the holy saga and legend, shaped and fashioned unconsciously by the spirit of a people or a fellowship, there is present the very same eternal Spirit of God, which Hebrew prophecy and poetry and history also manifest, that Spirit which, in every form of its expression, is the Spirit of revelation and truth.

Appendix XIII

RELIGIOUS ESSAYS, A SUPPLEMENT TO 'THE IDEA OF THE HOLY' (O.U.P.)

TABLE OF CONTENTS

INDEX

PRINTED IN GREAT BRITAIN
AT THE UNIVERSITY PRESS, OXFORD
BY CHARLES BATEY, PRINTER TO THE UNIVERSITY